MW01016394

Key Issues

ON THE WEALTH OF NATIONS
Contemporary Responses to Adam Smith

Key Issues

ON THE WEALTH OF NATIONS

Contemporary Responses to Adam Smith

Edited and Introduced by
Ian S. Ross
Professor Emeritus, University of British Columbia

Series Editor
ANDREW PYLE
University of Bristol

THOEMMES PRESS

© Thoemmes Press 1998

Published in 1998 by
Thoemmes Press
11 Great George Street
Bristol BS1 5RR, England

US office: Distribution and Marketing
22883 Quicksilver Drive
Dulles, Virginia 20166, USA

ISBN
Paper : 1 85506 567 3
Cloth : 1 85506 566 5

On the Wealth of Nations
Key Issues No. 19

Items from *The Correspondence of Adam Smith* (revised
edition, 1987), edited by E. C. Mossner and Ian S. Ross, and
Essays on Philosophical Subjects, edited by W. P. D.
Wightman, J. C. Bryce and Ian S. Ross (1980), general
editors D. D. Raphael and A. S. Skinner, are reproduced by
permission of Oxford University Press.

'Report on Manufactures, 1791' from *The Papers of
Alexander Hamilton*, vol. 10, edited by Harold C. Syrett.
Copyright © 1966 by Columbia University Press.
Reprinted with permission of the publisher.

British Library Cataloguing-in-Publication Data

A catalogue record of this title is available
from the British Library

Printed in Great Britain by Creative Print and Design Group

CONTENTS

IV. CRITICISM

V. ENTRY OF THE WEALTH OF NATIONS
INTO BRITISH POLITICS

b) France

c) Italy

d) United States Of America

ACKNOWLEDGEMENTS

Work on this book has been made agreeable by the co-operation of many individuals and institutions.

I wish to acknowledge with gratitude the permission given to me to publish in whole or in part material owned by Giles A. F. E. Adams, Esq., Woodford Lodge, near Kettering, Northants., England (letter from Lord Grenville to Pitt, 1800); Columbia University Press ('Report on Manufactures', 1791: *Papers of Alexander Hamilton*, ed. Harold C. Syrett, vol. 10); Professor Gabriella Gioli, University of Pisa (1819 edition of Francesco Mengotti's *Il Colbertismo*); Institut de France Bibliothèque (J.-B. Say's annotations to *Wealth of Nations*, 1789); Professor Hiroshi Hashimoto, Uji-shi, Kyoto, Japan (transcriptions of the Say annotations); Oxford University Press (extracts from the *Works and Correspondence of Adam Smith*, 1976–87); the Royal Society of Edinburgh as depositor and National Library of Scotland as repository (letter from John Millar to David Hume, 1776).

For friendly offices as the book progressed, I am most grateful to Professor Paul-Gabriel Boucé, Université de Paris III; Dr Iain G. Brown, National Library of Scotland; Mr Kenneth E. Carpenter, Harvard University Library; Professor Bernhard Fabian, Institutum Erasmianum, Münster; Dr Helena Frenschkowski and Professor Marco Frenschkowski, Hofheim; Professor Alan T. McKenzie, Purdue University; Mireille Pastoureau, Director, Institut de France Bibliothèque, Paris; Professor Hermann J. Real, Westfälische Wilhelms-Universität, Münster; Professor Angus Ross, University of Sussex; Herr Klaus Schmidt, Akademie der Wissenschaften: Index deutscher Rezensions-Zeitschriften des 18. Jahrhunderts, Göttingen; Dr habil. Peter Thal, Halle; and my editor at Thoemmes Press, Jane Williamson.

Members of my immediate family supported me with their most welcome cheerfulness, also forgiveness for my short-comings: Isla, Bettina, Andrew, David, and Marion. And my dear wife Ingrid was as always a tower of strength and resourcefulness, especially in helping me with German sources. Fergus Macpherson our cat and now Trixie the Airedale added much enjoyment and some excitement to days and nights spent writing up this project.

I. S. R.
Bardscroft, Gambier Island, British Columbia
14 October 1997

INTRODUCTION

An Inquiry into the Nature and Causes of the Wealth of Nation, was published on 9 March 1776, with Adam Smith's authorship of *The Theory of Moral Sentiments* (4th ed. 1774), which had first brought him fame as an author in 1759, also acknowledged.[1] It went through five editions in Smith's lifetime, and never seems to have gone out of print in English, as well as being translated into the world's leading languages. It is not in all likelihood the 'most important book that was ever written', as Thomas Henry Buckle claimed in 1857, 'looking at its ultimate results'.[2] Nevertheless, this characteristic product of the Scottish Enlightenment, appearing at a time of expanding markets and consumerism, as well as political revolutions, is a book that has shaped profoundly modern understanding of human nature engaged in economic processes, and the ongoing search for material welfare.

Smith defined wealth as the produce of a country's land and labour which supplies its inhabitants with 'all the necessaries and conveniences of life' (WN Intro. 1). He proceeds in his first Book to demonstrate that it is created by division of labour, animated by self-interest (WN I.ii.2), channelled in the human 'propensity to truck, barter, and exchange' (I.ii.1) and the 'desire

---

[1] References to Smith's Works are to the Glasgow edition, Oxford University Press, 1976–83, cited as WN = *An Inquiry into the Nature and Causes of the Wealth of Nations*, ed. R. H. Campbell, A. S. Skinner, and W. B. Todd, 2 vols., 1976, detailing book, section, and paragraph numbers; TMS = *The Theory of Moral Sentiments*, ed. D. D. Raphael and A. L. Macfie, 1976; EPS = *Essays on Philosophical Subjects*, ed. W. P. D. Wightman, J. C. Bryce, and I. S. Ross – general eds. D. D. Raphael and A. S. Skinner (includes Dugald Stewart's 'Account of Smith'), 1980; Corr. = *Correspondence*, ed. E. C. Mossner and I. S. Ross, 2nd ed., 1987, identifying letter nos. Biographical material for this Introduction is drawn from I. S. Ross, *The Life of Adam Smith* (Oxford University Press, 1995), which provides a full list of sources.

[2] H. T. Buckle, *History of Civilization in England*, 1857 (Henry Frowde: London, 1904), i.167; his annotated copy of WN 1839 is in the Newberry Library, Chicago.

of bettering our condition' (I.ii.28). His discussion takes up such central aspects of wealth as money, price, wages and profit, rent, and value. In the second Book, he presents his theory of the accumulation of wealth in the form of capital, countering the error of the contemporary French school of economists, the Physiocrats, who held that the manufacturing sector was unproductive.

Books I and II depict in an empirical way the processes of an ideal market economy, thus the theory of price distinguishes clearly between factors of production: land, labour, and capital; and the categories of return: rent, wages, and profit. Smith demonstrates understanding of the interdependence of economic phenomena, and builds a macroeconomic model incorporating ideas generated by the leader of the Physiocrats, Quesnay, and their ally Turgot. This model represents the factors as flows rather than stocks, with money, accumulating from rent, wages, and profits, exchanged for commodities, and 'circular flow' to be found in withdrawal of goods from the circulating capital of society through purchase, and simultaneously replacement through production of commodities. In addition, Smith showed awareness of the potential for growth by stating that outputs in given time periods could exceed previous performance, either by increasing the number of productive labourers or the power of those labourers. But these sources of increased output required additional capital, either to increase the wage fund or buy machines to 'abridge labour'. The source of this capital was

---

[3] Commentaries and books on Smith's economics are legion. Most useful for this Introduction have been the following: Adolph Lowe, 'Adam Smith's System of Equilibrium Growth' in *Essays on Adam Smith*, ed. A. S. Skinner and Thomas Wilson (Oxford University Press, 1975), pp. 415–25; and A. S. Skinner, *A System of Social Science*, 2nd ed. (Oxford University Press, 1995). Sources of the discussion here of economists, also economic theory and policy, are chiefly Joseph A. Schumpeter, *History of Economic Analysis*, ed. from MS by Elizabeth Boody Schumpeter, 1954; with a new introduction by Mark Perlman (Oxford University Press: New York, 1994); D. P. O'Brien, *The Classical Economists* (Oxford University Press, 1975); Jean-Claude Perrot, *Une histoire intellectuelle de l'économie politique des XVIIe–XVIII siècles* (Éditions de l'École des Hautes Études en Sciences Sociales: Paris, 1992) and Donald Winch, *Riches and Poverty: An Intellectual History of Political Economy in Britain, 1750–1834* (Cambridge University Press, 1996). Sources for tracking early responses to WN were mainly *Adam Smith: International Perspectives*, ed. Hiroshi Mizuta and Chuhei Sugiyama (Macmillan: London/Basingstoke, 1993) and the articles on Sartorius, Jakob, Garnier, and Mengotti in *Palgrave's*

'parsimony', which would yield net savings for investment (WN II.iii.17, 32).[3]

The first two Books of WN can be regarded as Smith's greatest achievement as an analytic economist. Never applying to his model the term *laissez-faire* (said to go back to the time of Colbert: (Stewart, Note I, EPS 345 n.), Smith called it the 'obvious and simple system of natural liberty' (WN IV.ix.51). Since catching the attention of Smith's first readers, such as those represented below, the 'simple' system's features of competition, free trade, and self-regulation through the market mechanism ('invisible hand': TMS IV.1.10; WN IV.ii. 9), within the limits of justice, have continued ever since to arouse keen support and equally vigorous opposition.

In Books III and IV of WN, Smith turns from analysis to historical evaluation of alternative economic systems to which he gives the names 'commercial' or 'mercantile', also to examination of the 'agricultural system proposed by the Physiocrats. This gives him an opportunity to mount a polemic against mistaken attempts of governments inspired by mercantilism to redirect and thwart economic activities through monopolies, bounties (e.g. for corn (grain) production), and drawbacks, against the Natural Law tendencies of the simple system of natural liberty. Opening with an account of the four stages of socioeconomic development, Book V offers constructive advice about the necessary curtailment of individual economic freedom in a commercial society to provide for our chief social needs: justice, defence, public works, religious establishments, and education. Such is the work to which the members of Smith's circle, his first critics, and contemporary politicians in Britain, also translators and commentators abroad made their responses introduced below.

I. *Letters by Members of Smith's Scottish Enlightenment Circle*

a) Hume was regarded by Smith as 'by far the most illustrious philosopher and historian of the present age' (WN V.i.g.3), and

Dictionary of Political Economy, ed. Henry Higgs, rev. ed. 1925–6 (Augustus M. Kelley reprints: New York, 1963), and on Smith, Anderson, Stewart, Lauderdale, Buchanan, J.-B. Say, and Hamilton in *The New Palgrave: A Dictionary of Economics*, ed. John Eatwell, Murray Milgate, and Peter Newman (Macmillan: London/Basingstoke, 1987).

his project of building a 'science of man' inspired Scottish Enlightenment authors. He certainly exerted a major influence on Smith's economics. His general observations threw light on the fundamental principles of human nature which operate to increase wealth, including 'avarice, or the desire of gain, ... an universal passion, which operates at all times, in all places, and upon all persons' ('The Rise of Arts and Sciences'). His *Political Discourses* (1752), in particular, made theoretical advances in sectoral analysis, specie-flow, and international trade theory. Additionally, he subjected the prevailing mercantilist or interventionist approach to economic policy to a telling critique.[4] In a sense, he was the ideal reader of WN. Alerted by a letter of 8 February 1776 that Hume knew WN had been 'printed long ago' and was mortally ill (Corr. No. 149), Smith must have awaited Hume's verdict of 1 April with eager and poignant curiosity.

b) Hugh Blair, who offered Smith his congratulations two days later, had no special knowledge of economics, but he was one of the most famous preachers of his era, with a special concern for the morality of a commercial society (*Sermons*, 1777–1801). The division of the 'science of man' he had taken up was criticism, and his *Lectures on Rhetoric and Belles-Letters* (1783), became a widely-studied textbook, especially in North America. He recalled Smith reading parts of WN to him, perhaps to get comments on the style, and he declared confidently that this book 'ought to be, and I am perswaded will in some degree become, the Commercial Code of Nations'. While praising Smith's style, he thought WN would be improved by the addition of an index, which was supplied in the third edition of 1784. Blair also called for a syllabus, outlining the main tenets of the book and citing the pages where they are 'handled and proved'. As part of the preface to what became the canonical French translation of WN (1st ed. 1802), Germain Garnier offered something like this feature in his 'Method of Facilitating the Study of Dr Smith's Work' (below pp. 213–24).

c) Writing to Smith on 8 April 1776, Principal William Robertson, Blair's colleague at Edinburgh University, reckoned

[4] A. S. Skinner, 'David Hume: Principles of Political Economy' in *The Cambridge Companion to Hume*, ed. David Fate Norton (Cambridge University Press, 1993), pp. 222–54.

that WN would bring about a 'total change in several important articles both in police [economic policy] and finance', if the English proved 'capable of extending their ideas beyond the narrow and illiberal principles introduced by the mercantile supporters of [Whig] Revolution principles'. Robertson's histories of Scotland, Europe, America, and India helped to alter Europe's awareness of its past and connections with the New World and the Orient, and gave him a place with Hume and Gibbon as one of the three leading historians of the age.[5] Referring to his current project, a *History of America* (1777), Robertson announced in his letter that he would often follow Smith as his 'Guide and interpreter' about the 'absurdity' of the British limitations on the American colony trade. One practical suggestion he made was that WN would benefit from '*Side-notes*, pointing out the progress of the subject in every paragraph'. Feeling like an 'architect commissioned to place a new building alongside some ancient masterpiece', Edwin Cannan eventually met this need with a 'marginal summary of the text' in his widely-used WN edition of 1904 (6th, 1950, p. vi).

d) Adam Ferguson, Professor of Moral Philosophy at Edinburgh University, and author of *An Essay on the History of Civil Society* (1767), which attracted much attention in Germany as a pioneering work in sociology, carried on a debate with Hume and Smith about the viability of civic humanist ideas in a commercial age. He alleged to Smith on 18 April that he had been too busy reading WN, as well as 'recommending and quoting it' to his students, to trouble his friend with letters. He wrote that he took Smith's side in criticizing the 'church, the universities, and merchants' (cf. WN IV.ii.c.9; V.i.f,g), but he refused to go along with him in discounting the worth of a militia (V.i.a.23). As a firm civic humanist, perhaps the 'most Machiavellian' of the Scottish thinkers of his time, he was convinced that a free people must be capable of defending their liberty in arms and not trust to hiring a standing army. Smith held that, as a result of division of labour and technological change, professional soldiers under

[5] *William Robertson and the Expansion of Empire*, ed. Stewart J. Brown (Cambridge University Press, 1997).

the direction of the civil leadership were needed to defend the state with the sophisticated firepower of the modern era.[6]

e) A final letter representing views found in Smith's circle was written by John Millar, Professor of Civil Law at Glasgow, and student, colleague, and friend of Smith. This one was addressed to Hume, probably some time in April 1776, after both men had read WN, and Hume had expressed to Millar criticisms of Smith's style. Millar, however, took up another issue, which more and more readers came to see as central to WN: '[Smith's] great leading opinion, concerning the unbounded freedom of trade'.

To be sure, Smith's approach to the study of law and government is adopted intelligently in Millar's books: *Observations Concerning the Distinction of Ranks* (1771; 3rd ed. enlarged, 1779) and *An Historical View of the English Government* (1787). Moreover, he was a stout upholder of political liberty, which led him to support the American revolution and the early stages at least of the French one. Nevertheless, Millar challenged Smith's advocacy of the unfettered market, arguing that where public interest warrants it, there should be regulation of trade to secure raw materials for home manufactures.

II. *Published Letter*

An early, well-informed reading of WN is reflected in a letter addressed to Smith from Richmond on 25 September 1776, and published shortly thereafter in London as a pamphlet of 48 pages. The writer was Thomas Pownall, a career civil servant who spent five years altogether in America, latterly as Governor of Massachusetts Bay colony, 1757–9. Serving as an MP, 1767–80, he occupied himself with the American crisis, generally by opposing coercion of the Americans and proposing conciliation, a stand favoured by Smith.

---

[6] J. G. A. Pocock, *The Machiavellian Moment* (Princeton University Press, 1975); Istvan Hont, 'The "Rich Country – Poor Country" Debate in Scottish Classical Political Economy' in *Wealth and Virtue: The Shaping of Political Economy in the Scottish Enlightenment*, ed. Istvan Hont and Michael Ignatieff (Cambridge University Press, 1983) pp. 271–315; Richard B. Sher, 'Adam Ferguson, Adam Smith, and the Problem of National Defense', *The Journal of Modern History*, vol. 61, no. 2 (1989), pp. 240–68. Vincenzo Merolle challenges the claim Adam Ferguson was 'Machiavellian' in *Scottish Studies Newsletter*, no. 7 (1997), pp. 12, 16–17.

Pownall's letter offered pertinent criticisms of Smith's economic analysis, which he believed affected the final synthesis of the 'obvious and simple system of natural liberty'. In particular, he questioned Smith's views on price, patterns of trade, restraints on trade, and the monopoly of the colony trade. His most telling point, perhaps, related to Smith's conduct of his argument, for he brings out that what are advanced as probable conclusions concerning the different ways of employing capital in one part of WN, subsequently are treated as 'absolute proofs' of the disadvantages of the monopoly of the colony trade. While praising Smith's enterprise in general terms, Pownall often scolds him sharply about his specific policy advice. He is far from satisfied that Smith's global free trade vision ('extensive commerce from all countries to all countries': IV.v.b.39) would be worth the social cost of abandoning the corn bounty, and the political cost of dismantling the British Empire. Pownall's responses to WN began a long tradition of argument over Smith's approach to agricultural support policies and free trade, extending to modern suspicions of such developments as the European Economic Union and the North American Free Trade Agreement.

III. *Review*
Smith's opinion of reviews fluctuated. On 26 June 1776, he wrote to Thomas Cadell, one of his publishers in London: 'send me all the criticisms [of WN] you can'. In 1780, he is reported as never speaking 'but with ridicule and detestation of *reviews*', and said, 'it is not easy to conceive in what contempt they were held in London' (*The Bee*, 11 May 1791). Possibly what soured him was not reviews of WN, but the reaction in the press to his letter praising the sceptic Hume for 'approaching as nearly to the idea of a perfectly wise and virtuous man, as perhaps the nature of human frailty will admit' (Corr. no. 178). This gave great offence to some Christians, and as he confessed on 26 October 1780, a 'very harmless Sheet of paper [on Hume's death] ... brought upon me more abuse than the very violent attack I had made upon the whole commercial system of Great Britain'. He summed up reviews of his 'violent attack' thus: 'I have upon the whole been much less abused than I had reason to expect' (Corr. no. 298).

Canvass of WN reviews is not very helpful for revealing how the book was being presented to the reading public. One scholar,

Richard F. Teichgraeber, III, has confessed his investigation into this subject was 'slightly mind-numbing'. His careful research suggested that reviewers towards the end of the century in Britain were overwhelmed by the sheer number of books with which they had to deal. Perhaps 16,243 titles alone were published in the London of the 1790s. The reviews were 'little more than descriptive catalogues of recently published books and hence provide little in the way of a systematic ordering of new knowledge'.[7]

This comment holds for the article on WN in a leading periodical, the *Monthly Review* (first part, below pp. 81–4). It was written by William Enfield, a dissenting minister who was tutor in belles-lettres and rector of Warrington Academy. At once effusive in praise of Smith and vague about the principles he is said to have investigated critically, it certainly reached a wide audience since the print-run of the *Monthly Review* in 1776 was 3,500 copies.[8]

IV. *Criticism*

a) *James Anderson on Smith's Agricultural Policy*

Anderson had extensive experience from the age of fifteen as an improving farmer, first at Hermiston, near Edinburgh, and at Monkshill, Aberdeenshire. He acquired some education in chemistry and other sciences, and wrote on a variety of topics from planting and drainage to chimneys, monsoons, and slavery. Smith called him a 'very diligent, laborious Man', which he certainly was for in addition to practising scientific agriculture and journalism, he helped to raise thirteen children. He made an impact as a development economist, and *inter alia* in his *Observations on the Means of Exciting a Spirit of National Industry* (1777), he set out to answer Smith's objection to the corn bounty.

---

[7] Richard F. Teichgraeber, III, '"Less Abused than I had Reason to Expect": The Reception of WN in Britain, 1776–90', *The Historical Journal*, vol. 30, no. 2 (1987), pp. 337–64, and 'WN and Tradition: Adam Smith before Malthus', t/s paper prepared for the 1988 ASECS Annual Meeting, Knoxville, Tennessee. See, also, Salim Rashid, 'Adam Smith's Rise to Fame: A Reexamination of the Evidence', *The Eighteenth Century: Theory and Interpretation*, vol. 23, no. 1 (1982), pp. 64–85.

[8] Derek Roper, *Reviewing before the 'Edinburgh' 1788–1802* (Methuen: London, 1978), p. 262 n.7.

   Anderson's criticism of Smith has at least two significant aspects. First, he was writing in the context of debate in Scotland over proposed legislation to increase the price of imported corn (grain). Opponents of this measure, and of the Corn Laws in general, had relied on Smith's thesis that free trade would force producers to adjust to the discipline of the market and thus consumers would benefit from movement towards a natural or, as we would say, equilibrium price. Anderson's point is that while this may hold true in general for manufacturers, who have the necessary economic flexibility, those rooted in the land and involved in agricultural production would be ruined by unprotected corn prices. Accordingly, he could not support Smith's across-the-board free market approach. This challenge to Smith, of course, caused him to be identified evermore strongly with the cause of free trade.
   Second, of importance for the history of economic thought, Anderson was led into developing a theory of rent which was incorporated into David Ricardo's 'corn model'. Thus he contributed to a successful extension of the analytic side of classical economics, in which relationships in the aggregate are represented in terms of applying labour and capital to produce corn.[9]

b) *Dugald Stewart's Reading of WN*
Stewart was a member of Smith's circle in his last years, and thus had the benefit of discussing Smith's ideas with their originator. Educated at the Universities of Edinburgh and Glasgow, he succeeded Adam Ferguson in the Moral Philosophy Chair at Edinburgh in 1785. He included a course on political economy inspired by WN in his eloquent and supremely successful lectures. Some of his students, for instance, Lord Palmerston, Lord John Russell, and the 3rd Marquess of Lansdowne, achieved great distinction in the framing the Reform and free trade legislation of the nineteenth century.
   He was an obvious choice to write an 'Account' of Smith for delivery to the Royal Society of Edinburgh in 1793, then publication with Smith's posthumous *Essays on Philosophical Subjects* in 1795. Since the 'Account' was frequently republished as an introduction to WN, its 'reading' of Smith's book (below pp.

[9] O'Brien (1975), pp. 38–40.

105–20) was highly influential in stressing its free trade message, and demonstrating the methodological link with TMS. However, writing during the violent stage of the French Revolution, he wished to distance Smith, and himself as commentator, from suspicion that WN threatened revolutionary contagion.[10]

c) *Lauderdale's Refusal to Accept Smith's Conclusions*
Also personally known to Smith was James, Lord Maitland, who succeeded his father as 8th Earl of Lauderdale in 1789. Perhaps inspired by his teacher at Glasgow, John Millar, when he became an MP he was a strong supporter of the Whig leader, Charles James Fox, and when he entered the House of Lords he developed republican sympathies and endorsed the French Revolution. In mid-life, however, he became and remained a diehard Tory, opposing most measures for economic and political reform, including relief for child labour and the parliamentary Reform Bill of 1832.

Though he wrote pamphlets on currency problems and the question of debt, his significant work on economic theory is to be found in his *Inquiry into the Nature and Origin of Public Wealth* (1st ed. 1804; 2nd, minor revisions, 1819). In large part, his book fleshes out positions taken in the notes to his copy of WN, held in Tokyo Keizai University Library, Japan.[11] He denies there is a natural harmony of interests such that maximizing private wealth brings maximum public wealth. He holds that exchange rather than labour creates value. He will not entertain the idea that division of labour brings about growth. He argues parsimony and saving often have a negative impact through creating over-investment and a capital glut. He thinks that parsimony mandated by governments, as in a sinking fund to retire public debt too rapidly, restricts aggregate consumption, reduces profits and capital values, and can cause economic distress. The extracts below (pp. 121–30) illustrate his major criticisms of Smith's theory of value and insistence on parsimony. These together with a similar counter-intuitive positions taken by Thomas Malthus in his *Principles of Political Economy*, Book II

---

[10] Emma Rothschild, 'Adam Smith and Conservative Economics', *Economic History Review*, vol. 45, no. 1 (1992), pp. 74–96.

[11] *Lauderdale's Notes on Adam Smith's WN*, ed. Chuhei Sugiyama (Routledge: London/New York, 1996).

(1820, 1836), brought to light shortcomings in the classical economic theory of consumption and production in relation to savings and investment.[12]

d) *David Buchanan and 'What Is Amiss' in* WN

David Buchanan was the son of the learned Montrose printer and publisher of the same name who published a series of miniature English classics. After working in the family business, the younger Buchanan turned journalist, specializing in articles on geography, statistics, and economics, mostly the latter. He contributed lengthy pieces on finance and agricultural economics to the *Edinburgh Review*. Founded in 1802, and a great improvement over its eighteenth-century predecessors, this periodical gave much space to political economy. Buchanan became editor of the *Weekly Register* in 1808, moved to the *Caledonian Mercury* in 1810, and then was editor of the *Edinburgh Courant* from 1827 until his death in 1848.

Following the example of William Playfair, who brought out the eleventh edition of WN in 1805 with an extensive apparatus, Buchanan in 1814 produced a new, annotated edition of WN in three volumes, with a fourth volume devoted to *Observations on the Subjects Treated of in Dr Smith's Inquiry*. This venture obliged Malthus to give up his plan for editing WN.[13] In his *Observations*, Buchanan focused on 'what is amiss' with WN in relation to its theory of rent, already raised as an issue by James Anderson, and the connexion Smith saw between wages and growth (below pp. 131–40). Smith in general held to a harmony of interests theory about landowners and other classes of society, and he had treated rent, the income of landowners, as a part of 'natural' price. He had also remarked, however, that landowners loved to reap where they had not sown (WN I.vi.8), suggesting their incomes from rent were unearned. Buchanan followed up James Anderson, and was joined by Ricardo, in developing a new theory of rent which represented it as a monopoly return to the privileged class of landowners, rather than part of 'natural' price. This pointed to the emergence of social conflict and curbs on progress. Buchanan also saw that Malthus's work on subsistence

[12] O'Brien (1975), pp. 229–34.

[13] Hitoshi Hashimoto, 'Malthus & WN – His Examination Papers & Inverarity Manuscript', *Kyoto Sangyo University Economic and Business Review*, no. 15 (1988), pp. 19–95.

and population suggested something was amiss with Smith's conclusions regarding the relationship between wages and growth. His general point was that all classes were 'liable to be warped by their own partial views, and when these are at variance with the public good, they seldom hesitate which to prefer' (WN 1814 ed. i.422n).[14]

V. *Entry of WN into British Politics*
The record of parliamentary debates suggests that only gradually and after a generation was WN taken to be an authority on economic policy. Bearing this out, Kirk Willis has computed from citations in Parliament that Smith runs a 'poor ninth or tenth in comparison with other economic authorities', such as Locke, Hume, Gregory King, Charles Davenant, Sir Josiah Child, Sir William Petty, Dean Josiah Tucker, and Arthur Young. Willis, however, does list three groups who invoked Smith's name: personal friends and acquaintances; leading specialists in public finance and economic policy; and radicals and Foxite Whigs (i.e. supporters of Charles James Fox), but he fails to show how individuals in these groups had power in Government, or were close to those in power – how they formed an influential élite.[15] The idea of a power-wielding élite making use of WN is pursued here, by illustrating how a series of Prime Ministers of Britain found in Smith's book economic theory or policy advice that affected their decisions: North, Shelburne, Pitt the Younger, and Grenville.

a) *North's Budget Measures*
Lord North entered the House of Commons within a year of coming of age. He spent almost all his adult life in Parliament and was Prime Minister for twelve years, throughout the crisis of the American revolutionary war, for whose disastrous outcome, from the British point of view, he must in large part be held responsible. Yet, he was a skilful parliamentarian, and he had a

---

[14] Winch (1996), pp. 351–2.

[15] Kirk Willis, 'The Role in Parliament of the Economic Ideas of Adam Smith, 1776–1800', *History of Political Economy*, vol. 11, no. 4 (1979), pp. 505–44.

good head for finances. In addition, he made himself accessible in an affable way to all MPs.[16]

North is shown in our extracts to have canvassed WN for ideas about revenue sources in 1778, with the short-term goal of replenishing his war chest. His successors used their budgets to increase revenue, but in the context of aiming at growth to be achieved by freeing trade and encouraging competition among merchants and manufacturers.

b) *Shelburne's 'Revision of the Whole Trading System'*
North probably met Smith in London in a casual way in the course of parliamentary business. Lord Shelburne (from 1784, 1st Marquess of Lansdowne) sought Smith's acquaintance and friendship, and became an avowed convert to Smith's principles. Feeling keenly his own lack of adequate education, he had placed his brother Thomas under Smith at Glasgow from 1759 to 1761, and probably in the latter year, he travelled with Smith to London. On this journey, Smith taught him his principles of political economy (see below p. 147).

Shelburne was a leading figure in the Opposition to North during the American war. With his chief supporters he entered Rockingham's Administration in March 1782, committed to bringing peace abroad and political and administrative reform at home. Some progress was made in restoring independence to the Irish Parliament and freeing Ireland's trade. Rockingham died on 1 July, and Shelburne was asked to become Prime Minister by the King.

In an innovative move, Shelburne announced the programme of his Administration in the summer of 1782. It included principles that are to be found in WN. For example, taxes were to be simplified and made more just in distribution, as Smith's canons required (WN V.ii.b.2–6). A revival of trade would be sought not through protection, but rather a general revision of customs, as WN had prescribed, to allow freer trade.

---

[16] The accounts of North, Shelburne, Pitt the Younger, and Grenville in politics are drawn from Sir Lewis Namier and John Brooke, *The History of Parliament: The House of Commons 1754–1790*, 3 vols. (Her Majesty's Stationery Office: London, 1964), supplemented by J. Steven Watson, *The Reign of George III* (Clarendon Press: Oxford, 1960), Paul Langford, *A Polite and Commercial People: England 1727–1783* (Oxford University Press, 1989), and Peter Jupp, *Lord Grenville 1759–1834* (Clarendon Press: Oxford, 1985).

For the negotiations in Paris, Shelburne had sweeping and far-seeing plans, which fitted in with the vision of WN. This is illustrated in relevant extracts (below pp. 147–51). First, from the King's speech, emanating from Shelburne or someone under his eye, opening the third session of George III's fifteenth Parliament, 5 December 1782, we have the announcement of a 'revision of our whole trading system … with a view to its widest possible extension', on the 'liberal principles' adopted earlier in the year for improving relations with Ireland. This essentially means instituting free trade in the empire.

The second extract comes from a speech of Shelburne's on 17 February 1783, defending the boundary proposed in the peace treaty for dividing Canada and the United States. He certainly adopts Smithian arguments: that defending the monopoly of North American trade was ruinously expensive to Britain; that merchants love monopoly; and 'with more industry, with more enterprise, with more capital than any trading nation of earth, it ought to be [Britain's] constant cry, let every market be open, let us meet our rivals fairly, and we ask no more'. But Shelburne could not make clear even to his Cabinet colleagues, far less Parliament as a whole, his vision of Britain thriving through free trade expansion whatever territory was ceded to the Americans, and it was judged that he was losing the peace as North had lost the war. When votes on the peace treaty went against him in the House of Commons, he resigned on 24 February 1783, and a Fox–North Coalition formed the Government.

c) *Pitt's 'Simple and Obvious System of Capital Accumulation'*
Securing an impressive parliamentary majority in 1784, William Pitt, younger son of the great leader of the Seven Years War against France, took up at twenty-five the work begun by Shelburne in making government more efficient and financially responsible, also in rebuilding public credit. Undoubtedly, Pitt was attracted by the ideas about economic growth in WN, which he is believed to have discussed with his cousin, William Wyndham Grenville, in 1784.[17] His 'approbation' of Smith was communicated by the MP Henry Beaufoy in 1786, and Smith wrote in answer that he discerned in the 'great outlines' of Pitt's administration, 'courage, activity, probity, and public spirit'.

[17] Jupp (1985), p. 48.

Signs of Pitt's response to WN can be perceived, perhaps, in the record of the reform-minded Parliament elected in 1784, also in the commercial treaty with France of 1786, and in his assessment in 1792 of the circumstances of economic growth in Britain. In this connexion, presented below (pp. 152–60) are the following pieces.

i) The first is an extract from Henry Mackenzie's 'Review of the Parliament of 1784', attesting to Smith's influence in 'showing how much was to be gained by restoring trade to its natural freedom', and claiming that the 'justice of his doctrines had been felt in France and Britain'. Mackenzie said his 'Review' had been 'anxiously revised and corrected' by Pitt himself (Mackenzie, *Works*, 1808: vii. 181).

ii) The second comes from a speech by Pitt stating some of the arguments for and against a commercial treaty with France initiating freer trade, which resulted in higher customs revenues, and helped to achieve this Prime Minister's 'miracle' of the reconstruction of the British economy. The arguments correlate with WN IV.iii.c.12–13, paragraphs inserted in the 'Additions and Corrections' to WN published on 20 November 1784, also in the third edition published simultaneously, believed to be the time when Pitt was discussing Smith's book with Grenville.

iii) The third comes from Pitt's speech on 17 February 1792 about economic growth of Britain. It pays a notable tribute to WN for its development and explanation of the operation of the principle of the 'constant accumulation of capital'.

It is not claimed here that WN was a policy manual for Pitt, but rather that its doctrines exerted a seminal influence on this outstanding British statesman of the era. We must certainly bear in mind Pitt's independent political judgment, for he did declare on one occasion that 'though always ingenious', Smith was 'sometimes injudicious'.[18]

d) *Grenville's Conviction of the 'Soundness of Smith's Principles of Political Economy'*

William Wyndham Grenville was well connected with the great political families of England. His father, George Grenville, was Prime Minister 1763–5 when the unfortunate Stamp Act was introduced which added so much to American ire against the

---

[18] Willis (1979), p. 515.

colonial administration. The elder Pitt was his uncle and the younger one his cousin, and as noted the cousins are believed to have read WN together in 1784. The letter presented below indicates that Grenville was by far the steadier believer in Smith's principles. Pitt brought him into his Administration to serve on the Boards of Trade and Control, and he took a prominent part in seeking new commercial relations with Ireland and France, also in funding the national debt securely, all policies endorsed in WN. Serving Pitt chiefly as Foreign secretary, he became Prime Minister for a year after Pitt's death. Conservative in defending family privilege, he resisted more parliamentary and economic reform, but supported the abolition of the slave trade.

Grenville felt free to lecture Pitt in this letter of 1800 because he obviously felt his chief was slipping away from WN's truths. Perhaps his remonstrations had the greater point because three years before there had been an unsuccessful attempt in Parliament to control the cattle trade by means of a private member's bill. Smith's old friend William Pulteney sought to persuade the Commons that the 'market should be left perfectly free to find its own level', and Pitt had ended the debate by declaring, 'it appeared better to follow the ordinary course of things . . . and to leave trade open and unfettered'.[19] The cattle trade was one thing, however, and that in corn (grain) was quite another. When war conditions affected supply from abroad and bad weather at home struck at harvests, disastrously so in 1799, there was much distress among farm workers and bread rioting in the cities. Pitt as a Prime Minister could not afford to be dogmatic about abandoning a protectionist policy in the short run. In the long run, and allowing for interruptions of wartime conditions, prices did stabilize. This was the context in which Grenville was prepared to be dogmatic about freeing the corn trade, claiming, perhaps with irony, that 'so a man ought to speak on such a subject when he thinks he has arrived at almost mathematical certainty upon it'.

A similar hardening of a theoretical position and definitiveness in policy application has been ascribed in the unfolding of the history of economic thought to James Mill (*The Impolicy of a Bounty upon the Exportation of Grain*, 1804, and *Commerce Defended*, 1808) and thereafter to his 'pupil' Ricardo, who

---

[19] Willis (1979), p. 521.

claimed that his all-embracing economic prescriptions were 'in the nature of mathematical truths'.[20]

VI. *Early Reception of WN Abroad*

a) *In Germany*

Books associated with the Scottish Enlightenment were of particular interest to German intellectuals seeking to free themselves from the cultural dominance of France and develop their own national culture. In the emerging field of economics, Hume's *Political Discourses* (1752) was valued in Germany, and the *Principles of Political Economy* (1767) by Sir James Steuart-Denham, showing familiarity at firsthand with German economic conditions, was regarded as a leading work. It was in this context, where there was some awareness of a Scottish tradition of political economy distinct from Physiocracy, that the first translation of WN was into German. We introduce here three critical responses: those of the first German translator; a reviewer of the second translation, whose qualified acceptance of Smith's ideas was highly influential; and a theorist who contributed to the reformulation of economics in Germany taking WN as a starting point.

i) The first translator, Johann Friedrich Schiller, cousin of the poet Friedrich Schiller, was the London agent of the Leipzig firm of Weichmann, which had become the leading publisher in Germany under the direction of Philipp Erasmus Reich. J. F. Schiller arranged to have English books sent to Germany and recommended books for translation.[21] He set to work on WN, aided by Christian August Wichmann, soon after its publication, and published the first volume (Books I, II) by the end of 1776.

The preface to the second volume (below pp. 167–8) gives reasons for delaying in its publication until 1778. Readers are told that WN was favourably received, and when a second edition was called for, Smith had wanted to include answers to some of his critics. Schiller procrastinated over his second volume for a few months after the appearance of WN ed. 2 on 28

---

[20] Terence Hutcheson, *The Uses and Abuses of Economics: Contentious Essays on History and Method* (Routledge: London/New York, 1994), pp. 53, 59.

[21] Bernhard Fabian, *Selecta Anglicana: Buchgeschichtliche Studien zur aufnahme der Englischen Literatur in Deutschland im achtzehnten Jahrhundert* (Harrassowitz Verlag: Wiesbaden, 1994), p. 25.

February 1778. Finally, Schiller decided to get his second volume out, and compare later Smith's first and second editions, then present the improvements in a supplement. He wrote that he owed further sustained work on WN (even to an 11th or 12th reading), not only to the German public and the Göttingen critics who had already compared the first volume of his translation with the original, but also to Smith whose personal friendship he counted among the happiest circumstances of his life. This is useful evidence about early reactions to WN and its first appearance in translation in the German book trade. Schiller moved to Mainz in 1784 to become a bookseller, and after his death his publisher did bring out in 1792 a third WN volume with corrections and additions based on the English 3rd edition of 1784, Smith's last substantive revision of his text.

ii) One of the critics to whom J. F. Schiller referred was Georg Friedrich Sartorius, later Professor of Philosophy then Politics at the University of Göttingen. This institution, founded in 1737 by King George II of Britain and Elector of Hanover, had built up a notable collection of books in English. As an outgrowth of research activities in the Library, professors and former students reviewed British books extensively in the *Göttingische Anzeigen von gelehrte Sachen*. For this periodical, Sartorius reviewed the first volume of the second WN translation, noting Smith had as yet had no influence in Germany (below pp. 169–71).

The new version completely overshadowed Schiller's. It was published in 1794–6 at Breslau by Christian Garve, with the help of Ober-Postkommissar August Dörrien. Garve had taught philosophy at the University of Leipzig, where he made an extensive study of Scottish Enlightenment authors. Until Kant's philosophy preoccupied the reading public, Garve was the leading writer in his field, and it is believed this helped to make his version of WN create a deeper impression in Germany.

Sartorius had already begun to lecture on Smith's economic principles from 1792, about the time Dugald Stewart was doing so in Edinburgh. The year before, Christian Jacob Kraus, Kant's colleague at Königsberg, had also begun to introduce WN to his students, including some who became top-ranking Prussian officials involved in economic reforms in their kingdom.

Sartorius was convinced that Smith's doctrine of free trade was true in the main, and he published a clearly organized summary of WN addressed to the general public: *Handbuch der*

Staatswirthschaft (1796), revised as *Elemente des National-Reichtums* (1806). In a further book inspired by Smith: *Abhandlungen, die Elemente des National-Reichtums und die Staatswirthschaft betreffend* (1806), Sartorius responded to Lauderdale's criticisms of the theory of value in WN; Smith's preference for parsimony over prodigality as conducive to growth; and his definition of public and private wealth. He also addressed the issue that bothered John Millar in 1776, at what point does the pursuit of self-interest have to be curbed by law for society's sake. His divergence from Smith about the need for state intervention in the market to safeguard public interest was reflected in the work of most German economists.[22]

iii) At Göttingen's great rival, the University of Halle, founded in 1694, Ludwig Heinrich von Jakob had begun teaching political economy in 1799 using Sartorius's *Handbuch*, which forced him to come to terms with WN itself. With a background in Natural Law and Kant's Critical Philosophy, and the experience of translating Hume's *Treatise of Human Nature* (1790–92), he could appreciate better than Sartorius the formal characteristics of WN, and retrieve its theoretical principles of economics. Since he believed these were hidden by Smith's presentation, he determined to publish his own textbook in 1805: *Grundsätze der National-Oekonomie oder National-Wirthschaftslehre* (extract below, from the 3rd ed. 1814, pp. 172–85). Jakob sought to make clear that his concern was not state economy (*Staatswirthschaft*), but rather, taking up Smith's subject-matter, the economic processes in a civil society of interacting individuals. Since he needed a name for this, he chose *National-Oekonomie*. Summarizing briefly its literature at the end of the Introduction to his *Grundsätze*, Jakob declares that Smith is the first writer to distinguish a theory of civil welfare from a science of government aimed at identifying sources of public finance. Jakob was highly influential in fostering the development of economic analysis in terms of universal principles, and thus contributing to a movement known as *Smithianismus*, which transformed the old

---

[22] The contributions of Sartorius, Jakob, and other contemporary writers to the history of economic thought in Germany are well covered in Keith Tribe, *Governing Economy: The Reformation of German Economic Discourse 1750–1840* (Cambridge University Press, 1988); see, also, David F. Lindenfeld, *The Practical Imagination: The German Sciences of State in the Nineteenth Century* (University of Chicago Press, 1997).

Cameralist tradition of economics associated with the German
Administrative Counsellors.

b) *In France*

As has been well said by Kenneth Carpenter, the story of French
translations of WN, and acceptance of the book into the French
literature of economics, is one of passage from peripheral publication to centrality in place of publication and the minds of
inquirers into political economy.[23]

The first translator to publish the whole work, identified as
'M***' on the title-page, remains anonymous. His version
appeared in 1778–9 in four volumes at The Hague, often chosen
for the publication of French books that might run afoul of the
authorities in France. WN was such a book, and a well-known
writer on economics, known to Smith personally, the Abbé André
Morellet, hoping to be first in the field in 1776, perhaps at the
prompting of Shelburne and Turgot, had translated an extract
early that year. He tried to get permission to publish this, but the
extract was seized by the police. WN's liberal message and criticisms of French economic policy were no doubt regarded as
dangerous by the royal censors.

Morellet eventually completed his translation, but it was never
published, because another Abbé, Jean Louis Blavet, already the
translator of TMS (1774), scooped his venture with a string of
publications: a version serialized in the *Journal de l'agriculture,
du commerce, des arts et des finances*, Jan. 1779–Dec. 1780; the
parts put together as a book, Paris, 2 vols., 1781 (twenty copies
only); an edition at Yverdon, in the Swiss territory of Berne,
thus free from censorship, 6 vols., 1781; an issue at Paris, 2
vols., 1788, covered with a *permission simple*; and a new edition,
considerably revised, Paris, 4 vols., 1800–1801, the only one
bearing the translator's name, given as 'Citoyen Blavet'. Blavet
persevered with his translation though Morellet and others told
him that WN would not take hold in France, because it required
'too much application and study'. But the times were a-changing.
When his version finally came from the periphery of his country
to the capital in 1788, on the eve of the Revolution, WN's liberal
doctrines aroused the enthusiasm of a writer in the *Mercure de*

---

[23] Kenneth E. Carpenter, '*Recherches sur la nature et les causes de la richesse des
nations* et politique culturelle en France', *Économies et Societés*, OEconomia,
Histoire de la pensée économique, Série P. E. no. 24: 10 (1995), pp. 5–30.

France of 22 March: 'One does not hesitate in putting these researches in the rank of productions which bring most honour to our age and the human spirit.' In the course of the next fourteen years, WN in various guises became the most frequently published work on political economy.

French responses to WN during this period are charted below (pp. 186–224) to reveal, first, the enthusiasm of a fourth translator at the outset of the Revolution; second, growing proficiency in understanding Smith's arguments noticeable in Smith's first French 'disciple'; and, third, insightful commentary introducing what became the canonical translation.

i) The fourth translator, who issued his work at Paris amid considerable publicity (4 vols., 1790–91: based on WN ed. 4, 1786), was the poet Jean-Antoine Roucher, who was guillotined in 1794. Unlike Morellet, he had no special background for translating Smith's work, other than knowing English well enough to publish a translation of James Thomson's long poem, *The Seasons*. There were two other issues of Roucher's translation at Neuchâtel (5 vols., 1792), and then a second edition was published at Paris in 1794. The translator's Advertisement breathes the spirit of a moderate revolutionary, asserting that a French version of WN 'is needed more than ever today when the National Assembly concerns itself with the means of regenerating public wealth squandered by great waste and prodigality'.

ii) Smith's first French 'disciple', Jean-Baptiste Say, was a moderate revolutionary like Roucher, but he survived the Terror to continue a career as a journalist and editor, politician (briefly under Napoleon when he was First Consul), owner and manager of a cotton-spinning factory, and writer on political economy. After lecturing on that subject for some years, he was given the first chair in France so designated at the end of his life in 1831. Say's schooling at the behest of his Protestant family in Lyons was thorough and modern, including study of the natural sciences. On completing it, he was sent to England for two years to learn business methods and gain fluency in the language. Returning to Paris in 1787, he was employed as secretary to Etienne Clavière, also a Protestant, who owned a life insurance company.[24]

---

[24] *J.-B. Say: An Economist in Troubled Times*, writings selected and translated by R. R. Palmer (Princeton University Press, 1997).

Clavière had an English edition of WN which he lent to young Say. He read it with ease because of his facility in English, and was so impressed that he ordered a copy of the 5th edition of 1789, whose three volumes he proceeded to annotate over the next thirteen years, perhaps most heavily in the three years before the publication of the first edition of his book, *Traité d'économie politique* (2 vols., 1802).

In all his work, however innovative, such as formulating the Law of Markets sometimes given his name, WN was his bedside book, to him, perhaps, 'a vast chaos of valuable ideas, mingled pell-mell with true insights' (*Traité*, 1802, p. vi), but a constant source of inspiration. His personal copy of 1789 replete with the annotations in his own hand was bequeathed to his son, Horace, and by him to a grandson, also an economist of note, Léon Say, who gave it to the library of the Institut de France on 7 January 1888. Nine of the notes were added to the 1843 edition of Germain Garnier's translation prepared by Say's follower, Adolphe Blanqui, editor of the *Journal de Commerce*, which also included notes by Buchanan, J. R. McCulloch, Malthus, Bentham, James Mill, Ricardo, Sismondi, and Storch. All of Say's notes have been transcribed by Hitoshi Hashimoto and presented in two articles dated 1980 and 1982.[25] By permission, a selection of these notes is offered below (pp. 188–202) to illustrate the direct responses of an intelligent, innovative political economist and successful businessman to the last edition of WN authorized by Smith himself.

iii) Germain Garnier was a deputy to the National Assembly deeply involved in constitution-making in the early stage of the Revolution. Clashing with the Jacobins, he fled from the Terror to Switzerland, where in 1794 he found solace translating WN. To the translation he added a Preface with three parts: an exposition of Smith's teaching compared with that of the French Economists (Physiocrats); a method for facilitating the study of WN; and a parallel between the wealth of France and England, assessed on Smith's principles and using data from 1798–1800 such as Pitt's revenue estimates.

---

[25] Hitoshi Hashimoto, 'Notes inédites de J.-B. Say qui couvrent les marges de la *Richesse des Nations* et qui la critiquent', *Kyoto Sangyo University Economic and Business Review*, no. 7 (1980), pp. 53–81, no. 9 (1982), pp. 31–133.

Garnier published his WN version in Paris in 1802 in five volumes, enhanced by a fine engraving of Smith based on the Tassie medallion of 1787, the first to be circulated, produced by B. L. Prevost. Garnier's translation became canonical: J. B. Say deemed it 'excellent' in the first edition of his *Traité* (1803), and Napoleon, who had made notes on Roucher's translation in 1791, took a copy with him into exile on St Helena. In 1822, it reached a six-volume second edition, with the addition of notes and new observations. Re-edited extensively for publication by Adolphe Blanqui in 1843 in two volumes, in Guillaumin's *Collection des principaux économistes*, with notes by many political economists, this was the WN translation that carried Smith's ideas farthest across Europe. Germain Garnier's grandson, Joseph, Perpetual Secretary of the Société d'économie politique, then revised the text further for an edition in 1859 (3 vols.), and again for a fifth edition in 1881 (2 vols.) This last has become the WN edition of reference in French, and as such it is presented by Daniel Diatkine, in the Flammarion edition of 1991 (2 vols.) He notes that new work on WN translation into French is being done by Paulette Taïeb under the direction of J.-M. Servet.

To represent Garnier's insights into WN, we have chosen to offer two of his introductory pieces, 'Short View of the Doctrine of Smith, Compared with that of the French Economists' and his 'Method of Facilitating the Study of Dr Smith's Work' (below pp. 203–24). Their inclusion in editions of WN was recommended by the *Monthly Review* critic of Garnier's translation in 1802, and the practice continued from 1806 until 1868 at least.

c) *In Italy*
Smith's reputation in Italy was established through news of WN as the masterwork of a 'great philosopher of the first degree', and articles appeared about it from 1777 onwards in such journals as the *Diario economico di agricultura, manifatture e commercio* (Rome: 1776–7), *Giornale enciclopedico* (Vicenza), and *Novelle letterarie* (Florence: 1781). Luigi Riccomanni, in the *Diario*, was perhaps the first writer to try to come to terms with Smith, finding in WN confirmation of his own viewpoint that real wealth lay not in coin, but in improved agriculture and manufactures, also in widespread productive employment. The first Italian translation of WN came from Naples in 1790, but though the

anonymous translator wrote in his preface that it was based on the English original, it seems that the Abbé Blavet's version of 1779–80 was the source. The first Italian translation was not widely diffused in Italy, and though editions in English did circulate, for the most part Blavet's editions were the best known.

Soon after the appearance of WN, Smith's ideas were debated in the academies and societies of the enlightened, in Italy as elsewhere hotbeds of arguments over the best means for social, political, and economic reform. In 1791, the Royal Economic Society of Florence set this question: whether in legislation favouring manufactures, there should be control of commerce in raw materials, or perfect liberty of natural commerce in these materials? The submission declared the winner on 13 June 1792 and much reprinted, reaching a fourth edition in 1819, was by the economist and statistician, Francesco Mengotti. He was a Fellow of the Royal Academies of Georgofili and of Science, Letters, and Arts of Padua, who served as an administrator in the Venetian provinces under the French and Austrian governments. His piece was entitled, *Il Colbertismo*.[26]

This writer follows Smith in criticizing Colbert's approach in favouring the industry of the towns more than that of the country, and even being willing to 'depress and keep down that of the country' by forbidding grain exports (WN IV.ix.3). Mengotti like Smith holds both that economic systems will succeed best to the extent natural liberty prevails as an organizing principle, and that there is a natural order of economic development with agriculture playing the leading role, followed by manufactures, then foreign trade (cf. WN III.i.8). The extract presented below (pp. 225–34) illustrates Mengotti's grasp of Smith's teaching.

d) *In the United States of America*

Most of the founding fathers of the United States of America were acquainted with WN as a formidably-argued book on political economy. In Alexander Hamilton, however, Treasury Secretary under Washington as first President, we find the closest student and most outspoken critic of Smith's ideas in the new republic. In 1782 he had declared that belief in the self-regulation of trade

---

[26] Gabriella Gioli, *Gli Albori dello Smithianismo in Italia* (Università degli Studi di Firenze, Facoltà Economia e Commercio: Firenze, 1972).

without government intervention was a 'wild speculative paradox'. He is said to have written an extended commentary on Smith's book in 1783, though this was subsequently lost.[27] Setting himself the task of placing American public credit and the national economy on a sound basis, he prepared plans for a revenue service, a national bank, and a mint.

The climax of his efforts in this direction was the communication to Congress on 5 December 1791 of a 'Report on the Subject of Manufactures'. This relies on Smith's ideas about economic growth in general arising from the division of labour, the harmful effects of monopolies, and the benefits of competition. With respect to infant manufactures, he turns to criticism, arguing against Smith's concept of the 'invisible hand', raising the problems of unequal terms of exchange and fluctuating demand which tend to hurt an agricultural nation. Presented below (pp. 235–47) are passages revealing the following viewpoints. First, Hamilton held that perfect liberty of commerce would be an ideal state of affairs, but it is far from characterizing the general policy of nations. Second, he argued that the United States and Europe could not exchange on equal terms: to attempt this would be to confine his country to agriculture. Third, he cites Smith's argument that government encouragement of manufactures favours producers over consumers, but he contends that in the long run protection will result in lower prices as manufactures become established. His 'Report' emphasized the benefits of tariffs to protect infant industries. Basically, the new republic became and remained tariff-minded, at least as far as the powerful Northern states were concerned.

This fact was noted by the German economist Friedrich List, who had studied and admired Alexander Hamilton's views about encouraging national industry. Soon after his arrival in America, he published *Outlines of a New [American] System of Political Economy* (1827), taking up Hamilton's ideas. This book foreshadows his better known book, *Das nationale System der politischen Ökonomie* (1841), and in both he opposes Smith's 'cosmopolitical economy'. In these books, as Japanese scholars put it, 'Smith was viewed from behind'. This means Smith has been perceived from the point of view of a country which has not

---

[27] *The Continentalist*, no. V, 18 April 1782; E. G. Bourne, 'Alexander Hamilton and Adam Smith', *Quarterly Journal of Economics*, April 1894.

achieved Britain's stage of economic growth, and which specifically in the industrial sector requires protection and state capitalism. Today's debates over the successful performance of the postwar German economy and of the turmoils in the newer Asian economies, as opposed to the sluggishness in the Anglo-American economic domain, have their roots in the stand List took opposing Smith's 'obvious and simple system of natural liberty'.[28] The Anglo-American establishment of economic advisors, perhaps most prominently in the Reagan–Thatcher years, but also under the Clinton and New Labour administrations, has continued to proclaim something like the Smithian call for worldwide free trade. But one way or another the powerful message of Smith's economic vision has been relayed by criticism or advocacy from country to country.[29]

[28] Noboru Kobayashi, 'James Steuart, Adam Smith, and Friedrich List', Science Council of Japan: Third Division, Economic Series no. 40 (Tokyo, 1967); James Fallows, *Looking at the Sun: The Rise of the New East Asian Economic and Political System* (Pantheon Books: New York, 1994).

[29] *The Rise of Free Trade*, ed. Cheryl Schonhardt–Bailey, vol. 4, *Free Trade Reappraised: The New Secondary Literature* (Routledge: London/New York, 1997).

ABBREVIATIONS

BM   British Museum

Corr.   *Correspondence of Adam Smith*, ed. E. C.
            Mossner and Ian S. Ross, second revised edition
            (Oxford, 1987)

Fay   C. R. Fay, *Adam Smith and the Scotland of his
            Day* (Cambridge, 1956)

HL   *The Letters of David Hume*, ed. J. Y. T. Greig,
            2 vols. (Oxford, 1932)

NLS   National Library of Scotland

Rae   John Rae, *Life of Adam Smith* (London, 1895)

RSE   Royal Society of Edinburgh

Small   John Small, 'Biographical Sketch of Adam
            Ferguson', *Royal Society of Edinburgh
            Transactions*, vol. 23 (1864), pp. 599–665

THE AUTHORS

Letters by Members of Smith's Scottish Enlightenment Circle

LETTER FROM DAVID HUME*
1 April 1776

Address: To Adam Smith Esqr
MS., RSE ii. 56; HL ii. 311–12.
Edinburgh, 1 Apr. 1776
Euge!¹ Belle! Dear Mr Smith: I am much pleas'd with your
Performance, and the Perusal of it has taken me from a State
of great Anxiety. It was a Work of so much Expectation, by
yourself, by your Friends, and by the Public, that I trembled
for its Appearance; but am now much relieved. Not but that
the Reading of it necessarily requires so much Attention, and
the Public is disposed to give so little, that I shall still doubt
for some time of its being at first very popular:² But it has
Depth and Solidity and Acuteness, and is so much illustrated
by curious Facts, that it must at last take the public Attention.
It is probably much improved by your last Abode in London.
If you were here at my Fireside, I shoud dispute some of your
Principles. I cannot think, that the Rent of Farms makes any
part of the Price of the Produce, but that the Price is determined
altogether by the Quantity and the Demand.³ It appears to me
impossible, that the King of France can take a Seigniorage of
8 per cent upon the Coinage. No body would bring Bullion to

---

* From *Corr.*, no. 150, pp. 186–7. The notes of the original editors have been
  retained here and in the letters from Blair, Robertson, and Ferguson.

¹ Greek for 'Well done!'

² The *Gentleman's Magazine* ignored WN, and it received only a two-page
  review in the 1776 *Annual Register*. This is thought to have been written
  by Burke but this evidence is lacking.

³ At WN I.vi.8, Smith states that the rent of land constitutes a third part of
  the price of most kinds of goods, but notes later that rent enters into the
  composition of the price of commodities in a different way from wages
  and profit (I.xi.a.8). Hume's criticism foreshadows that of Ricardo:
  The Principles of Political Economy and Taxation, ch. xxiv, and
  Buchanan.

the mint:[4] It woud be all sent to Holland or England, where it might be coined and sent back to France for less than two per cent. Accordingly Neckre[5] says, that the French King takes only two per cent of Seigniorage. But these and a hundred other Points are fit only to be discussed in Conversation; which, till you tell me the contrary, I shall still flatter myself with soon. I hope it will be soon: For I am in a very bad State of Health and cannot afford a long Delay.

I fancy you are acquainted with Mr Gibbon: I like his Performance extremely and have ventured to tell him, that, had I not been personally acquainted with him, I shoud never have expected such an excellent Work from the Pen of an Englishman.[6] It is lamentable to consider how much that Nation has declined in Literature during our time. I hope he did not take amiss the national Reflection.

All your Friends here are in great Grief at present for the Death of Baron Mure,[7] which is an irreparable Loss to our Society. He was among the oldest and best Friends I had in the World.

I wrote you about six Weeks ago,[8] which I hope you received: You may certainly at present have the Subject of a Letter to me; and you have no longer any very pressing Occupation. But our Friendship does not depend on these Ceremonials.

D. H.

---

[4] In WN IV.vi.20, 'of Treaties of Commerce', Smith stated on the authority of Bazinghen's *Traité des monnoies* (1764), that the coinage in France increases the value of a mark of standard gold bullion, by the difference between 671 livres 10 deniers, and 720 livres; or by 48 livres 19 sous and 2 deniers. This works out at a seignorage of slightly over 7% (not 8% as Hume claimed). But Hume's criticism was just, for Garnier in his translation of WN (1802: v. 234) points out that the mint price referred to by Bazinghen remained in force a very short time. When it failed to bring bullion to the mint, higher prices were offered, and at the time of the publication of WN, the seignorage amounted to approximately 3%.

[5] The reference is to Jacques Necker's *Essai sur la législation et le commerce des grains* (1775), which Smith cites, e.g. at WN V.ii.k.78. See Letter 159, n. 5.

[6] The first volume of *The Decline and Fall of the Roman Empire* was published by Strahan on 20 February. Hume congratulated Gibbon on 18 March (HL ii. 309–11), in a letter which the author said 'overpaid the labour of ten years'. Gibbon's book sold better than WN (Rae 286).

[7] Baron Mure died at Caldwell on 25 March 1776, of gout in the stomach.

[8] Letter 149, dated 8 Feb. 1776.

LETTER FROM HUGH BLAIR*[1]
3 April 1776

MS., NLS 1005 fols. 21–22ᵛ; Fay 39–40 (in part).
Edinburgh, 3 Apr. [1776]
My Dear Sir
   I Cannot forbear writing to Congratulate you upon your
Book. I have just finished it; and though from what you read
to me some years ago, and from the great Attention which I
knew you had bestowed on the Subject, I expected much, yet
I Confess you have exceeded my expectations. One writer
after another on these Subjects did nothing but puzzle me. I
despaired of ever arriving at clear Ideas. You have given me
full and Compleat Satisfaction and my Faith is fixed. I do think
the Age is highly indebted to you, and I wish they may be duly
Sensible of the Obligation. You have done great Service to the
World by overturning all that interested Sophistry of Merchants, with which they had Confounded the whole Subject of
Commerce. Your work ought to be, and I am perswaded will
in some degree become, the Commercial Code of Nations. I
did not read one Chapter of it without Acquiring much Light
and instruction. I am Convinced that since Montesquieu's

---

* From *Corr.*, no. 151, pp. 187–90.

[1] Hugh Blair (1718–1800), leader among the moderates of the Edinburgh
ministers, successively incumbent of the Canongate Kirk, Lady Yester's, and
the High Kirk of St. Giles (after 1758); famous as a preacher and literary
critic; appointed Regius Professor of Rhetoric and Belles-Lettres at Edinburgh, 1762; remembered for his preface (anon.) to Macpherson's
Fragments of Ancient Poetry (1760), *Critical Dissertation on the Poems of
Ossian* (1763), *Lectures on Rhetoric and Belles-Lettres* (1783), and *Sermons*
(1778–1801). Blair followed Smith and Robert Watson in lecturing on
rhetoric at Edinburgh. He was shown by Smith 'part of a manuscript treatise
on rhetoric', presumably a version of the later LRBL, and he incorporated
ideas from it in his own lectures. Also, he is reported as making use of
Smith's ideas on jurisprudence in his sermons, but Smith did not complain,
remarking: 'He is very welcome. There is enough left' (Rae 33, quoting
indirectly Henry Mackenzie).

Esprit des Loix, Europe has not received any Publication which tends so much to Enlarge and Rectify the ideas of mankind.

Your Arrangement is excellent. One chapter paves the way for another; and your System gradually erects itself. Nothing was ever better suited than your Style is to the Subject; clear and distinct to the last degree, full without being too much so, and as tercly as the Subject could admit. Dry as some of the Subjects are, It carried me along. I read the whole with avidity; and have pleasure in thinking that I shall within some short time give it a Second and more deliberate perusal.

But have I no faults to find? There are some pages about the middle of the Second Volume where you enter into a description about the measures we ought at present to take with respect to America, giving them a representation etc.[2] which I wish had been omitted, because it is too much like a publication for the present moment. In Subsequent editions when publick Measures come to be Settled, these pages will fall to be omitted or Altered. But in the mean time they will go into the Translation of your work (unless, which perhaps might deserve your Consideration, you write to prevent it) into French, and may remain in Europe unaltered. By your two Chapters on Universities and the Church,[3] you have raised up very formidable adversaries who will do all they can to decry you. There is so much good Sense and Truth in your doctrine about Universities, and it is so fit that your doctrine should be preached to the World, that I own I would have regretted the Want of that Chapter. But in your System about the Church I cannot wholly agree with you. Independency was at no time a popular or practicable System. The little Sects you Speak of, would for many reasons, have Combined together into greater bodies, and done much Mischief to Society. You are, I think, too favourable by much to Presbytery. It Connects the Teachers too closely with the People; and gives too much aid to that Austere System you Speak of,[4] which is never favourable to the great improvements of mankind.

---

[2] WN IV.vii.c. 75–9.

[3] WN V.i.f. and g.

[4] According to Smith the 'austere system' of morality was favoured by the 'common people' and the 'liberal' or 'loose' one by the people of fashion: see WN V.i.g.10, also 34 and 37.

But the chief Improvement I wish for in the next Edition is that you take some method to point out in what parts of the Book we may find out any thing we wish to look for. You travel thro' a great Variety of Subjects. One has frequently occasion to reflect and look back. The Contents of your chapters are so short as to afford little direction. An Index (which however will be Necessary) does not fully Supply the want.⁵ My Idea is this; That at the beginning or end of the work you should give us a Syllabus of the whole; expressed in short independent Propositions, like the Syllabus's we are in use to give of our College Lectures; with references under each, to the pages in which these propositions are handled and proved. The Benefit of this would not only be that it would lead us to any part of the work we wanted to Consult, but (which would be a much higher advantage) it would Exhibit a Scientifical View of the whole System; it would impress your Principles on our Memory; it would show us how they hang upon one another, and give mutual Support and Con[s]istency to the Fabrick; it would gather together the Scatter'd Ideas which many of your Readers will form, and give them something like real improvement. I do not know whether I have made you clearly understand my Idea. But I am Convinced that something of this kind would be a great and material improvement of your work. Ten or fifteen Additional pages would comprize it all; and they would be the most Valuable pages of the whole. Pray think of this. I want exceedingly to have it done. It would give both more eclat and more usefulness to your System.

This has been a fortunate Season. Gibbon has given us an Elegant and Masterly Book. But what the Deuce had he to do with Attacking Religion?⁶ It will both Clog his Work, and it is in itself Unhistorical, and out of place. I heartily wish him to go on; but for Gods sake let him for the future keep off that ground as much as possible.

Your Friends here are well; except (how miserable it is that we must make that exception!) poor D. Hume.⁷ He is declining

---

⁵ An index was added to the 3rd edn. of WN in 1784; see Letter 242 addressed to Thomas Cadell, dated 18 Nov. of that year.

⁶ Chs. 15 and 16 of *The Decline and Fall of the Roman Empire*.

⁷ 'In spring 1775', Hume wrote, 'I was struck with a Disorder in my Bowels, which at first gave me no Alarm, but has since, as I apprehend it, become mortal and incurable' (*My Own Life*, 18 Apr. 1776).

Sadly. I dread, I dread—and I shudder at the prospect. We
have suffered so much by the loss of Friends in our Circle here
of late,[8] that such a blow as that would be utterly over-
whelming. We have often flattered our Selves with the prospect
of your Settling amongst us in a Station that would be both
Creditable and Usefull. But I own that I have less prospect of
that than I had. I Cannot believe but that they will place you
at some of the great Boards in England. They are Idiots if they
do not: Tho perhaps you might pass your days as Comfortably
at some of our Boards here.[9] Wherever you are, God bless you.
The D[uke] of B[uccleuch] your friend goes up, I hear it said,
next week. I ever am, with great respect and Esteem

My Dear Sir
Your Affectionate and Faithful
Hugh Blair

[8] Baron Mure and Lord Alemoor.

[9] Smith was made a Commissioner of Customs for Scotland in January 1778.

LETTER FROM WILLIAM ROBERTSON*
8 April 1776

Lady Dorothea Charnwood, *An Autograph Collection*
(London, 1930), 121–2.
North Murchiston, 8 Apr. 1776
My Dear Sir
   Though I am little disposed to write letters, and nobody, I
know, is less apt to expect them than you, I cannot rise from
finishing my first reading of the *Inquiry*, full of the new ideas
and knowledge which it has communicated to me, without
expressing somewhat of the cordial satisfaction which one
naturally feels upon contemplating any uncommon and meri-
torious exertion of a friend. As I knew how much time and
attention you had bestowed upon this work, I had raised my
expectations of it very high, but it has gone far beyond what
I expected. You have formed into a regular and consistent
system one of the most intricate and important parts of
political science, and if the English be capable of extending
their ideas beyond the narrow and illiberal arrangements introduced by the mercantile supporters of Revolution principles,
and countenanced by Locke and some of their favourite
writers, I should think your Book will occasion a total change
in several important articles both in police[1] and finance. All
your friends here have but one opinion concerning your work.
Perhaps, however, when we have the pleasure of seeing you,

---

* From *Corr.*, no. 153, pp. 192–3.

[1] At the opening of his Lectures on Jurisprudence, Smith said: 'The four great
objects of law are justice, police, revenue, and arms.' Later came a definition:
'Police is the second general division of jurisprudence. The name is French,
and is originally derived from the Greek πολιτεία, which properly signified
the policy of civil government, but now it only means the regulation of the
inferior parts of government, *viz.*: cleanliness, security, and cheapness or
plenty' (LJ(B), 5, 203; ed. Cannan, 3, 154).

we may venture to discuss some articles of your Creed, and to dispute others, but in the spirit of meekness, non ita certandi cupidi, quam propter amorem. None of your friends, however, will profit more by your labours and discoveries than I.[2] Many of your observations concerning the Colonies are of capital importance to me. I shall often follow you as my Guide and instructor. I am happy to find my own ideas concerning the absurdity of the limitations upon the Colony trade established much better than I could have done myself. I have now finished all my work, but what relates to the British Colonies, and in the present uncertain state into which they are thrown, I go on writing with hesitation.[3]

As your Book must necessarily become a Political or Commercial Code to all Europe, which must be often consulted both by men of Practice and Speculation, I should wish that in the 2d Edition you would give a copious index,[4] and likewise what the Book-sellers call *Side-notes*, pointing out the progress of the subject in every paragraph. This will greatly facilitate the consulting or referring to it. I hope now that your Book is off your hand, that we may have the pleasure of seeing you in Scotland. Our society here has suffered cruel loppings. Mr Hume declines so fast, that I am under the greatest sollicitude about him. If he does not recruit with the return of good weather, I shall become very apprehensive about his fate. I

[2] Evidence exists about Robertson making use of Smith's ideas at an earlier stage in his career. David Callander of Westertown who heard Smith's lectures on jurisprudence *c.* 1757–8 averred that 'Dr Robertson had borrowed the first volume of his History of Charles V. from them as every student could testify'. The reference is to the first vol. of the *History: A View of the Progress of Society in Europe from the Subversion of the Roman Empire to the Beginning of the Sixteenth Century*. According to Callander, Smith said Robertson 'was able to form a good outline but he wanted industry to fill up the plan' (EUL MSS. La. ii. 451–2, quoted in Scott 55–6).

[3] In the first eight books of his *History of America* (1777), Robertson gave 'an account of the discovery of the New World, and of the progress of the Spanish arms and Colonies there'. The last two books dealt with the history of Virginia to 1688 and of New England to 1652. In the preface he promised he would return to the British colonies when the 'civil war with Great Britain terminated', but he did not do so.

[4] See Letter 151 from Hugh Blair, dated 3 April 1776, n. 5.

need not say to you what a loss we shall all suffer. Believe me
My Dear Sir ever to be

Your affectionate and faithfull friend
William Robertson

LETTER FROM ADAM FERGUSON*
18 April 1776

Small 621; Rae 138 (in part).
Edinburgh, 18 Apr. 1776.
My Dear Sir,

  I have been for some time so busy reading you, and recommending and quoting you, to my students, that I have not had leisure to trouble you with letters. I suppose, however, that of all the opinions on which you have any curiosity, mine is among the least doubtful. You may believe, that on further acquaintance with your work my esteem is not a little increased. You are surely to reign alone on these subjects, to form the opinions, and I hope to govern at least the coming generations. I see no addition your work can receive except such little matters as may occur to yourself in subsequent editions. You are not to expect the run of a novel, nor even of a true history; but you may venture to assure your booksellers of a steady and continual sale, as long as people wish for information on these subjects.[1] You have provoked, it is true, the church, the universities, and the merchants, against all of whom I am willing to take your part; but you have likewise provoked the militia, and there I must be against you.[2] The gentlemen and peasants of this country do not need the

---

* From *Corr.*, no. 154, pp. 193–4.

[1] Hume thought WN required 'too much thought to be as popular as Mr Gibbon's [History]' (HL, ii. 314), and Strahan concurred: 'What you say of Mr Gibbon's and Dr Smith's book is exactly just. The former is the more popular work; but the sale of the latter, though not near to rapid, has been more than I could have expected from a work that requires much thought and reflection (qualities that do not much abound among modern readers) to peruse to any purpose' (12 Apr. 1776, RSE Hume MSS.) Ed. 1 of WN was exhausted in six months.

[2] In general, Smith argued a militia would be inferior to a professional standing army, since modern war made demands ill-trained soldiers could not meet, but with a prophetic eye on America he noted a militia long in the field could become the equal of a standing army: WN V.i.a. 23 and 27.

authority of philosophers to make them supine and negligent of every resource they might have in themselves, in the case of certain extremities, of which the pressure, God knows, may be at no great distance. But of this more at Philippi. You have heard from Black of our worthy friend D. Hume. If anything in such a case could be agreeable, the easy and pleasant state of his mind and spirits would be really so. I believe he will be prevailed on at least to get in motion, and to try the effect of Bath, or anything else Sir John Pringle may recommend.[3] I have said more on this subject to Mr Gibbon who, if you be found at London, will communicate to you. If not, I hope we shall soon meet here. And am, etc.

Adam Ferguson

Ferguson was a leader in the campaign to get a Scottish militia: *The Proceedings in the Case of Margaret, called Peg, only Sister of John Bull* (1761). In 1775, he enthused to Alexander Carlyle about seeing the Swiss militia under arm.

[3] This month of April, Sir John Pringle persuaded Hume to come to London for a medical examination and then to try the waters at Bath and Buxton. Hume left Edinburgh on 21 April, meeting Smith and John Home the dramatist two days later at Morpeth. Smith continued on to Kirkcaldy to see his ailing mother, while his companion returned to London with Hume.

LETTER FROM JOHN MILLAR*
April 1776

[*MS.*, NLS MS.23156, no.38]
Glasgow, Sunday [?Apr. 1776][1]
My Dear Sir
   I am afraid your criticisms on Smith's Style are not altogether
without foundation—tho' I think you rather severe.[2] There is
something in Smith's Style that appears as *original*, as there
is in the thought—and the one is exceedingly well adapted to
the other. I own however that, notwithstanding all the pains
he has taken, there are many of his positions which I have
great difficulty in admitting—and some where I am not sure
in what latitude he means to establish them. In particular his
great leading opinion, concerning the unbounded freedom of
trade, I have but a vague notion how far it is true, or how far
he means to say it ought to be carried.[3] I should be glad to
know what is your view of this point.—I admit that government should be cautious of regulating trade; because those
who direct the administration are commonly but bad judges

---

* A previously unpublished MS from the National Library of Scotland. The
 notes are added by the present editor.

[1] WN ed. 1 was published on 9 March 1776, and Hume had read it and
 wrote to Smith about it by 1 April. He left Edinburgh to travel to London
 for medical reasons on 21 April, returning in time to give a dinner for his
 friends on 4 July. It seems likely that Millar was responding to comments
 from Hume, and would write to him in the month following WN's publication.

[2] Hume concerned himself with the style of his fellow Scottish literati (see
 Ross 1995: 291), but may have been responding to Smith's avowal in WN:
 'I am always willing to run some hazard of being tedious in order to be
 sure that I am perspicuous; and after taking the utmost pains that I can to
 be perspicuous, some obscurity may still appear to remain upon a subject
 in its own nature extremely abstracted' (I.iv.18). Say complained about the
 obscurity and abstraction of Smith's treatment.

[3] The reference is to WN's 'obvious and simple system of natural liberty'
 (IV.ix.51), but Smith recognized that, in the form of freedom of trade, it
 had irresistable opposition from the 'prejudices of the publick' and the
 'private interests of many individuals' (IV.ii.43).

of those matters, so that when we talk of the wisdom of the nation we often make use of a very violent figure of speech. I also admit that regulations with respect to trade are not easily enforced, and the attempt to enforce them is generally attended with much expense. But still, nothwithstanding these two considerations, may there not be cases where a regulation of trade is proper? I imagine the point may be determined in the affirmative or negative, according as we find that the interest of every merchant and manufacturer coincides in all cases with that of the Public, or otherwise. We may suppose that mercantile people will generally understand their own interest. And if their private interest always coincides with that of the Public, they may be safely left to trade as they please. But I doubt whether there be not some branches of trade, very profitable to the merchant, which are hurtful to the public, or at least, among different branches equally profitable to the private undertaker, there be not some much more beneficial to the Public than others. If this be true, then a regulation of trade must often be highly expedient. I shall figure one case.— The question occurs whether a trade of importing wines be more beneficial than another for importing raw materials. The respective merch[an]ts in these branches will consider [only] their own profits—which may be greater [in the] wine-trade than in the other—tho' [the other] seems more beneficial to the Public. In this case therefore the good trade will be given up for a bad one—unless the Government should interfere. Perhaps the instance I have pitched upon is not so good as some others that might be mentioned.—You will observe that I am present setting aside the case of Infant manufactures, which Smith makes an exception to his general rule.[4]—I find I have got no time for the law questions you put—which I shall answer soon.[5]

Yours

J. Millar

---

[4] Smith touches on protection for infant manufactures at IV.ii.13, and discusses two major qualifications to his doctrine of free trade at IV.ii.23–36: for protection of defence industry (a justification of the act of navigation); and taxation of foreign imports when similar home products are taxed. Pownall and Hamilton (below) argue the infant manufacture case for materials produced at home.

[5] Perhaps these concerned the terms of Hume's will which he modified in codicils at this time.

Published Letter

LETTER FROM THOMAS POWNALL*[1]
25 September 1776

Richmond, 25 Sept. 1776

Sir,

When I first saw the plan and superstructure of your very ingenious and very learned Treatise on the Wealth of Nations, it gave me a compleat idea of that system, which I had long wished to see the publick in possession of. A system, that might fix some first principles in the most important of sciences, the knowledge of the human community, and its operations. That might become *principia* to the knowledge of politick operations; as Mathematicks are to Mechanicks, Astronomy, and the other Sciences.

Early in my life I had begun an analysis, of *those laws of motion* (if I may so express myself) which are the source of, and give direction to, the labour of man in the individual; which form that reciprocation of wants and intercommunion of mutual supply that becomes *the creating cause of community*; which give energy, motion, and *that organized form* to the compound labour and operations of that community, *which is government*; which give source to trade and commerce, and are the forming causes of the instrument of it, *money*; of the effect of it in operation, an *influx of riches*, and of the final effect, *wealth and power*. The fate of that life called me off

---

* *A Letter from Governor Pownall to Adam Smith, LL.D., F.R.S., being an Examination of Several Points of Doctrine, laid down in his 'Inquiry into the Nature and Causes of the Wealth of Nations'* (London, 1776). From *Correspondence of Adam Smith,* edited by E. C. Mossner and Ian S. Ross, revised edition (Oxford, 1987), Appendix A, pp. 337–76. The notes of the original editors have been retained.

[1] See *Correspondence,* Letter no. 182, Adam Smith to Governor Pownall, dated 19 Jan. 1777. This text, with the errata corrected, is reprinted from the copy in the British Library. Pownall's WN citations were from ed. 1, 1776. These have been converted to vol. and page ref. to ed. 1, and each is followed by the Glasgow Edition form. Citations and editorial notes are placed within square brackets.

from study. I have however at times (never totally losing sight of it) endeavoured to resume this investigation; but fearing that the want of exercise and habit in those intellectual exertions may have rendered me unequal to the attempt, I am extremely happy to find this executed by abilities superior to what I can pretend to, and to a point beyond that which the utmost range of my shot could have attained. Not having any personal knowledge of the author, or of the port which I now understand he bears in the learned world, I read your book without prejudice.—I saw it deserved a more close and attentive application, than the season of business would allow me to give to it; I have since in the retreat of summer studied it: you have, I find, by a truly philosophic and patient analysis, endeavoured to investigate *analitically* those principles, by which nature first moves and then conducts the operations of man in the individual, and in community: And then, next, by application of these principles to fact, experience, and the institutions of men, you have endeavoured to deduce *synthetically*, by the most precise and measured steps of demonstration, those important doctrines of practice, which your very scientifick and learned book offers to the consideration of the world of business.

Viewing your book in this light, yet seeing, as my reasoning leads me to conceive, some deviations which have misled your analysis, some aberrations from the exact line of demonstration in the deductive part; and considering any errors in a work of that authority, which the learning and knowledge that abounds in yours must always give, as the most dangerous, and the more so, as they tend to mix themselves in with the reasoning and conduct of men, not of speculation, but of business—I have taken the liberty, by stating my doubts to you in this Letter, to recommend a revision of those parts which I think exceptionable.

If these doubts should appear to you to contain any matter of real objection, I should hope those parts might be corrected, or that the bad consequences of those positions, which I conceive to be dangerous, may be obviated. When I first wrote these observations, I meant to have sent them to you, by the interposition of a common friend, in a private letter; but, as I think these subjects deserve a fair, full, and publick discussion, and as there are now in the world of business many very ingenious men, who have turned their minds to these speculations, the making this publick may perhaps excite their ingenuity, and thus become the means of eliciting truth in the most important of all sciences. It may animate even your spirit of inquiry, and lead to further researches. It is not in the spirit of controversy, which I both detest and despise, but in that of fair discussion that I address this to you.

When, in your investigation of those springs, which give motion, direction, and division to labour[2]—you state '*a propensity to barter*'; as the cause of this division: when you[3] say, 'that it is that trucking business which *originally* gives occasion to the division of labour;' I think you have stopped short in your analysis before you have arrived at the first natural cause and principle of the division of labour. You do indeed[4] doubt, 'whether this propensity be one of those *original principles* in human nature, of which no farther account can be given; or whether, as seems more probable, it be the necessary consequence of the faculties of reason and speech.' Before a man can have the propensity to barter, he must have acquired somewhat, which he does not want himself, and must feel, that there is something which he does want, that another person has in his way acquired; a man has not a propensity to acquire, especially by labour, either the thing which he does not want, or more than he wants, even of necessaries; and yet nature so works in him, he is so made, that his labour, in the ordinary course of it, furnishes him in the line in which he labours, with more than he wants; but while his labour is confined in that particular line, he is deprived of the opportunity to supply himself with some other articles equally necessary to him, as that which he is in the act of acquiring. As it is with one man, so is it with the next, with every individual, and with all. Nature has so formed us, as that the labour of each must take one special direction, in preference to, and to the exclusion of some other equally necessary line of labour, by which direction of his labour, he will be but partially and imperfectly supplied. Yet while each take a different line of labour, the channels of all are abundantly supplied.

Man's wants and desires require to be supplied through

[2] [i. 16; I.ii.1.]

[3] [i. 18; I.ii.3.]

[4] [i. 16; I.ii.2.]

many channels; his labour will more than supply him in some one or more; but through the limitation and the defined direction of his capacities he cannot actuate them all. This limitation, however, of his capacities, and the extent of his wants, necessarily creates to each man an accumulation of some articles of supply, and a defect of others, and is the original principle of his nature, which creates, by a reciprocation of wants, the necessity of an intercommunion of mutual supplies; this is the forming cause, not only of the division of labour, but the efficient cause of that community, which is the basis and origin of civil government; for, by necessarily creating an inequality of accumulation, and a consequential subordination of classes and orders of men, it puts the community under that form, and that organization of powers, which is government. It is this principle, which, operating by a reciprocation of wants in nature, as well as in man, becomes also the source to that intercommunion of supplies, which barter, trade, and general commerce, in the progress of society, give. It is not in the voluntary desires, much less in a capricious '*propensity to barter*,' that this first principle of community resides; it is not a consequence of reason and speech actuating this propensity, it is interwoven with the essence of our nature, and is there in the progress of, and as part of that nature, the creating and efficient cause of government; of government as *the true state of nature* to man, not as an artificial succedaneum to an imagined theoretic state of nature.

The pursuing of the Analysis up to this *first principle*, does not immediately, I agree with you, 'belong to the subject of your inquiries;' for the doctrine contained in the second chapter of your first book, seems only noted *en passant*, but is no where, either in the course of your Analysis, used, nor applied in the subsequent explications. But as some thirty years ago, I had made this Analysis of the [5]*Principles of Polity*; and as I have, in the practical administration of the powers of government, found, that those powers on one hand do, as from the

---

[5] [London, 1752]. A little Treatise which I wrote when I was very young, and which is very imperfect and incorrect in its manner and composition; but such in the matter and reasoning, as frequent revision and application of the principles to matters in fact, have confirmed me in the conviction of as true, although different from the common train of reasoning in those who follow Mr Locke's phrases rather than his arguments.

truest source, derive from these principles of nature, and that the liberties of mankind are most safely established on them: and as I think that great danger may arise to both, in deriving the source of community and government from passions or caprice, creating by will an artificial succedaneum to nature, I could not but in the same manner, *en passant*, make this cursory remark.

Having established and defined this first operation of man in community, that of *barter*, you proceed to consider the *natural rules* by which this is conducted; what it is which gives *value*; what it is which *measures* the relative or *comparative value*, and hence the doctrine of *price*: and by the intervention of these, the *introduction of money and coin*. As in the former doctrine, I thought you had not pursued the analysis to the real sources of nature; so here, on the contrary, I think you have stretched your doctrine beyond the garb of nature. Some of your more refined doctrines have rather subtilised ideas, as they lie in your mind, than analised those distinctions which lie in nature. On the first reading the eight first chapters of your first book, in which these matters are treated of, before I came to the use and application of your doctrines in the explication of practice and business, I began to apprehend, that some dangerous consequences in practice might be deduced from theory, instead of those sound and beneficial doctrines which derive through experience, by a true analysis of nature and her principles. I thought I saw, that many mischievous impertinent meddlings might take rise from a distinction between *a natural* and *a market price*. As I had been used to hold that only to be the measure of exchangeable value, which the world generally takes and uses as such, money formed of the precious metals: I could not but apprehend, that many extensively dangerous practices might arise from your laying aside, in your Analysis of Money, the idea of its being A DEPOSIT. I saw, that that *theory of metaphysicks*, led to a destructive *practice in physicks*; to the practice of creating a *circulation of paper*, and of calling such circulation, money; and of introducing it as such. In your doctrine, that 'labour is the measure of exchangeable value of all commodities,' connected with your mode of explanation of the wages of labour, the profit of stock, the rent of land, and the effect of the progress of improvements, I thought I saw great danger, that Theory, in the pride of rectitude, might harden its heart against the real, though relative, distresses, which the labourer and the landed gentry of a country do suffer, and are oppressed by, *during the progress* of improvement, in consequence of a *continuing influx of riches*; and might therefore depreciate, or even endeavour to obstruct, all those current remedies which give comfort and relief to these distresses, and alleviate even those which cannot be remedied.

Although[6] the demand for those who live by wages must naturally increase with the increase of national wealth; and consequently the price of wages rise in proportion to the rise of every thing else; so as that the labourer will in the end partake of the general riches and happiness of the publick. Although[7] the rise in the price of all produce is in the end no calamity, but the *forerunner* of every publick advantage: Yet as those prices do *forerun*, and must, during the progress of improvement, *always forerun*; wages and rent must always continue *at an under-value* in the comparison. They will indeed rise also, but as this foreruns, they can only follow, *sed non passibus œquis*. The labourer, and he who lives on rent, therefore, must always, though improving, be unable to improve so fast as to emerge from a continued distress: if this distinction, that a flowing encrease of wealth, although it is the forerunner of every advantage to the publick in general, and *in the end* to every individual, yet is the continuing cause to the continued distress of the labourer, and of him who lives by rent, is not carefully attended to. If the state of the circumstances of distress, which continues to oppress those classes of the community, are not constantly adverted to with feeling, and with exertions of precaution and benevolence, we shall, in the triumph of our general prosperity, be the constant oppressors of those who have the best title to share in this prosperity.

Under these ideas and apprehensions I did very carefully and repeatedly, before I proceeded to the applied doctrines contained in the latter book, revise the analytic part of the former. When I came to the doctrines applied to practice, and the businesses of the world, I found that my cautions had not been unnecessary, and that my apprehensions, that some such consequences might be drawn from it, were grounded: I found

[6] [i. 85; I.viii.21.]

[7] [i. 286; I.xi.l.1 2]

also what I did not from the principles expect (nor as yet do I see how they derive from them, as any part of the chain of reasoning) that in the course of the doctrines you hold, you are led to disapprove the law giving a bounty on corn exported; and also to think, that the monopoly, which we claim in the American trade,[8] 'like all other mean and malignant expedients of the mercantile system,' without in the least increasing, doth on the contrary diminish the industry of the country, in whose favour it is established; and doth, although it may have the seducing aspect of a *relative advantage*,[9] subject the nation, its trade and commerce, to an absolute disadvantage. I hope you will not think, that I misunderstand, or mean to mis-state, your position. You allow, and very fully explain the great advantages of the colony trade, but think that the monopoly is the reason why, great as it is, we do not derive so great advantages from it to the nation and to the landed interest, and to the community in general, as we might have done, had it not been crampt and perverted by the monopoly.

In the many occasions which I have had to view this monopoly, I own, although I have seen some errors in the extension of the *measure*, further than is expedient or necessary, yet I do not see the malignancy of the principle of a monopoly; nor while I have lived amidst the daily proofs of the *relative advantage* which it gives to the mother country, by its colonies, over all other foreign nations, I have not been able to discover, nor have your arguments, although so methodically and so clearly drawn out, been able to explain to me, that absolute disadvantage which you think it subjects us to.

Although I agree entirely with you, having also previously read the same opinion in Mr Necker's Treatise, *sur la Legislation & le Commerce des Graines*, that the bounty which our law gives to the exportation of corn, has not been the sole cause which hath rendered corn cheaper than otherwise it would have been; but, on the contrary, hath, in each direct instance, given it some small advance in the general scale of prices: Yet, considering that so far as it does this, and gives relief to the relative oppression which the landed interest must continue to feel under *a continued influx of riches*, and an

[8] [ii. 217; IV. vii.c.56]
[9] [ii. 201; IV. vii.c.26]

advancing rise in the prices of every thing else; I think it one of the wisest measures for a country like England that could be devised.

I think with you, that many of our laws and regulations of trade are practical errors, and mischievous. I think that, while they seem to be founded on our navigation act, they mistake the spirit of it, and no less mistake the real interest of the nation: yet I cannot but hold these to be errors only, as they deviate from the true principle of the act of navigation, which is a different thing from the acts of trade.

Having prefaced thus much as to the several doctrines on which I have conceived some doubts, I will now, following the order of your work, state those doubts. When I found you discarding *metallic money*, that intervening commodity which having, by common consent, acquired a value of its own, hath been hitherto esteemed a common known measure of the value of all other things, from being any longer such common measure, and by a refinement of theory, endeavouring to estab-lish in its place 'an abstract notion,' *that labour was the common measure of all value*; I did not only doubt the truth of the position, but, looking to the uses that might be made of the doctrine, hesitated on the principle. If labour be the only real and ultimate measure of value, money is but the instru-ment, like the counters on the checkquer, which keeps the account; if this be all the use of money, then *circulation*, or even *an account opened with a banker* (according to a practice in Scotland, as described by you) is to all uses and ends as good as money. If it is not necessary, that the common measure should have some known permanent value in itself, so as to be a deposit of that absent value which it represents, as well as measures, so as to convey to all who possess it an absolute power of purchase, then indeed the circulating instrument, the machine that circulates, whether it be a paper or a leather one, or even an account, without any *deposit*, is equal to all the uses and end of money, is that which we may safely receive for the future. As I have been mixed in the business of a country, where the evils of this doctrine and practice have been severely felt, and where it was my duty to watch, that nothing was imposed upon the publick as money, but what was either in itself a deposit, or was established on a fund equal to a deposit, and what had *all* the uses of a permanent known measure in all cases of circulation; I could not but read this leading doctrine of your's with great caution and doubt. I must doubt, whether it be labour simply which creates and becomes the measure of value, when I find other component parts mixed in the most simple idea of value: I cannot conceive, that equal quantities of labour are absolutely of equal value, when I find the value of labour both in use and in exchange varying in all proportions, amidst the correlative values of these components' parts; I cannot suppose labour to be the ultimate measure, when I find labour itself measured by something more remote.—You say very properly in the major of your syllogism, that when the division of labour has once thoroughly taken place, it is but a very small part of the necessaries and conveniences of life, with which a man's own labour can supply him. But when we come to the minor proposition of it, we must consider also the objects on which labour is employed; for it is not simply the *labour*, but the *labour mixed with these objects*, that is exchanged; it is *the composite article, the laboured article*: Some part of the exchangeable value is derived from the object itself; and in this composite value, which is the thing actually exchanged, the labour bears very different proportions of value, according to the different nature of the object on which it is employed. Labour, employed in *collecting* the *spontaneous produce* of the earth, is very different in the composite exchangeable value of the fruit collected, from that which is employed on raising and collecting the *cultured fruits* of the earth. Labour, employed on a rich, cleared, subdued and fruitful, or on a poor and unkindly soil, or on a wild uncleared waste, has a very different value in the composite object produced in the one, from what it bears in the composite value of the other. As the object then makes part of the composite value, we must consider, in the exchangeable value, the object also, as a component part. Whose then is the object? Who has acquired, and does possess, the object or objects on which the labour may be employed? Let us take up this consideration under these first scenes of man, which are usually called a state of nature, somewhat advanced in the division of labour and community. Previous to the employing of labour, there must be some acquisition of objects whereon to employ this labour; a strong and selfish man, who will not labour, sits, we will suppose, idly under a tree, loaded with the spontaneous fruits of nature; an industrious, but weaker man, wants some part of those to supply his necessity, the idler will not let him collect the fruit, unless that other collects also enough for both. Or if, still more churlish and more selfish, he will not let him who is willing, by his labour, to collect a sufficiency for *his* use, unless the labourer collects also more than sufficient for the idler's present use, sufficient for his future use also. Does the labourer here command or exchange, by his labour, any part of the labour of the idler? Certainly not. In this state a *division of the objects* on which labour must be employed, and with which it must be mixed, as well as a division of labour hath taken place; and therefore the labourer must be able, by his labour, to command in exchange a certain portion of these objects which another hath, as well as a certain part of that other's labour. It will not relieve this doubt by saying, as Mr Locke (treating of right) says, that there can be no *right of possession*, but by a man's mixing his labour with any object; because we are here not considering the matter of right, but the matter of fact: nor will it answer to say, that the acquisition itself is an act of labour, because I have here stated the case of a churlish sluggard idler, strong enough to maintain himself in idleness, by commanding not only the actual labourer, but certain *greater or lesser quantity of that labour*, according as his selfish churlish temper leads him to press upon the necessity of the weaker. Suppose the same idler, in this division of the objects of labour, to have got possession of a fishing lake, or a beaver-pond, or in a sandy desart of a spring; or of a spot of fruitful ground, amidst a barren country; or of a ford, or particular position, which commands a fine hunting-ground, so as to exclude the labourer from the objects whereon his labour must be employed, in order to form that laboured article which is to supply his wants. You see, that the means of commanding the *objects of labour, as well the labour* of another, make part of the supply whereby a man must live, whereby he may be said to be rich or poor. Even you yourself (I hope you will excuse the expression under which I quote it) say, with rather some degree of confusion in terms, 'that every thing is really *worth* to the man who has *acquired it*, and who wants to dispose of it, or exchange it for something else; the toil and trouble which it can save to himself, and which it can impose upon other people.' This expresses the conclusion which I draw from the case I have stated, and not your position, that labour is the *measure*, and that it is labour which is exchangeable for *value*: it is, on the contrary, the mixture of the labour, and the objects laboured upon, which produces the composite value. The labour must remain unproductive, unless it hath some object whereon to exert itself, and the object is of no use unless laboured upon. The exchange therefore is made by A keeping a part of his labour mixed with a part of the object, and B using a part of his objects rendered useful by the labour of A mixed with them. The consequence therefore in your syllogism cannot fairly conclude, that the value of any commodity to the person who possesses it, and who means not to use or to consume it himself, but to exchange it for other commodities, *is equal to the quantity of labour*, which it enables him to purchase or command. On the contrary, it is a composite value of the object and labour mixed, and takes part of its value from each of the component parts. It is not therefore labour (which is but one of the component parts of the exchangeable commodity) which gives the exchangeable value, but *the labour and the object mixed*, the compounded laboured article, in which the labour bears all possible proportions to the correlative value of the two component parts, according as the possessor of the object, or the exertor of the labour, or the common general course of the estimation of mankind shall settle it. Real value, if any such thing there be different from market value, is *the mixed composite laboured article*, not labour simply.

You have, Sir, made a very proper distinction of *value in use*, and *value in exchange*. That labour which varies in its productive power, according as it is differently applied, and according to the object it is employed upon, must certainly vary in its use, and equal quantities of it must be in such different circumstances of very unequal value to the labourer. *Labour in vain, lost labour—Labour which makes itself work*, (phrases which, to a proverb, express some species of labour,) *cannot be* said to be *of any use* to the labourer. He who would shave a block with razor, will labour in vain. He who sows on a rock, or on a barren sand, or in a drowned morass, will lose his labour. He who sheers his hogs, will have great cry and little wool, and only make himself work: but labour will still vary more in its *exchangeable value*; equal quantities of labour will receive very variable degrees of estimation and value. In the first operation of barter of labour (the value of the objects being, for the sake of argument, laid aside) we will suppose A to say to B, you shall have as much of the surplus of my labour on the article M, as you will exchange for the surplus of your labour on the article Δ. By this, A 'means to save as much of his toil and trouble to himself, and to impose as much upon B, as he can.' B means the same. What then is to be the real standard of measure? Not labour itself. What is to give the respective estimation in which each holds his labour? Each alternatively will be disposed to estimate his own most valuable, and to each 'the labour of the other will sometimes appear to be of greater and sometimes of smaller value[10].' This value cannot be fixed by and in the nature of the labour; it will depend upon the nature of the feelings and the activity of the persons estimating it. A and B having, by equal quantities of labour, produced equal quantities of two of the most necessary articles of supply, whose values, in the general scale of things, vary the least; each having a surplus in the article which his labour has produced, and each likewise having an equal want of what the other has produced. This *quantity* of labour, although stated as *equal*, will have very different *exchangeable values* in the hands of the one or the other, as A or B are *by nature* formed to make a good bargain in the common adjustment of the barter. He who has not an impatience in his desire on one hand, or a soon-alarmed fear on the other of losing his market; who has a certain firmness, perseverance and coldness in barter; who has a certain *natural* self-estimation, will take the lead in setting the price upon the meek and poor in spirit; upon the impatient and timid bargainer. The higher or lower value of these equal quantities of labour, will follow the one or the other spirit. The value is not equal, and is not fixed in, nor depends upon, the equal quantity of the labour, it is unequal and differs, and is fixed by, and derives from, the different *natures of the persons* bargaining. The exchangeable value of equal quantities of labour, stated equal in all circumstances, is not only not equal in this first instance, between that of A and B, but may, in other comparisons, vary both in A and in B individually. The exchangeable value of B, although inferior in barter with A, may acquire an ascendant value, and be superior in barter with C. This difference and this variation will run through every degree in the utmost extent of the markets: nay, the same person will, in different habits, relations

[10] [i. 39; I.v.8, also, see l.iv.13].

and circumstances of life, estimate that labour (which shall be stated to be absolutely equal) as of very different value; he will, on different occasions, estimate his 'ease, liberty, and desire of happiness' differently. Equal quantities of labour, equal, I mean absolutely, and in every respect, will acquire and derive very different values both in use, and in exchange both in respect of the person by whom such is exerted, as well as in respect of the person who barters for it, from the objects with which it is mixed. Respecting the person by whom it is exerted, if a day's labour always produces a day's subsistance, the value in use is always the same; if it doth not, the value in use must vary. In respect of exchangeable value, labour will sometimes give value to things which, in themselves, had little or no value: in others, it will derive value from the things with which it is mixed; it will itself have an exchangeable value from its compounded value, that is, from the proportion of value which it bears in the composite laboured article.

What is thus varying in a relative value, must require some correlative, which, while this measures other things, in return will measure it; that which is itself measured by something more remote, cannot be the final measure or standard. It cannot[11] therefore be 'alone the ultimate and real standard by which the value of all commodities can, at all times and places, be estimated and compared: it is not their *real price*.' I must therefore conclude, in a proposition which I quote from yourself, where I wish you had let the business[12] rest; 'That there can be no accurate measure, but that exchangeable value must be settled by the higgling and bargaining of the market, according to that sort of rough equality, which, though not exact, is sufficient for the carrying on the business of life.'

You confess, that this proposition of your's: '*That labour is the measure of the value, and the real price of all commodities,*' is '*an abstract notion.*' As such I should not have taken any notice of it; but you endeavour to establish it as a leading principle, whereby I think a *practical one*, which mankind hath universally and generally acted upon, may be in dangerous speculations distinguished away. If the common forensick idea, that money which, in the common acceptation of it, hath

[11] [i. 39; I.v.7.]

[12] [i. 37; I.v.4.]

actually been used to measure, doth in strict truth measure as 'a common intervening commodity', both labour and all other things, and their relations, is to be considered as a mere practical notion, and we are in reasoning to look to some abstract notion, as the real standard. What do we, but pervert our reasoning from distinct notions in practice, to 'abstract notions,' and subleties in theory: as I apprehend that these theories have been, and fear they may and will again be used, if admitted into the reasoning of the world, to very mischievous and destructive schemes; as I think that they remove old bounds, and erase old and solid foundations, and may be applied to the building paper castles in the air; as they lead to speculations, which swerve from the idea of *pledge and deposit in money matters*, and tend to create *an imaginary phantom of circulation*, erected on the foundation of credit and opinion of trust only, I have taken the liberty of stating my doubts upon it.

While I have thus doubted, whether labour is the ultimate measure and standard of the exchangeable value of all commodities, I should be willing with you to admit, that corn will not universally answer as such a measure had not you yourself,[13] in another part of your book seemed to think, that 'the nature of things has stamped upon corn, *a real* value, which no human institution can alter; and that *corn* is that regulating commodity, by which the real value of all other commodities must *be finally measured* and determined.' Gold and silver, you say, varying as it doth in its own value, can never be an accurate measure of the value of other things. There is then, according to what I have always been used to think, and what from your Treatise I find myself confirmed in, no one commodity that will measure all others, but that all are to one another in their reciprocal value *alternate measures*; and that *gold and silver* is only the common and most general, almost the universal, measure, so found to be, and so used by the general experience and consent of mankind, as *that intervening commodity* which will most uniformly become *a common measure*, at the same that it doth (as being a deposit of value, which all mankind have agreed to receive) *give universal power of purchase*.

[13] [ii. 101; IV.v.a.23.]

As I think that there is no real measure of value, so I think there is no fixed natural rate of value, or real price distinct from the market price. I think, that the doctrine which states the two definitions as an actual existing truth, and as a practical distinction formed for business, not true on one hand, but on the other a dangerous proposition.

You say,[14] 'That there is in every society or neighbourhood *an ordinary or average rate* both of wages and profit, in every different employment of labour and stock;' these average rates you call 'the *natural price*, at the time and place in which they commonly prevail.'

The actual price at which any commodity is *commonly sold*, is called its market price.

I clearly see the distinction in definition; but I do not learn how the ordinary average rates, or price paid for labour, or for the use of land or stock, or for any commodity in the neighbourhood, where it comes from the first hand, in the first act of bargain and sale, is any more natural than the price which it finds and bears in any other succeeding act of bargain and sale, at the time and place wherever it is sold. What is it, in the first instance, which settles these average rates, which you call natural, but the competition of the effectual demand, compared with the supply, and founded on some proportion whereby the price paid for labour, stock or land, will enable the seller to purchase an equivalent quantity of those necessaries and conveniences which his state of life requires? If, from this first operation of bargain and sale, the commodity, by means of carriage, and the collection, storage, and distribution of the middle man, goes to a succeeding and more complicated value with these adventitious articles of expence added to it: Is not the price which is here, also the price at which it here commonly sells, and which is in like manner precisely determined equally, that ordinary average rate and *natural price* as the former? Or rather, is not the price in the first operation of bargain and sale *equally a market price* as the latter, settled by that higgling and barter which doth and must regulate it in all times and in all cases? The refinement which, using different expressions, as in one case calling it 'the ordinary average rate,' and in the other, 'that price at which it

[14] [i. 66; I.vii.1.]

is commonly sold,' is a distinction of words without scarce a difference in idea, certainly none in fact and truth. If there be any such thing as a natural price, both are natural; if not, which I rather think both are the artificial market price, such as the act of higgling and barter can settle on the reciprocation of wants and mutual supply. What else is it in *nature* which settles the ordinary average rates, which you call the natural price? This price '*naturally* increases,' as adventitious circumstances mix with the commodity brought to sale. The encreased market price encreases by the adventitious circumstances of labour in carriage, of risque, storage, and the middle-man's profit. This encrease is *naturally* regulated by the ordinary and average rates of these added circumstances in their time and place; and on these the competition, compared with the supply, doth as naturally in one case as in the other create the market price; which may be called, if you choose to call the former so, a natural price; but both are, in fact, equally in their time and place the market price. When therefore you say,[15] 'that the natural price is the *central price*, to which the prices of all commodities are perpetually gravitating'; I must own that I receive the metaphor of the proposition with great apprehensions of the uses in practice, which the doctrine may lead to. If any one, who has got a lead in business, should adopt your distinction of *natural and market price*; and, following the delusion of your metaphor, should think, that, as in nature, all market prices do perpetually gravitate to the natural *central price*, so the circuiting motion of all market prices should be made to take and keep this direction round their center; (perfectly satisfying himself, that as he ought not, so he does not, meddle with the *natural prices* of things:) he may, through a confusion and reverse of all order, so perplex the supply of the community, as totally to ruin those who are concerned in it, and intirely to obstruct it. He may render trade almost impracticable, and annihilate commerce. That the succeeding prices of the secondary operations of bargain and sale are regulated by the same rules and laws of barter as the first; and that the outset of the first will give direction of motion, as well as motion to all succeeding operations, regulated by the same laws of this motion, is certainly true; and that it will (while in

[15] [i. 70; I.vii.15.]

the ordinary course of things) keep this motion equable by the respective average rates in their time and place; that the violence and artifices of man will ever and anon try to warp and misrate it, is certainly true; and a truth well worthy of constant attention—not with a view to interfere and intermeddle with the *market prices*, under any theory of regulating them by some supposed natural *central price*, but to obstruct and oppose all interference and meddling whatsoever; and upon this truth to maintain in the market an universal freedom, choice and liberty.

Although, as I have stated my opinion above, I think, that the general course of all prices, or that correlative value between commodities must depend upon, and derive from the reciprocal higgling of bargain and sale, and are not measured by labour: Yet so far as they depend upon, or are mixed with labour, there is some natural scale below which they cannot go; which scale takes its level from the quantity of subsistence which such labour will procure. The plain and homespun wisdom of our ancestors, therefore, did not attempt to measure the prices of things by any *abstract notion of labour being that measure*, but they measured labour itself[16] 'by the plenty or dearth of provisions,' or the subsistance, according to the laboured productive effects of nature from time to time. Although therefore I agree with you,[17] 'that the *common wages* of labour *depends* every where *upon the contract* made between two parties, whose interests are by no means the same;' yet in that,[18] 'a man must always live by his work, and that his wages must at least maintain him.' There is a scale of rate below which the price of labour cannot by any contract or bargain be lowered.

That the prices of wages do continually increase with the advancing prosperity of any community, and that they are the highest in those communities, who are advancing with the most rapid velocity, is a truth, a comfortable and an encouraging truth: yet as prices of wages follow but with slow and loaded steps, in proportion to the quick motions of the rise of the prices of all other things, if some care and attention is not given to aid the motion of the rise of wages, in some measure

---

[16] Vide the several statutes of labourers.

[17] [i. 81; I.viii.11.]

[18] [i. 83; I.viii.15.]

to keep it above the lowest scale, which it can subsist by; we may, in the triumph of prosperity, and in the pride of rectitude, see the poor labourer, of the lower classes, under a continued state of helpless oppression, amidst the prosperity of the community in general; but of the nature, and of the manner of regulating these, I shall have occasion to treat in another place, and on another occasion.

As value or price is not any fixed *natural* thing, but is merely the *actual* correlative proportion of exchange amongst all commodities; *so that intervening commodity which* does in fact most commonly, or on common result, and by common consent, *express this correlative proportion*, is *the common measure* of this value: It is not an abstract notion of *labour*, 'but *money*[19] (as 'Mr Hume says) which is *by agreement* the common measure.' 'This common measure does not barely express the proportion of value between commodities when brought together in the act of exchange, but is that something, that most common intervening commodity, which mankind hath generally and universally agreed shall not only express this act of exchange, and the relation of reciprocal value under which it is made, but which is in fact an universal equivalent deposit of value, which gives, in all places and at all times, with all persons, a power of purchase, and is in fact and truth that intervening commodity, which, as a common measure, exchanges without actually bringing the things exchanged into barter. The thing which we thus express in abstract reasoning by the word *money*, is *by use* universal, by general and common consent, *the precious metals applied as this practical common measure*, the uses which it hath, and the purposes to which it is applied amongst the acts and things of the community, gives it *a value in its exchangeable operations*. This idea of money is fixed by *old bounds* of common consent and universal practice; and as I am not willing *to remove old bounds*, fixed in a real foundation, to follow an abstract notion[20] 'on Dædalian wings through the air;' I will here next take the liberty to state the reasons which make me hesitate

---

[19] *Essay on Money*, p. 321. [*Essays*, 1764, 1767 edns. Hume wrote 'money is nothing but the representation of labour and commodities, and serves only as a method of rating or estimating them', *Phil. Wks.* (1875), iii. 312, 'Of Money'.]

[20] [i. 389; II.ii.86.]

to follow you in those regions of theory. Although you tell me, that it is not the metallic money which is exchanged, it is the *money's worth*; that money may be the *actual* measure of this exchange, but that it is the labour which the money represents and sells and purchases, which is the *real measure*. Yet when my ideas lead me in the very line of your analysis to conceive, that labour is not, no more than any other commodity, the ultimate measure, but is the thing measured; that when measured against subsistance, it is actually measured by that subsistance. When I consider, that although it is the money's worth which is exchanged, yet it is the money which measures and exchanges it. I cannot but think it nearest even to abstract truth, and safest in practice, to abide by *the old bounds* of that idea which mankind hath generally and universally fixed, *that money* IS THE COMMON MEASURE, to be which adequately, and in all its *uses*, it must be a DEPOSIT also.

In your account[21] of the origin and use of money, you very properly state, that 'every prudent man in every period of society (after the first establishment of the division of labour) must naturally have endeavoured to manage his affairs in such manner, as to have at all times by him, besides the peculiar produce of his own industry, a certain quantity of some one commodity or other, such as he imagined few people would be likely to refuse in exchange for the produce of their industry.' If in the doing this, all, led by any thing in the nature of any commodity itself, or by some coincidence of reasoning and consent, should agree upon any one commodity in general, which would be thus generally and universally received in exchange, *that*, in the most refined strictness of abstract reasoning, as well as in decisive fact, would become that[22] *intervening commodity* which would measure the exchangeable value, and be the real instrument of actual exchange in the market. It would not only be that *measure*, but it would become a *real* as well as *actual deposit of value*, and would convey to whomsoever possessed it, a general, universal and effective power of purchase.

When next then I inquire, what this intervening commodity

[21] [i. 28; I.iv.2.]
[22] [i. 37; I.v.6.]

is—I find,[23] that metallic money, or rather, 'silver', is that which, by the general consent of mankind, has become that deposit, which is the common measure; this is a general effect of some general cause. The experience of its degree of scarceness, compared with its common introduction amidst men, together with the facility of its being known by its visible and palpable properties, hath given this effect. Its degree of scarceness hath given it a value proportioned to the making it A DEPOSIT; and the certain quantity in which this is mixed with the possessions and transactions of men, together with the facility of its being known, had made it A COMMON MEASURE amongst those things. There are perhaps other things which might be better applied to commerce as *a common measure*, and there are perhaps other things which might better answer *as a deposit*; but there is nothing, except [the precious metals, or rather] silver, known and acknowledged by the general experience of mankind, which is *a deposit and a common measure*. Paper, leather, or parchment, may, by the sanction of government, become a common measure, to an extent beyond what silver could reach; yet all the sanction and power of government never will make it an *adequate* deposit. Diamonds, pearls, or other jewels, may, in many cases, be considered as a more apt and suitable deposit, and may be applied as such to an extent to which silver will not reach: yet their scarcity tends to throw them into a monopoly; they cannot be subdivided nor amassed into one concrete; and the knowledge of them is more calculated for a mystery, or trade, than for the forensic uses of man in common, and they will never therefore become a common measure.

'The quantity of this deposit, and the general application of it to several different commodities, in different places and circumstances, creates a correlative proportion between it and other objects, with which it stands compared, and from this proportion forms *its own scale*; this scale derives from the effect of natural operations, and not from artificial imposition. If therefore silver was never used but by the merchant, as the general measure of his commerce and exchange, *coin* would be (as it is in such case) of no use; it would be considered as bullion only. Although bullion is thus sufficient for the measure

---

[23] Vide *Administration of the Colonies* [ed. 5, 1774], vol. i, ch. v.

of general commerce, yet for the daily uses of the market something more is wanted in detail; something is wanted to mark to common judgment its proportion, and to give the scale: government therefore here interposes, and by forming it into COIN gives the scale, and makes it become to forensic use AN INSTRUMENT in detail, as well as it is in bullion A MEASURE in general.'

It is here, Sir, that I think your Analysis, subtilised by too high refinement, deviates from the path in which the nature of things would have led you. Quitting the idea of money being A COMMON MEASURE, and totally leaving out all idea of its being a DEPOSIT, your Analysis leads you to conceive no other idea of it but as CIRCULATION, or, as you distinctly express it, a CIRCULATING MACHINE; and of course, according to these principles, considering it as an instrument, you state it in your account *amongst those instruments which form the fixed capital of the community.* The result of which in fair reasoning is, that as these machines cost an expence (which must be either drawn from the circulating capital of the community, or from its revenue by savings) both to erect them and to maintain them; so every saving which can be made in the erection or maintenance of such a machine, will be advantageous to the circulating capital, the source of materials and wages, and the spring of industry. In this line of deduction you come to the result in practice, and say,[24] that 'the substitution of paper, in the room of gold and silver money, replaces *a very expensive instrument* of commerce with one much less costly, and *some-times* equally convenient; *circulation* comes to be carried on by *a new wheel*, which it costs less both to erect and to maintain than *the old one*.'

As my reasoning hath many years ago impressed it strongly on my mind, that money is a COMMON MEASURE and must be a DEPOSIT, and *in coin an instrument* of the market; and as many years experience in a country of paper hath convinced me, that if any instrument of the exchange of commodities, other than that which, while it measures the correlative values in circulation, is founded on a DEPOSIT, equivalent at all times to the conversion of it into money, shall be introduced, it will be a source of fraud, which, leading by an unnatural influx of

[24] [i. 350; II.ii.26.]

riches to luxury without bounds, and to enterprize without
foundation, will derange all industry, and instead of substantial
wealth end by bankruptcies in distress and poverty.

So far as *circulation* can carry on the exchanges of commodities in the community, so far paper bills of credit, or even
accounts opened, may do in the room of the metallic money;
but without a deposit, which is adequate and equivalent in all
times and places, and with all persons, to this conversion of
it, I have no sure foundation, that I do possess, in all times
and places, and with all persons, *the power of purchasing or
of accumulating as I like*. Although I have all the trust and
confidence in the world in the credit of this circulating machine
of paper, yet it has not the universal extent in, nor the operation of all the uses of money, although therefore it may be
'*sometimes equally convenient*;' it is not that intervening commodity which hath *all the uses of money*,[25] universally and
adequately. Circulation, even where no paper money or credit
exists, must always much exceed in its total of exchange the
sum total of the money deposit, how much that is, experience
in the fact can alone determine: paper may certainly, without
any danger, encrease this power of circulation, if it does not
exceed what the deposit will answer while it is in circulation,
and is created *on such a fund, as will finally convert it into
money*. So far as paper, by the extent of the uses, and the
absolute security and exchangeable conversion of it into metallic money, *can be and is made a deposit*, so far it may safely
measure as money, and become a convenient instrument; but
in that this security is always more or less uncertain; in that it
depends on the prudence and probity of the money makers,
it is always liable to exception, abuse and failure. So far forth
as it is defective in its fund, the creation and use of it must be
always hazardous, and hath been generally ruinous; and
however distant and remote the end may be, *must* be a fraud
in the end. In a world of enterprize, where *trust and credit* is
substituted *in the stead of fund* and prompt change, paper
money loses the very essence of a deposit; unless I have a
deposit, which gives me an absolute actual power of purchasing, in all times and places, in all events, to all intents and
uses; or that which is absolutely ready and immediate change

[25] [i. 351; II.ii.29.]

for such deposit. The bill which I have, may or may not, here or there, now and then, *sometimes* not always, maintain in me *the power of purchasing*, or of real hoarding or banking as I like. General, universal, permanent consent of all mankind, has, from *actual experience* of its uses, given to *metallic money* a permanent and absolute value: partial, local, temporary agreement, founded *in opinion of trust and credit*, can give to paper but a partial, local, temporary ideal value, which never will be a real and universal deposit; it may become to certain local temporary purposes a *circulating machine*, but money is something more: this paper is not that intervening commodity, which all mankind hath universally agreed to be *that common measure which is a deposit*; such alone is money in the strict as well as common acceptation of the word and idea.

So far as paper money can be so contrived as to have, while it is in circulation, *all the uses* of money; or is so founded, that it can in all moments and in all places be taken out of circulation by conversion into metallic money at its nominal value, so far it will be equal to money both as a measure and as a deposit. But so far as it is defective in any one use, however much it may excel in any other use, it will and must depreciate below the real value of the metallic money, which it is supposed to represent; so far as in any point of time or place the power of converting it into metallic money is remote, so far is it ideal, unsubstantial, and no deposit. Although with a fund of 20,000*l*. a banker, or the treasury of a government, may circulate 100,000*l*. yet as whenever, for any reason, or by any event, it becomes necessary to take that 100,000*l*. out of circulation, the banker or the treasury can but pay 20,000*l*. or four shillings in the pound, that circulation must end in a fraud.

Where, in the circulation of capital, paper money is substituted instead of metallic money, you allow, that it will not answer in its uses to foreign trade. I, for the same reason, add, it will not *pay taxes*, so far as those taxes are to *supply expences incurred or laid out abroad*. If great variety of *reabsorbing glands* did not in Scotland take up, in the course of circulation, the amount of the taxes levied on that part of the kingdom, their paper money could not pay that amount.

Just as much gold, as paper circulation becomes a substitute for, may be spared from circulation, and will become, as you truly say, a new fund for commerce, and will go abroad in foreign trade: if it is employed in a commerce of luxury or consumption, it is in every respect hurtful to society; so far as it purchases raw and rude materials, or provisions or tools, and instruments to work with, it may be beneficial. You think that, however individuals may run into the former, bodies and societies are more likely to actuate the latter. Yet in countries where a superabundant quantity of paper money hath taken place, where the power of creating this money hath advanced faster in its creation and emissions than the labour, industry and abilities of the inhabitants would have produced it, this *artificial plenty* hath always encouraged a commerce of luxury; an over-trading; a multitude and disproportionate number of shop-keepers; extravagant expences in idle land-holders; more building than can be supported; and all kinds of ambitious and dangerous projects. '[26]The commerce and industy of a country, you must acknowledge, and do candidly confess, though they may be somewhat augmented, cannot be altogether *so secure*, when they are thus, as it were, suspended upon the *Dædalian wings of paper money*, as when they travel *on the solid ground of gold and silver*. Over and above the accidents to which they are exposed from the unskilfulness (I *would here add the fraud also*) of the conductors of this paper money, they are liable to several others, from which no prudence or skill of the conductors can guard them.'—You indeed reason from the *abuse*, but all these arguments do equally derive from the *defect* of this paper money. As it creates an *influx of riches*, which does not spring from industry, which is not the effect and produce of useful labour; it creates, with aggravated circumstances, all that distress which the real useful labourer and real man of property, the land-owner, must feel, even under an influx of real riches; it gives motion and velocity to this influx, without producing any real *deposit* whereon the *riches*, which it pours in to circulation, *may be funded as* WEALTH. The landholder lives for a while under oppression and distress; he then, raising his rents beyond what the real stock will bear, lives in a delusive abundance of luxurious expence, but is finally ruined. The successor, who purchases him out, succeeds by the same disease to the same ruin. The labourer, and all who live on fixed stipend, are under a continued series of oppression. The false wealth only of

[26] [i. 389; II.ii.86.]

adventurers, jobbers, and cheats, become the riches of the country; that real deposit, which would be a fund of real wealth and real supply in case of distress, will be chaced away. The phantom of circulation, which is substituted in its place, will, instead of coming in aid, fail, and vanish on the first alarm of distress.

'[27]An unsuccessful war, for example, in which the enemy got possession of the capital (*who does not tremble as he reads?*) and consequently of that treasure which supported the credit of paper money, would occasion *a much greater confusion* in a country where the whole circulation was carried on by paper, than in one where the greater part of it was carried on by gold and silver. The usual instrument of commerce *having lost its value*, no exchanges could be made but by barter or upon credit. All taxes having been usually paid in paper money, the prince would not have wherewithal either to pay his troops or to furnish his magazines; and the state of the country would be much more irretrievable, than if the greater part of its circulation had consisted in gold and silver. A prince, anxious to maintain his dominions in a state in which he can most easily defend them, ought, upon this account (*and I add upon all others*) to guard not only against the excessive multiplication of paper money, which ruins the very banks that issue it, but even against that multiplication of it, which enables them to fill the greater part of the circulation with it.'

I was willing to oppose, in your own words, this fair description which you give of the dangerous state of a country which abounds in *circulation of riches*, instead of a deposit, which is *wealth*, as an antidote against the delusions of this powerful temptation: and as I think the dose ought to be repeated, I will repeat it in the words of the very clear-minded and ingenious Mr Hume.[28]

'He has entertained (*he says from similar reasons as above stated*) a great doubt concerning the benefit of banks and paper credit, which are so generally esteemed advantageous to every nation. That provisions and labour should become dear, by the encrease of trade and money, is, in many respects, an inconvenience, but an inconvenience that is unavoidable, and

---

[27] [i. 389; II.ii.87.]

[28] Hume's third *Essay on Money* [*Phil. Wks.* iii. 311.].

the effect of that publick wealth and prosperity, which is the end of all our wishes. It is compensated, however, by the advantages which we reap, from the possession of those *precious metals*, and the weight which they give the nation in all foreign wars and negotiations. But there appears no reason for the encreasing that inconvenience by *a counterfeit money*, which foreigners will not accept in any payment, and which *any great disorder in the state will reduce to* NOTHING.'

It is for these reasons, because I am not for *removing old bounds*, and that I wish to preserve the old general established opinion, that money is a *common measure*; because I am unwilling to receive that *new and delusive friend* CIRCULATION, instead of *the old and steady one*, MONEY, which being a DEPOSIT, will stick by us in all times, that I have taken the liberty to examine this part of your Analysis, and to wish, if you should be persuaded to revise it, that you would enquire, in the real track of nature, whether that commodity, by the intervention of which the exchanges of all commodities may in all times and cases be actuated, must not, *in truth as well as in fact*, be that common measure in the use of which all mankind have universally agreed, and must not be a deposit, which the metallic money alone is: and whether, where paper circulation is not so proportioned to the deposit as that, that deposit is always ready to exchange it during its circulation; is not established on such a *fund* as will *absolutely exchange it*; whether, I say, such paper circulation is not a delusion that must finally, however remotely, lead to a fraud.

By what I have said above I do not mean to say, that paper is not useful; I think, that under such due regulations respecting the FUND, which is to exchange it, the USES to which it is to be applied, and the QUANTITY in which it may be safely issued, as will make it a common measure and a DEPOSIT, it is not only generally beneficial, but that the greatest advantages may be derived from it to the publick.

If now, Sir, by these principles, as I have stated them, as they are found in the FUND and the USES, you examine all the schemes of paper circulation from that of the bank of Amsterdam, founded on a real deposit, to that of the Scotch banks, founded on[29] trust and confidence, without any actual

---

[29] [i. 351; I.ii.28, also § 41 et seq.]

deposit; if you examine the paper money, and the operations of that wise and prudent institution, the loan-office of Pensylvania, examine the foundation and the succeeding operations of the bank of England, you will find, that you have a fixed canon, by which you may precisely mark what are real, what delusive; what may be beneficial, what will be ruinous in the end. Whereas, if no other idea but that of *circulation* enters into our notion of money; if it be conceived to be nothing more than *a circulating machine*, under that conception every delusive fraudulent credit, which every adventurer can establish *on a deceived and betrayed confidence*, may set in motion a circulation, that may on every ground be justified even in the moment of its bankruptcy. And even those just and wise precautions, with which you have endeavoured to guard this circulation against fraud, may tend to give an opinion of confidence to this circulation, when it shall be so guarded, which in any case it ought not to have, unless it can be so framed as to have *all the use* of money in circulation, and be so *funded* as in the end to be a real deposit.

It is impossible to pass over those parts of your learned work, wherein you treat of labour, stock, and land; of wages, profit, and rent; of the monied prices of commodities, and especially your very curious and scientifick Treatise on the Precious Metals applied as Money; it is impossible to read those parts respecting the effects of the progress of improvement in the community, of the nature, accumulation, and employment of stock, without reiterating the idea and the wish expressed in the beginning of this letter, of seeing your book considered as INSTITUTE OF THE PRINCIPIA *of those laws of motion*, by which the operations of the community are directed and regulated, and by which they should be examined. In that part, however, which explains the different effect of different employment of capital, wherein you seem rather to have engrafted some foreign shoots, than to have trained up, in the regular branchings of your Analysis, to propositions fully demonstrated, I will beg to arrest your steps for a moment, while we examine the ground whereon we tread; and the more so, as I find these propositions used in the second part of your work as data; whence you endeavour to prove, that the monopoly of the colony trade is a disadvantageous commercial institution.

After having very justly described the four different ways in which capital stock may be employed—first, in drawing from the elements of earth and water the rude, the spontaneous or cultured produce; next, in working these materials up for use; next, the general exchange or trade of these commodities, conveyed from place to place as they are wanted; and, lastly, the retail distribution of them to the consumer. After having divided by fair analysis the general trade or commerce, described under the third head, into three different operations—that is, the home trade; the foreign trade of consumption, and the carrying trade. After having shewn the just gradation of beneficial employ of capital, which these different operations produce, and how truly beneficial each in its respective *natural* gradations is,[30] 'When the course of things, without any constraint or violence, naturally introduces it;' you lay and prepare a ground of contrast, from whence in your fourth book to prove, that the establishment of a monopoly in the colony trade, by perverting this *natural order and gradation of operations* in commerce, hath rendered the commerce of such colonies less beneficial than they might otherwise in general have been; I am here marking only the order of your argument, not trying the force of it. In the order of this argument, I think I discover an essential misconception of that branch and operation of commerce, which is in nature *circuitous*, and as such beneficial; but which you conceive to be and call *a round-about commerce*, and as such of course, and in the nature of things, disadvantageous. Your argument goes to prove, that the monopoly, instead of leaving the direct trade to its full and free operation, instead of suffering the round-about trade (as you call it) to take up the *surplus only* of capital which that produces, and next the carrying trade naturally to absorb what the others disgorge, doth force capital, which might have been more beneficially employed in a direct trade, into a round-about trade; which is too commonly mistaken for the carrying trade of Great Britain.

I mean, in its place, to examine this your argument, in your application of it to the actual subject. I will here, in the mean time, with your leave, make an assay of the truth of its combination; for it appears to me, that in treating *a circuitous commerce* as *a round-about trade*, you confound two things

[30] [i. 453; II.v.32.]

the most distinct in their nature, and the most different in their effect of any two that could have been put together.

A CIRCUITOUS TRADE or commerce is that by which receiving, *with the due profits of return of capital*, some article of trade or some commodity, *which is better to go to market with than money*, I go to market with that commodity so received; and perhaps again with some other in like manner received; and perhaps again with a third, making by each operation my due profits, annexed to each return of my capital; and finally a greater superlucration of profit than I could have done by the same number of direct trades; and consequently either a greater revenue, or a greater accumulation of capital, that may again employ more productive labour.

A ROUND-ABOUT TRADE, on the contrary, with lost labour, with waste of expence, and unprofitable detention of capital, sends to market some commodity (as the proverb well expresses it) *by Tom-Long the carrier.*

We will suppose, that the British merchant or factor hath sold his British manufactures in Virginia, in which he vested his capital; and that he has it in speculation, whether by taking money, a bill of exchange, or some commodity, which is ready money's worth in the British market, he shall make a direct return of his capital, and its simple accretion of profit; or whether by taking such commodities, as by an intermediate operation in his way home, he may derive an intermediate adventitious profit from, before the same is again reinvested in British goods for the Virginian market.

In the first case, his capital may be said to return with its profit directly; in the second, although it may make a circuit, and be detained awhile in its way home, yet it is not detained, nor goes out of its way *unprofitably* to Great Britain; for by the superlucration, arising from the intermediate operation, it gives proportionably either a greater revenue, or as an encreased capital employs more productive labour.

We will suppose a second case taken up on this speculation, that he either receives corn by barter, or by purchase invests what he has received in that commodity, with which, instead of coming directly home, he calls in his way at Cadiz or Lisbon; the sale of his corn there returns him his capital with a second accretion of profit. Here again he speculates in like manner, and determines to invest this accumulated capital in wines, fruits, etc. which at the home market will again return his

capital, with farther accretion of profit. Has not every movement of this circuitous trade been a different operation? Has
not each operation made a distinct return of capital? Has not
each return given its peculiar profit? Has any expence been
wasted? Any labour lost? Has there been any detention of
capital unprofitably to Great Britain, while, at its return, it
affords either more revenue, or, as capital, employs more productive labour than otherwise it would.

Let us in another line suppose, that this merchant or factor
receives tobacco, rice, indigo, or peltry, which he brings directly
home; with these commodities at the British market he speculates, whether he shall take ready money there for them, which,
vesting in British manufactures, or foreign manufactures
bought with British produce, he will return directly to Virginia
again with. Or whether these commodities, which represent
his capital, with its accretion of profit, might not still more
encrease it, if he himself sent them to that market where they
are purchased for consumption. We will suppose, that his prudence directs him to the latter conduct. He sends them then to
Russia or to Germany. They there return him his capital, with
another accretion of profit. We will suppose, that he re-invests
his capital with hemp or flax for the British, or in linnens for
the American market. He is by this operation enabled to go
back again to America, either with Russian or German manufactures, bought with British commodities, or selling what he
bought of Russia or Germany in the British markets, with a
still more increased quantity of British manufactures than what
any direct trade between America and Great Britain could have
purchased. Here again the same questions may be asked, and
must receive the same answers.

On the contrary, wherever there is a *round-about trade*, there
the commercial operations are obstructed, and the advantages
greatly defalcated, if not, in many instances, entirely lost. The
obliging the merchant to bring rice from the southern latitudes
northward to Great Britain, which rice must go back again
south to its market in the southern parts of Europe and the
Streights, was a round-about trade, it was labour lost, it was
a waste of expence, an unprofitable detention of capital, and
the commodity was sent by *Tom Long the carrier* to market.
The monopoly therefore, in that case, where it created a round-
about trade, hath been relaxed. Sugars are in the same case;
and a like relaxation, under peculiar regulations relating to

that peculiar article, have been recommended, and might be safely and beneficially given. There are some parts of the tobacco crops, which, in the assortment, might be admitted to somewhat a similar liberty without danger, but with benefit. Nay, *that intermediate operation of the circuitous trade*, mentioned above, which obliges the Virginian tobacco to come to England before it goes to Germany, and the German linnens also to come to England before they go to America, *is a round-about trade*, a needless and very disadvantageous operation, in which some relaxation ought to be made. I can see, that the English merchant may lose a commission, but labour and expence would be saved to the community. In like manner the obliging the West India ships, which, since the interruption of the American trade, load staves, lumber and corn in England, which articles are brought from foreign parts, is obliging them to take up these things by a round-about trade; whereas, if they were permitted to ship, in British shipping only, these articles at the foreign markets directly for the West Indies, many inconveniencies, which the British part of the community experiences, might be avoided, and both labour and expence saved to the community at large. If salt fish, which is intended for the southern markets, was obliged to be brought northward first to England, and so go round about to the south, its proper market, it would create a round-about trade. If these ships loading with salt for their back carriage were obliged to come round by England, it would create a round-about trade, and in either case would waste labour, and might lose all the profit of the capital employed. The monopoly therefore does not take place in this.

The permitting, in certain cases stated, and under certain regulations specified, the Americans who go with fish directly to the Streight, Spain, or Portugal, to purchase there, if purchased of British merchants, certain articles, and to carry the same, so purchased, directly back to America, so far as it would avoid the round-about trade, persevering, and even extending at the same time the British market, has been for twelve or fourteen years successively recommended.

I think in general on this subject, that wherever the monopoly would create a round-about trade, it should not take place; and that wherever it hath occasioned any such round-about operation, it should be relaxed; always however keeping in view this object and end, namely, that so far as our colonies are to be considered as an institution, established and directed to encrease the naval force of our marine empire, and so far as that force derives in any degree from the operations of their commercial powers, so far that monopoly, which engrafts them upon our internal establishment, is indispensible, and ought never to be departed from or relaxed. The sovereign power, which hath the care of the defence and strength of the empire, ought never to permit any the most flattering idea of commercial opulence to come in competition with the solid ground of strength and defence. In this way of reasoning I find myself joined by you, who reason in the same way, and almost in the same words, when speaking of the act of navigation you say, that, 'although it be not favourable to foreign commerce, or to the growth of that general opulence which might arise from it, yet, as defence is of much more importance than opulence, it is the wisest of all the commercial regulations of England'. On the ground and deriving my reasoning from the same principle, I say, that the monopoly is of the same spirit; is not only wise, but is also necessary, and that it is not the monopoly, but the injudicious undistinguishing application of it, without that reason which alone can justify it, and in channels where it necessarily creates a round-about trade, which renders it disadvantageous, not only to the colonies, but to the general community of the empire.

As no round-about trade, unless where the obliging the colony trade to submit to such, is necessary to the system of defence, should be occasioned, but should even, where it has taken place, be relaxed, so, on the contrary,[31] I have always thought, that a circuitous operation in the colony trade, as the thing which of all others tends most to increase and extend the American markets for British manufactures, should be allowed and encouraged, provided that trade in its circuition keeps its course *in an orbit that hath Great Britain for its center.*

Having thus shewn, simply to the point of stating the case, not arguing it, that a circuitous commerce and a round-about trade are two very different and distinct things, having very different operations and very different effects: having shewn that the circuitous trade is very advantageous, while a round-

---

[31] Vide *Administ. of the British colonies*, vol. i, ch. viii.

about trade is always detrimental, but that the circuitous commerce of the colonies is not that hurtful round-about trade
which you treat as occasioned by the monopoly, I will now
proceed to examine, under their several heads, your application
of the principles which you lay down in your analysis, as what
directs your synthetic reasonings on the commercial institutions which have taken place in the British œconomy.

Although I perfectly agree with you, that the *restraints on
the importation* of such foreign goods as can be produced
cheaper at home are useless; and that the laying restraints on
the importation of such as cannot be made so cheap at home,
answers no good end, but may be hurtful; although I allow,
that these measures, as a kind of institution of monopoly in
favour of internal industry in preference, or to the exclusion
of the produce of foreign industry coming to it, does not always
tend to encourage the home industry, but, on the contrary,
gives a false turn to it, puts it on a false ground and profit,
and may have the effect of forcing an unprofitable labour: yet
I am unwilling to quit the principle of encouraging the first
efforts of home industry, if employed on home commodities in
the home market, as I think the principle, applied only in cases
where it is wanted, may be very beneficial; I had rather, in
my notions of political œconomy, abide by the principle, and
examine, upon each application of it, how it does or does not
operate to encourage a profitable industry, skill and habit in
peculiar branches of labour, which the society has to learn,
and which learnt will be profitable. If a society, which once
used to send abroad its rude produce to purchase manufactures
made of that very rude produce so sent out, and which it knew
not how to work up, had never been, by some adventitious
aid, over and above what the sources of the first efforts of its
industry could have given, encouraged to begin in trials of
its skill; if the individual is not, while he is learning his trade,
and the skill of working profitably in it, supported in part, he
can never attempt to learn it; if the society does not pay for
the learning, it can never have it; although it be true that at
first the *apprentice* (for by that name I will express the first
efforts of a manufacture) is not employed to the greatest advantage, because he might buy the articles which he is learning to
make, cheaper than he can make them; although the community pays this difference; although these efforts, thus
artificially forced, are at first disadvantageous and unprofitable

to the community: yet by his industry being so directed to, and
so supported in a line of labour, which he could not naturally
have gone into, nor could have supported himself by, these
first efforts, which the community pays for, do by repeated
exercise produce skill, which in time will work as well, and
enable the home manufacturer (if his labour is *employed on
native home rude produce*) to sell as cheap, and soon cheaper,
than the foreign workman and manufacturer; his labour then
will become profitable to himself, and advantageous to the
community of which he is a part. It was thus our woollen and
hardware manufacturers were first encouraged and supported;
but the very same principle, and the same reasoning upon it,
hath always led me to a persuasion, that no aids of a monopoly
in the home market, nor no bounties, can ever force a manufacture founded and *employed on foreign rude material*. It is an
attempt, by robbing Peter to pay Paul, to establish a trade, the
natural profit of which cannot support the establishment, and
the loss of which must be made up to it by payments from the
society at large. Against such your principle, in the full force
of its arguments, stands unanswerable. Such is the linnen
manufacture wrought on foreign line and flax; such is the silk
in some degree; this last, however, so far differs, as that rude
material may be imported full as cheap as any rival country in
Europe can raise it.

You think, the restraints upon the importation of live cattle
and corn an unreasonable and ungenerous monopoly, for that
the grazing and farming business of Great Britain could be but
little affected by a free importation of these, and not in the
least hurt. As, on the contrary, I think, any change in this part
of our system might be attended with the most important
consequences, especially to a class of people who bear the chief
burthen of all the taxes, and are the support of the state of the
community. I own, I tremble for the change, and should hope
this matter may be a little more thoroughly explored, in all
the effects of its operation, before any such idea becomes a
leading doctrine.

You have with clear and profound reasoning[32] shewn, that,
in an improving state of the community, the prices of cattle
and of butchers meat, and the lesser articles of the supply must

[32] [i. 274ff.; I.xi.1, Second Sort of Rude Produce.]

start, and continue to rise until they come to such a rate, as shall make it worth the farmer's while to cultivate the land, which he rents, to the purposes of breeding and feeding such cattle, and to the raising these other articles for the market; this you properly call *the natural progress of improvement*, and these rising values *the natural course of prices*. If a free importation of cattle and of these lesser articles should be allowed, this *adventitious supply* coming from countries which have great wastes for breeding cattle, which do not pay such heavy taxes, and which are not arrived at that degree of improvement in which this country is found, such importation *must derange this scale of natural prices, and must arrest this progress of improvement in its course*. If such foreign country can breed and feed, and afford to import and bring to market cattle and these lesser articles cheaper than our grazer can, the grazing business at home must cease. Well—but say you, if under these circumstances grazing will not answer, the land will be broken up for tillage. But here again, if a free importation of corn, on a like plan, derived from such reasoning on these principles, is, as you recommend, permitted, that branch of business, not capable of farther extension, and met at market by such importation, will be at a stand, and finally become retrograde; we shall be obliged to give up all our improvements, and return to our wastes and commons. In order to obviate in some measure these objections, a kind of distinction is made between the importation of lean and fat cattle. The importation of lean cattle would not, says the argument, hurt, but benefit the feeding farms. The breeding farms, however, would be ruined; and there is a link of connection, which so allies the whole progress of country business in one chain of intercommunion, that all in the end would suffer and be undone.

A second palliative used to obviate these objections, which naturally arise against this idea of giving up our system of restraints on importation of cattle,[33] is, that the importation of *salt provisions* could never come in competition with the fresh provisions of the country. To try how this would operate, let us suppose that the Victualling-Office, as the law now stands, is in the ordinary course of taking great quantities of

[33] [ii. 41; IV.ii.19.]

cattle, and in the extraordinary demand which war occasions, takes off a proportionate encreased number; this of course raises the price of the grazers sales, and countervails, in some measure, with the landed interest, the burthen of the encreased taxes. But if a free importation of salt provisions is to take place as a settled system, the English grazer, while the war encreases his burthens, and raises the price of every article which he purchases, is himself met at the market by a competition brought against him from a country that does not bear this encreased burthen; and he cannot therefore find that *natural scale of price*, which the maintenance of his business and relative state in the country requires; he must be ruined, and the land soon rendered incapable of paying its rents, and of raising those very taxes.

In the same train of reasoning you think, that a free importation of corn could very little affect the interest of the farmers of Great Britain, because the quantity imported, even in times of the greatest scarcity, bears so inconsiderable a proportion to the whole stock raised. From this argument, founded in fact, you think the farmers could have nothing to fear from the freest importation; and you reproach them on the account of the system of restraint against free importation of corn, as forgetting the generosity which is natural to their station, in demanding the exclusive privilege of supplying their countrymen. If here, Sir, you had weighed well a distinction which Mons. Necker[34] has, with exquisite precision, explained, you would have spared this reproach. It is not the ratio of the quantity of corn exported or imported, and the quantity of the whole stock raised, but the ratio between the *surplus* and this quantity exported or imported, which creates the effect; it is not a ratio of $\frac{1}{571}$, but a ratio of $\frac{1}{15}$, which acts and which operates on the market; it is not the $\frac{1}{571}$ part but the $\frac{1}{15}$th part which would operate to the depression of the market and the oppression of the farmer.

Chearful under the burthen of the taxes, and spiritedly willing to pay them in support of his country, he only wishes to enable himself to do so from his industry, and the natural profits of it at his own market, without having that market loaded from an external supply, and depressed by a

[34] *Sur la législation et le commerce des grains* [1775].

competition from countries which are not in that state of improvement, and do not pay those taxes, which he must add to his price, if he is to live and pay them; he does not desire the *exclusive* supply, but a fair and equal market on the natural scale of prices, which shall give vent to his supply; this surely he may do without reproach. On the contrary, were it possible to suppose that the country gentleman could be persuaded to change the system, and give up the security which the restraint on importation gives him in his interest, he would deservedly incur the real reproach of having lost that practical sense, which the country gentlemen have always hitherto been found to have, when they come to real business.

But I think you rather misrepresent our system of restraint on importation of corn; it does not absolutely prohibit corn from being brought into the country, and does not establish *an exclusive supply* in the country land-owner; it only restrains such an importation as may either in quantity or price injure the free and fair vent of our own supply in our own market, at such prices as the general state of the improvement of the community and the scale of prices, which is the natural consequence, require.

From the consideration of our restraints on importation of corn, whose operations act as a bounty, you proceed to the consideration of the direct BOUNTY which our system gives *on the exportation of corn*, to which you make the like, but stronger objections. As you seem on this subject to have adopted the reasoning which[35] Mr Necker uses, and to have copied it closely; and as his book, as well as your's, will carry great authority with it, I will in this place examine both your objections *ensemble*.

Contrary to the common use made of the popular argument in favour of the measure, you both say, the measure has a direct tendency *in the instant* to raise the price of corn in the interior market, and to enable the merchant to introduce it into the foreign market at a lower price. What you say is fact, and the truth rightly understood; and yet while this measure encourages a plenty, overflowing with a constant succession of surplusses, it hath a tendency, *in a series of times taken together*, to lower the price. That our measure of the bounty

---

[35] *Sur la législation et le commerce des grains.*

has not been the sole cause of lowering the price of corn, Mr Necker gives a decisive proof in fact, which you[36] copy. That the general lowering of the price of corn is not owing to the English measure of *the bounty on exportation*, is (he says) plain, because the same general lowering of the price has taken place in France in the same period, where a direct contrary system, *a total prohibition of exportation* hath invariably prevailed till very lately. You add to his argument an assertion, 'that it raises however *not the real but nominal price only*, and is of no use to the landed interest.' There is perhaps (you say) but one set of men in the whole commonwealth to whom the bounty either was or could easily be serviceable, these are the corn-merchants; it loads (you add) the publick revenue with a very considerable expence, but does not in any respect encrease the real value of the landed man's commodity.

Mr Necker has also said that the bounty is not necessary; for if there be a surplus, and the foreign market wants it, it will have it without the aid of the bounty. The difference only is, that if the merchant finds that he cannot export it at the price of the British market, so as to carry it to the foreign market, he must wait till it falls in price in England, or rises in the foreign market, as many shillings per quarter as the bounty would give: *then* he will be equally able to export it *without* as *before with* the bounty. In a corollary of which argument you join him in saying, as he had said, that if the surplus quantity may be, by the aid of the bounty, thus exported when corn is at a high price, the surplus of a plentiful year will always so go out, as not to come in aid to relieve the scarcity of a defective one.

After having (in a manner indeed which rather has reference to the effect it might have in France) reprobated the measure of granting a bounty on the exportation of corn, he gives an opinion, in which I own I was surprized to find you following him; that if an encouragement is necessary to agriculture, it should be given *not on the exportation, but on the production*.

I will first state what I think to be the real operations and end of the bounty on corn exported, and then consider the positions above, not by way of reply, but by comparison on

---

[36] [Vol.i.248; l.xi.g.11, see also V.v.a.21–2.]

fair examination, mark wherein they deviate and differ from the real state of the case.

Any country rising in that progressive state of improvement, by which England for near a century hath been rising, must have experienced *a continued influx of riches*; that continued influx must have and hath created *a continued progressive rise of prices*. If the continuation of the influx was arrested in its course, however great *the quantity of* riches which hath come in, however great the glut of money; yet, after it hath spread itself in all parts, and found its general level, *all* prices will be proportionably raised; the original proportions which they held, before the start of prices, will be restored; all therefore, however high, will be but *nominal,* and a greater or a less quantity of the precious metals will be totally indifferent; but the case is very different, while the influx is in continuance. During its operation it starts the prices of things, but of different things with very different velocity in the motion of the rise. Objects of fancy, caprice, luxurious use, and the lesser articles of food, which bore little or no price, while the necessaries must always have born a certain price, even what may be called a high price in a poor and unimproved state of the community, will, when the progression of improvement begins, start first in price, and with a velocity that will continue to *forerun* the velocity of rise in the price of necessaries. The relative proportion of the scale of prices being changed, the difference of the prices is real, and corn will be always last and lowest in the scale. Although the price of corn may and will rise, yet not rising in proportion to other things, and the rents of land and the wages of labour depending on the price of corn, the price of every other thing must not only rise before rent and wages can start in price, but must continue *so to forerun* in their rise, that the landed man and labourer must be in a continued state of oppression and distress: that they are so in fact, the invariable and universal experience of all improving countries, actuating manufactures and trades, demonstrates. In the end all must equally partake of the general prosperity; corn must rise in price; rents must rise; wages must be encreased: but during the continuance of the influx there must be a partial distress, which, although relative, is not the less but the more aggravated from being relative, others being in the actual enjoyment of a prosperity which the landed man can but look up to and hope for in the end. If the operation was short, and if the influx soon spread itself into a level, it would not be of much moment in what order the scale of prices arose. In a country where the land-workers and owners are few, in proportion to those employed in trade and commerce, as in rich commercial countries of small extent, there this effect is soon produced; there the landed interest cannot suffer much from the disproportionate velocity of the rise of prices, however accelerated, but in a trading and commercial country, *of large extent*, the spreading and level of the inflowing riches must be an operation of so long time, and the effect so far removed from the first cause, that the land-worker and owner can never receive a proportionate relief, much less the benefit of an equable scale of prices, *while that cause is in operation*. If the influx be a continued encreasing operation, the scale will always be ascending. In a country circumstanced as thus described, if the legislator is ever to intermeddle, or can ever do any good by meddling in these matters, his interference should be directed to relieve this oppressed order and class of the community. The English measure of the bounty does this, by aiding in its first effect the relative, and therefore *real price* of the produce of the land *without obstructing the natural effects* of the advancing and improving state of the community. It relieves the relative distress, which the acceleration of the inflowing of riches occasions to the land-worker; it helps to accelerate the rising of the price of his commodity, and in some measure guards them from a greater distress, which they would otherwise feel: as it is, the traders and merchants eat out the landed man: they do suffer, but much less than they would do. In a country of this sort the velocity of the influx of riches (especially if *an artificial influx* by paper money is added to the real one) may have even too much acceleration, if care is not taken at the same time to accelerate also the distribution of these riches into every channel and duct. In such a country as England, but more especially in France, if commerce be encouraged by the force of any artificial spring, if a disproportionate and[37] *more than natural* influx of riches comes in upon it, how much

---

[37] Either by an undue creation of paper money, or by the bringing in great quantities of money amassed by conquest or by rapine, as was the case in Rome, by the money brought from Asia; as was the case in Britain, by the money brought from Indostan.

soever (when this influx may in the end have taken its whole
effect and spread itself into a level) the land and labourer must
necessarily share in the general prosperity, yet if care is not
taken to give acceleration to the motion of the landed interest,
in some proportion to the motion of the advance of commerce,
and the influx of riches, the landed interest must remain under
a continued depression of circumstances. Under this relative
depression the land-worker, while he is buying every thing he
wants at an advanced price, requires some adventitious force
or spring to aid the velocity of the rise of the price of his
commodity which he hath to sell. The wisdom of our ancestors,
men of business, acting not from selfish and ungenerous
motives, not from any jealousy of commerce, but from feeling
and experience, gave this very encouragement, and gave it, in
the very way in which it could have the truest effect; in which
it could do the least harm, and the most good. They encouraged
the landworker without checking the operations of commerce,
or retarding the progress of improvement: and while in the
direct instant they effected by the bounty a rise of price to
the saleable commodity of the landworker, and gave that
encouragement, which was thus become necessary; yet they so
gave the bounty, as that in the remote effect it would prevent
the enhancing of the general price, because the bounty encouraged the raising not only a surplus, but a succession of
surplusses. They converted these surplusses even of our food
into an article of commerce, and encouraged, and made it the
interest of the corn merchant to trade with it in every part of
the world.

Thus acted the homely understanding of the country
gentlemen *upon practice*; men of refined and great abilities,
speculating in the closet, *decide upon theory*, that it would
have answered the same ends better to have given the bounty
not on exportation, but on production.

As the bounty on exportation goes only to the surplus
exported, and as a bounty on production must have gone to
the whole quantity raised, which measure do you, who made
the objection, think would load the publick revenue most? But
unless there was an assured constant vent by exportation of
any surplus that should be raised, such a bounty as you and
Mr Necker recommend, would never encrease the quantity, or
raise a surplus, (for say you, B. IV.C.V. p. 123. [IV.v.b.36])
'unless the surplus can in all ordinary cases be exported, the

grower will be careful never to grow any more than what the bare consumption of the home market requires, and that market will be very seldom over-stocked, but will be generally understocked.' To what end, say I, should the farmer work; it would be only making to himself work, to lose profit, for the more he raised, the less would be the price.

On the contrary, the bounty on the exportation, at the same time that it doth (as you and Mr Necker justly observe) actually and directly raise the price of the commodity, it raises (I say) *not the nominal* but the *real* price, for it brings that price which was *relatively* too low, nearer to the level of the general scale of prices: At the same time that it is (as you truly say) serviceable to the corn-merchant, it enables him, without lowering the price of corn below the rate at which the farmer in the country can afford to produce it, to throw it into the general circulation of the commerce of Europe at an average rate which suits that commerce. This tends to encrease, and does encrease the quantity raised, and yet preventing on one hand a discouraging fall, or a disproportionate inhancement of price on the other, keeps that price equable; and by creating a succession of surplusses, obviates your fear, that the exportation of the surplus of the plentiful year should prevent the use of a surplus, which should relieve, and come in aid to, the defects of a scarce one; for it doth actually, by the succession of surplusses, which the high prices of the home market will always first command, provide against such scarcity, which point the regulations in the permanent corn law, of the 13th of G. III. on this head do still more effectually secure.

Let us now try how your's and Mr Necker's objections to the English measure of granting a bounty on corn exported bear against these operations.

Let us try Mr Necker's first objection, viz. that it is a measure unnecessary, because, says he, if there be a surplus which the foreign market wants, it will take it off, as soon as the home price falls, or the foreign prices rise, as many shillings in the quarter of corn as the amount of the bounty comes to. We shall find, that if no surplus of wheat, for instance, can go out and flow in the channels of the European market, at a higher price than 32 shillings per quarter, (the general average price of wheat in Europe) there will be no such surplus; the farmer in the present improved state of England, loaded at the same time as it is with taxes, cannot afford to raise wheat at that price: And if the British merchant did wait till the English wheat did sink to that price, he might better never export it; he would find, that the Dutch, Hambrough or Dantzic merchant had got to market before him, and had forestalled it. On the other hand considering that, at the very lowest estimation, the farmer cannot raise wheat at a lower average rate than 37 shillings per quarter, the bounty adds the five shillings, per quarter, which is just sufficient on one hand to enable the merchant to give the farmer a living price, and on the other to carry it to the foreign market at the average rates of that market; so that if the encouragement of the farmer, and of the supply be proper, and if 'the business of the corn-merchant be in reality that trade, (as you say) which, if properly protected and encouraged, would contribute the most to the raising of corn.'[38] This measure of a bounty on export is every way not only beneficial, but necessary: although you have said, in one place, that it is serviceable to the corn merchant *only*, yet in this view you yourself find, that this trade of the corn merchant 'will support the trade of the farmer, in the same manner as the wholesale dealer supports that of the manufacturer.'

The next objection in which you and Mr Necker join, is, that the doing any thing to raise the price of *corn* (as you express it, of *subsistance*, as Mr Necker rather more logically) in the home-market, must of course raise the expence of our manufactures, and give advantage to the rival manufactures of every part of Europe against us. This objection takes rise from a total mis-stating of the case.

If corn was the first article which started in price, so that all other commodities followed it, then indeed both your positions would be true; first that so far as respects the home market, we should only raise the *nominal* price for all rising proportionably, there would be no alteration in the *ratios of the scale*: this would therefore be of no use to the farmer on one hand, but by raising *all the articles of subsistence and supply*, our manufactures must become too dear for the average rates of the general market. But the contrary is the fact. Corn is the last of all the articles of the market which starts in its price, and rises always with the slowest motion. It is only in consequence of all other commodities having arisen, that a rise in

---

[38] [ii. 116; IV.v.b.18.]

this becomes necessary, and when it does begin to rise, it follows with such unequal motion, that some encouragement becomes necessary, as a spring to aid the velocity of its rise in proportion to other things. It is not the rise of the price of corn, but the general improved state of the country, raising the rates of all things, and the burthen of taxes successively accumulated, which raises the price of our manufactures. On the contrary, encouraging the raising of corn by a good price in the direct instant, creates a plenty: a plenty, with a succession of surplusses, keeps down the price, taken in a general series of times; and in some measure it tends also to lower the price of manufactures, by the number of hands which plenty of subsistance, if I may so express myself, always creates.

Seeing then nothing narrow, invidious, selfish, or ungenerous in our system of restraints and bounties on our corn trade, considering it as a necessary, wise and beneficial system, interwoven into the general œconomy of our agriculture, manufactures and commerce: persuaded that a certain sober conviction of experience, arising from practice, first suggested the truth, I cannot but hope, that the same wisdom which gave the bounty, will operate with the country gentlemen, to doubt every speculation of closet doctrine, and to oppose, on every occasion, every the most distant attempt to lower, or to confine within narrower limits this bounty.

You have made several observations on, some objections to, and give rather a hasty and summary judgment on the general system of our corn laws: I have made some remarks on these parts also, but I shall reserve these to another place, where I shall have occasion to examine all the regulations relative to the supply of the community with bread-corn, and to the manner in which the surplus of that supply is converted into an article of commerce.

I will now proceed to the consideration of your opinions and doctrines respecting the *monopoly of the colony trade*.

You allow,[39] 'this colony-trade to be very advantageous, though not by means, yet in spight, of the monopoly, and that the natural good effects of it more than counterbalance to Great Britain the bad effects of the monopoly; so that, monopoly and all together, that trade, even as it is carried on at

---

[39] [ii. 214; IV.vii.c.50.]

present, is not only advantageous, but greatly advantageous.'
Although you allow this, yet while you consider our colonies
'rather as a cause of weakness than of strength', 'as a source
of expence not revenue'; while you say, that[40] 'the invidious
and malignant project of excluding other nations from any
share' in our colony-trade depresses the industry of all other
countries, but chiefly that of the colonies, without in the least
encreasing, but on the contrary diminishing, that of the country
in whose favour it is established; that, in order to obtain a
relative advantage, that country not only gives up an absolute
one in this trade itself, but subjects itself to both an absolute
and relative disadvantage in every other branch of trade
wherein this monopoly does not operate. While you say this,
you conclude,[41] 'that under the present system of management,
Great Britain derives nothing but loss from the dominion which
she assumes over her colonies.' In consequence of this doctrine,
you are not only for breaking up the monopoly, but for a
dismemberment of the empire,[42] by giving up the dominion
over our colonies. This prompt and hasty conclusion is very
unlike the author of 'the Treatise on the wealth of nations,' it
savours more of the puzzled inexperience of an unpracticed
surgeon, who is more ready with his amputation knife, than
prepared in the skill of healing medicines. If we lose our colonies, we must submit to our fate; but the idea of parting with
them on the ground of system, is much like the system which
an ironical proverb recommends, '*of dying to save charges*'.
When superficial importants talk, write, or vend such their idle
crudities, one is not surprized; unworthy of notice they are
neglected: but when a man, who, like yourself, hath joined
practical knowledge to the most refined spirit of speculation,
can suffer himself so to be mislead, an examination of those
speculations, or at least of their consequences, as they lead to
practice, is due to him and to the world: I will therefore
examine your objections to the monopoly, and the reasoning
whereon you found them, by the actual operations and effects
of this colony-trade, acted upon by this monopoly.

But first I cannot but observe, that a round assertion, 'that

[40] [ii. 196; IV.vii.c.18.]

[41] [ii. 224; IV.vii.c.65.]

[42] [ii. 224; IV.vii.c.66.]

our colonies have never yet furnished any military force for the defence of the mother country, and that they have been a cause rather of weakness than of strength', is such as should have followed only from a deduction of facts: and I will beg leave to suggest to you some facts that induce me, and may perhaps you also, to be of a very different opinion. That very naval force, which by their armed vessels they are now so destructively exerting against our West-India trade and transports, they did very effectively in the two late wars, especially in the last, exert to the ruin of the West Indian commerce of France and Spain, and to the almost total obstruction of all communication of those countries with their respective colonies. If you have not heard of what they did then, judge of it by what they are able to do now, against the whole undiverted power of their mother country.

The mother country, with her own immediate force, must always meet the immediate force of its enemies, wherever exerted. If therefore France sent its European forces to America, Great Britain, with her European force, must meet them in that field. If the strength of our colonies, exerted against the colonial strength of France or Spain was effective; or if it was ready to serve where it could best serve, and where most wanted; if it was not only equal to its own defence, but did act against the enemy offensively also, with effect, it did bring forth 'a military force for the defence of the mother country.' The military force of the province of Massachusett's Bay not only defended the dominions of the mother country in that province, but for many years exerted itself in defending Accadia or Nova Scotia. In the war which ended by the peace of Aix la Chapelle, the military force of that province took Louisburg and Cape Breton, an acquisition which purchased for the mother country that peace. So far as my assertion may go in proof, I will venture to assert, that had France during the last war effectuated a landing in Great Britain, and had been able to maintain themselves there until an account of it should have arrived in New England, I should have been able to have brought over, or sent from the province, Massachusett's Bay (perhaps joined by Connecticut also) 'a military force for the defence of the mother country'.

On the point of revenue, I will also beg leave to repeat, because I have now still stronger reason for it, an assertion which I made in parliament, that before we went to decided war, a revenue might have been had upon compact, on terms which would have established the constitutional sovereignty of this country, regulating at the same time the trade and naval powers of the colonies, if those terms might have gone, at the same time, to the securing the rights of those colonies as granted by the government of that mother country. As to the ways and means of coming at the *grounds of agreement*, and the nature of that revenue and compact, an explanation never will be withheld, if ever again events shall render them practical. The colonies did always raise a revenue in support of that establishment of internal government, which the mother country had set over them; I do not say that I approve the manner in which they applied it. As to their raising, while *under a state of minority*, farther taxes, *except port duties*, for the *external purposes of the empire at large*, I will give no opinion, but submit it to your judgment, who have thoroughly considered the different fructuation of surplus produce expended in revenue, or vested in circulating capital, for further improvements, which further extend the British market in America, to decide, which of the two were, in that state, most beneficial to the mother country. I reason here in the line in which you consider the subject, the line of political œconomy, not of administration of government.

Your objections to the monopoly endeavour to prove, that; in *the invidious and malignant project* (as you stile it) of excluding as much as possible all other nations from any share in the trade of our colonies, Great Britain sacrifices, in a great degree, an absolute advantage, to enjoy in a lesser degree a relative one: that if the trade had been free and open, the industry of the colonies would not only have been less cramped, but the source of all the advantages deriving to Europe, from the settlement of Europeans in America, would have been more abundant and more productive of advantage: and that, although Great Britain had sacrificed a relative advantage which she derived from the exclusive trade, she would yet have had a greater absolute advantage; as an explanatory proof you instance in the monopoly of the article of tobacco. The market opened for this article would, you think, *probably* have lowered the profits of a tobacco-plantation nearer to the level of a corn-farm; the price of the commodity would *probably* have been lowered, and an *equal quantity* of the commodities, either of England or of any other country, might have *purchased a greater quantity* of tobacco than it can at present. I will suppose with you, that by this new arrangement, and the consequential *new ratio in the scale of* prices betwixt Europe and America, that Great Britain as well as other countries would have derived a great absolute advantage: yet as these other countries would have derived the same advantage from our colonies, this fancied absolute advantage could be but merely *nominal*; for although England thus got more tobacco for a less quantity of British commodities, yet as other countries also got the same on the same terms directly from Maryland or Virginia, what Great Britain thus got would not only be less in value, but would run the risque of being a drug upon her hands. In giving up therefore the relative advantage which she enjoyed by her exclusive trade, *while she gained a nominal*, she would lose every *real* advantage. Besides, there is surely some management to be observed in the culture of an article of produce, whose consumption hath arisen from whim and caprice into an habitual, but not a necessary use: instead of encouraging an unbounded produce of this, it were best, *probably*, that it should be limited. I am sure it is an absolute advantage to Great Britain, that Virginia and Maryland should find it most to their advantage to cultivate tobacco, rice, indico, or any other exotick commodity, than that by bringing the profits of a tobacco-plantation nearer upon a level with those of a corn-farm; they should find their advantage in raising corn to the rivalling us at the European markets in our home commodity, and to the depression of our agriculture. So far therefore as this argument goes, it demonstrates to me, at least, that by quitting the relative, *a real* advantage, we should not even gain a *nominal* advantage, but should run every risque of losing every advantage, both relative and absolute, real and nominal, which is to be derived from this source restrained, and at the same time of setting up a rival culture against our own agriculture. If you see the matter in this light in which it appears to me, you will, I am sure, feel how dangerous it is to vend these novelties of speculation against the sober conviction of experience.

Your argument goes on to state, that there are *very probable reasons for believing*, that although we do sacrifice this absolute advantage (which would, *it is supposed*, probably be drawn from a free and open trade) for a narrow mean relative advantage; yet we do not possess even this relative advantage, without subjecting ourselves, at the same time, both to an absolute and to a relative disadvantage in almost every other branch of trade of which we have not the monopoly.

It strikes me as material, and I am sure, therefore, you will excuse me making, in this place, one remark even *on the manner* of your argument, and how *you stretch your reasoning nicely*. You in words advance upon the ground of *probable reasons for believing* only, you prove by probable suppositions only; yet most people who read your book, will think you mean to set up an absolute proof, and your conclusion is drawn as though you had.

You proceed to describe these absolute and relative disadvantages.

The monopoly of the colony trade, wherein the English merchant was enabled to sell dear and buy cheap, gave a rate of profit in that trade much above the level of profit in any other, and would therefore never fail of drawing capital from those other branches into this, as fast as it could employ such. This double effect of drawing capital from all other branches of trade, and of raising the rates of profit higher in our internal trades than it would otherwise have been, arose at the first establishment of the monopoly, and hath continued ever since. Having thus stated the effect, you proceed to prove them to be bad and disadvantageous.

By drawing, not through the natural effects of trade, but by the artificial operations of the monopoly, capital from other trades, and other branches of trade in Europe, which were greatly advantageous both in a commercial and in a political view, this monopoly, it is *probable* (you say) may not have occasioned *so much an addition* to the trade of Great Britain, *as a total change in its direction*.

First, as to the assertion, that capital has been drawn from certain trades and certain branches of trade in Europe, and turned by the monopoly into the colony trade, which without this would not have been so diverted; that (I answer) is a matter of fact, which must not be established by an argument, *à priori*—but on an actual deduction of facts. As I did not find the latter in your book, I looked into the only records which we have of the progressive state of our commerce, in a[43] series

---

[43] A very useful collection, published by Sir C. Whitworth, M.P. [*State of the Trade of Great Britain in its imports and exports progressively from the year 1697* (1776)].

of returns of the imports and exports of Great Britain, as made to parliament. I cannot ascertain in our European trade that fact which your theory supposes. The tides and currents of commerce, like that of the ocean over which it passes, are constantly shifting their force and course, but this comes not up to your fact. I find no deprivation, but an encreased state of our European trade; and at the same time an immense multiplied encrease of our colony trade, and of every branch of commerce connected with it. Supposing, however, that this fact was true, that there hath been a *total change* in the direction of our trade, by drawing capital from several of the European trades, and by employing more of our general capital in the colony trade than would naturally have gone to it, had all trade been free and open: yet that supposition will never, against fact, prove, that this monopoly, thus employing more capital in, and deriving more profits from the colony-trade, hath occasioned a privation of advantage to the trade of Great Britain in general—Fact contradicts that position. Well, but as Great Britain cannot have sufficient capital to actuate all, it must occasion a privation in some of the branches of its trade; for, although there may not be an absolute decrease in certain branches, there is a relative one, as they have not increased in the proportion in which they would have done. This is again argument, *à priori*, in matters of fact, wherein it cannot act as proof; however, for the sake of your argument we will even suppose it, and ask the question, what then? To which, in my way of reasoning, I should answer, that as in the division of labour no one man can actuate all the branches of it, so in the division of the commerce of the world, no nation nor no capital can carry on all the branches of it in every channel in which it flows. That country then which, while it does less in those branches of trade wherein least is to be gotten, but has the command in that which exceeds all others in profit, doth surely draw the greatest possible advantage from commerce. This part then of your argument proves to me, assisted by the reasoning which you use in other parts of your work, the very reverse of the conclusion which you here draw from it.

You say in the next place, that this monopoly has contributed to raise and keep up the rates of profit in all the different branches of the British trade higher than they would naturally have been, or, which is the same thing, to prevent them from falling so low as they would otherwise have fallen; and that this forced height of profit hath subjected the country, where it takes effect, both to an absolute and to relative disadvantage in every branch of trade, in which it has not the monopoly. I could here answer in general by your own reasoning, as you use it in the case of the profits of grazing and corn land; as when the state of the community is such, that it occasions a greater call for, and consequently a greater profit on the one than the other; that other will soon be converted into the one which is in demand, and will give the greater profits, till both come to a level: so in commerce, under whatever regulations, either those which the natural wants or the political institutions of men establish, it is carried on, will always shift about, and endeavour to flow in those channels wherein most profit is to be had. That country then which is under those fortunate and powerful circumstances, and has the wisdom so to profit of those circumstances, as to be able to maintain a monopoly of the most profitable channels; and be able to maintain, at the same time, (notwithstanding the clog of its high rates of profits) a share of other branches of trade, even where it is undersold, has surely acquired *that ascendency in trade and commerce*, which is always better understood than explained. But I will not rest within these entrenchments, I will meet your argument in your open field.

You say,[44] that in consequence of these high rates of profit, under which our commodities and manufactures must be brought to market, we must in our foreign trade 'both buy dearer and sell dearer, must both buy less and sell less;' but I deny the consequence, 'that we must profit less,'[45] because, although those high rates may confine the extent, yet raising the profit of the dealing, we enjoy as much, and produce in trade as much, as if we did more business of less profits: all is kept equal and level as to the foreign trade, and our colony trade goes on, the mean while, in a still more rapid prosperity. Your conclusion therefore, 'that it is in this manner that the capital of Great Britain has partly been drawn, and partly driven from the greater part of the different branches of trade, of which she has not the monopoly; from the trade of Europe in particular, and from that of the countries which lie round the

---

[44] [ii. 201; IV.vii.c.27.]
[45] [ii. 219; IV.vii.c.59.]

Mediterranean sea,' is neither deducible from your argument, *à priori*, nor will you find it justified by fact.

Yet again that we, who think well of the monopoly, may not derive any support from thinking, that as the colony-trade is more advantageous to Great Britain than any other, so the capital being forced into that channel, is of more advantage to the country than if employed any other way. That we may not avail ourselves of this comfort, you proceed to shew it to be 'a natural effect of this monopoly; that it turns our capital from a foreign trade of consumption with a neighbouring into one with a more distant country; in many cases from a *direct trade* of consumption *into a round-about one* and in some cases from all foreign trade of consumption into a carrying one.' And as in the analytick part of your work you have shewn, that the direct trade of consumption, especially that with a neighbouring country, maintains the greatest quantity of productive labour, by the direct and frequent returns of its capital; that a round-about trade is always less advantageous, and the carrying still least so of all; you draw your conclusion, that therefore the operation of the monopoly, thus acting, turns our capital into channels where it employs less productive labour than it would naturally have done, if the trade was left to its free and natural operations. By your first position you mean, that it hath turned the capital from the European trade to the North American and West Indian trade, from whence the returns are less frequent, both on account of the greater distance, but more especially on account of the peculiar circumstances of America. An improving country, always dealing beyond their capital, must wait to pay their debts by their improvements, by which means, although the merchant may repay himself by the profit he puts upon his goods, and by other means, yet the capital of Great Britain is detained and withheld; and, thus detained, prevented from maintaining such a quantity of productive labour as otherwise it would do. In answer to this state of the argument (which I hope I have stated fairly) I say, that that part of our capital, which is some while withheld in America and does not return directly, is not withheld unprofitably to Great Britain: like that portion of the harvest which is detained for seed, it is the matrix of a succeeding and encreased production; by operating to advance still farther these improvements, and consequently the population of these countries, it is *creating and extending a new market*, whose demand for our productive labour calls forth that labour faster and to more advantage, than the same capital directly returned and vested in British goods could do; as it encreases this market in a constant progression, it calls forth more *manufacturers*; gives a spring to *agriculture*; and extends the *commerce* of Great Britain.

Well but, say you, 'secondly, the monopoly of the colony-trade has, in many cases, forced some part of the capital of Great Britain from a direct foreign trade of consumption into a round-about one.' Wherever it does so, that is an error in the system, it should be corrected and amended, so far as is consistent (as I said above) with the establishment of the unity of empire in all its orders and subordination of orders. I have in a former part of this letter, and many years ago on other occasions, pointed out some of these errors and their remedy; but I must beg here to apply those distinctions, which, in my remarks on the analytick part of your work, I shewed to exist in nature and fact, *between a circuitous and a round-about trade*; and to observe, that where your objections are pointed against the circuitous operations of our colony-trade, they do not act with effect; for these are always advantageous, and should be even more encouraged than they are. Such a series of such circuitous operations as create and extend the market, accumulating by each operation a fresh profit, return home not only (by this accumulated capital) with the means of employing more manufacturers, but with having created[46] an encreasing demand for more and more manufactures. The encreasing market of our improving colonies, still more and more rapidly improved by the circuitous trade, must, while we have the command of that market, multiply British manufacturers; these manufacturers thus multiplied[47], 'constitute (as you state it

---

[46] This is what, in *The Administration of the British colonies*, vol. i, ch. viii, I call creating and securing 'an encreasing nation of appropriated customers;' which idea you, from that superiority that speaking *è cathedra* always inspires, treat with sovereign contempt; 'it is, (you say) a project fit only for a nation of shop-keepers, governed by shop-keepers.' This idea, however, upon the closest and strictest analysis is the only one I can find precisely to define the relation which a commercial country bears to its colonies, and to express that institution of policy, in our act of navigation, which you rather too lightly and too contemptuously call (p. 222) 'a truly shop-keeper proposal'.

[47] [ii. 215; IV.vii.c.51.]

truly) a new market for the produce of the land, and most advantageous of all markets, the home market, for corn and cattle.'

Another objection yet remains, that in many cases the colony-trade becomes, by means of the regulations of the monopoly, merely a *carrying trade*. This carrying trade, which you describe as a defect, would be so, if the carrying was the only part in which our capital was employed, and the hire of the carriage the only profit that we derive from it, but instead of that, joined as it is with the circuitous trade, it becomes, in a political as well as a commercial view, a beneficial part of the operations which employs our own shipping.

Having gone through your argument of objection, you close with some corollary observations, as deriving from it. You think, that the unnatural spring applied to the colony-trade, has destroyed the natural ballance which would otherwise have taken place amongst all the different branches of British industry, and that the direction of it is thus thrown too much into one channel. The idea then of a blood vessel, artificially swelled beyond its natural dimensions, strikes your imagination, and you are brought under an apprehension of some terrible disorder. As this disorder did not seize Great Britain in the case you supposed,[48] you then search out five unforseen and unthought-of events (to which I could add another very perfectly foreseen and thoroughly understood) which fortunately occurred to prevent it. As I am no *malade imaginaire* in politicks, and have no fears of those[49] 'convulsions, apoplexy, or death,' which have been so often predicted, I know not how to go seriously, against fact into reasoning upon them. That our trade has felt, on a great and sudden shock, no such convulsions or apoplexy, but that its productive powers continue to be actuated, and its circulation to run *in some other channels*, though our American artery is obstructed, proves, that this was not our principal, much less our sole great channel of commerce; some part, perhaps great part, of our circulation passed through it into other remoter vessels, which is now perhaps full as properly with more profit to the British merchant, poured through more direct channels. In

---

[48] [ii. 211; IV.vii.c.45.]

[49] [ii. 210; IV.vii.c.43.]

short, the whole state of our trade, as it stands in fact, and is found in effect, is to me a proof in point against your case in theory.

'⁵⁰The effect of the monopoly (you say) has been not to encrease the *quantity*, but to alter *the quality* of the manufactures of Great Britain, suited to a market from which the returns are slow,' instead of keeping on in an old trade, 'from which the returns are frequent.'

If we consider the effect which the opening a *new market under a monopoly*, or in *a free trade*, hath on a commercial country, we shall find, if it be a market which calls for some new assortment of manufactures of a *quality different* from the ordinary and accustomed sort, in which that commercial country dealt before this new demand was opened, that *a free and open market*, into which the operations of a competition comes, *is more likely to alter the quality of the manufactures*, than where any commercial country possesses that market under a monopoly. In the former case they must watch and suit every call, every fashion, and even caprice of their free customers; in the latter case they will oblige *their appropriated customers*, to take off such goods as they please to send them, altho' the sorts do not in quality entirely suit that market; they will under this monopoly, carry this so far as to drive the country, which is subject to the monopoly, into smuggling, not only on account of the price, *but merely to get* goods of a quality which suits them. Your information in the practick, as well as theoretick knowledge of our commerce, will be able to supply proofs of this fact from many revolutions of our manufactures in different periods of our commerce. It is not therefore *the effect of a monopoly*, so much as it would be *the effect of a free and open trade, to alter the quality* of the manufactures of Great Britain. We will then next enquire, *how this monopoly operates as to the increase or not of the quantity.* In the first step we are agreed, that *this increasing market of appropriated customers* doth at this one entrance *encrease the quantity* of manufactures demanded. Let us next enquire, how 'the surplus produce of the colonies, which (you justly say⁵¹) is the *source of all of that encrease of enjoyments and industry,*

⁵⁰ [ii. 216; IV.vii.c.55.]
⁵¹ [ii. 193; IV.vii.c.9.]

which Europe derives from the discovery and colonization of America,' operates under a monopoly, or would operate under a free and open trade to encrease the quantity of British industry and manufactures. The articles of this produce are (it is needless to enquire how) become of accustomed demand in the markets of Europe, not only for its more pleasurable enjoyment, but in the line of industry also. So far as Great Britain hath the monopoly of these articles, she will become *a necessary trader* in these markets. She will not go to such markets with these articles only; she will make up a cargo with assortments of her manufactures also; the one will necessarily introduce the others; and if the first cannot be had without the latter it will introduce those others, where, from the disadvantages of a high scale of prices, they would not otherwise have been introduced; so that *our monopoly* of these American sources of enjoyments and industry to the Europeans, *doth not only tend to encrease* the quantity of our industry and manufactures *partially, but absolutely.* As they are interwoven with our general commerce, they do actually tend to introduce and carry on our commerce in our manufactures, even under those disadvantages, which you have described as the effects of the monopoly; this is one ground of that *ascendancy in commerce*, which I rather referred to, than described as enjoyed by Great Britain.

As to the fact about the returns of capital, if you will compare notes between the merchant trading in British manufactures to Germany, and the merchant trading with British manufactures to America and the West Indies, you will find the returns of the latter upon the whole (if these goods go no farther than North America, or our West Indies) not slower than those from Germany. Credit has, even before the present war, been extended in Germany, and shortened towards America: inquire after this fact in Norwich, London, and the other great manufacturing places, and you will find it so.

That the productive labour of Great Britain is kept down by the monopoly; that this monopoly prevents its affording revenue so much as it might; and that rent and wages are always less abundant than otherwise they would be, is a corollary or propositions neither proved by reasoning nor established by fact. That the monopoly, raising the rates of mercantile profit, discourages the improvement of land, is still more aberrant from the line of reason, and more directly contrary to fact: the reason you give is, that the superior profits made by trade will draw capital from improvements in land. It will so in the first instance, but as this encreasing advanced interest of trade 'constitutes a new market for the produce of the land,' the rates of the price of the produce of the land will so rise, and so raise the profits made by improvements, that, although at first, as I have shewn above, it suffers a relative depression, the application of capital to it will of course and necessarily become a very advantageous employment of such: but the new and daily encreasing market of America, of which we have the monopoly, raising the rates of profit in trade, draws after it the daily ascending rates of that land, which supplies this market and the workmen in it; and is the very thing coincident with a general prosperity, that hath given such a spring to agriculture in this country.

When you say in another wreath of this corollary, that the high rates of profit necessarily keep up the high rate of interest, which *è contra* must lower the value of land, I answer, that the rate of interest does not necessarily depend on the rates of profit made by money, but on the proportion of demand for the use of it to the quantity which, and the velocity with which, the *influx* of riches, in consequence of an advancing mercantile prosperity, brings it into circulation. High profits themselves will occasion money to come in to the market which wants it; high profits, and an increasing demand, will open and give birth to a secondary source by paper circulation: so that the major of your syllogism is not founded in reason; nor is the conclusion, that the natural encrease of rent, and the rise in the value of land, is retarded by the effects of the monopoly, fact. I do here distinguish the effects of the monopoly from the effects of the trade itself: this, like all other advantageous applications of capital, where great mercantile profits are to be gotten, accelerates the rise of the profits of trade faster than those of land; but those of land are in the effect raised also by it; and although in a slower degree of velocity to that of the rise of mercantile profit, *yet not in a retarded but accelerated velocity also.*

Upon the whole, I fully and perfectly agree with you, that any regulation which gives a *confined course of direction*, and keeps in that line of direction any operation, must check and destroy part of the *vis motrix*, with which the body moving would fly off in a *direct course*. Just as the central force, which confines any body to circulate round that center in any given orbit, doth check and diminish part of the projectile force with which it would have flown off from that orbit: So the monopoly, which requires the colony-trade to observe Great Britain as its center, doth certainly check and diminish part of that *commercial activity with which it is at all points in exertion to fly off in a tangent.* Although I agree in this truth, yet being taught to think, that all separate communities, until some commercial millenium shall melt down all into one, must ever seek to give such a specifick direction to the operations of their own specifick powers, as shall maintain the separate and *relative state* of existence in which each community is placed; and knowing it to be an universal law of nature, that in any machine, part of the original *momentum* must always find itself diminished in proportion as it becomes necessary to give a *specifick direction* to its operation: So I consider the losing or lessening part of the productive activity, which the culture and commerce of the colonies might give *in a direct line, that is, to the world at large,* but not to Great Britain especially, as analogous to that law of nature; as the very essence of that combination of force, and consequential specifick direction, which confines it circulating in an orbit round Great Britain as its center; and as the precise state of that theorem, which no politician in the one case, any more than any true mechanick in the other, would deny as untrue, or condemn as wrong.

I cannot therefore but remain, and do fancy, that every sober man of business will remain in the persuasion and conviction, confirmed by experience, that while the monopoly of our colony trade gives as such to Great Britain, in its *relative state* of existence in the world, a *relative advantage* in the commercial world; Great Britain doth not lose unnecessarily any absolute advantage, nor doth subject itself to either absolute or relative disadvantage, in all other branches of commerce in which it hath not the monopoly: That it employs our capital, upon the ballance of the whole, to the greatest advantage, and conspires in the means, together with other branches of trade, of drawing forth our utmost productive industry: And that under the true system of a monopoly, Great Britain might derive from the dominion which she had in her colonies (of which dominion they were, in their due subordination, part) *force, revenue, and every commercial advantage.*

These are the matters in which I think your book has erred.

I have examined them with a view to such discussion, as may occasion a review of them; because I do really think, that your book, if corrected on these points, planned and written as it is, might become an institute, containing the *principia* of those laws of motion, by which the system of the human community is framed and doth act, AN INSTITUTE *of political œconomy*, such as I could heartily wish, for the reasons given at the beginning of this letter, that some understanding Tutor in our Universities would take up, as a basis of lectures on this subject.

I should here have proceeded to the consideration of your plans of the system, which you think Great Britain should adopt in her future conduct towards America; but the present state of events suspends all political discussion on that head. If future events shall ever lay a rational, sound and true ground of colonial government, the proposing of such may then be proper, and shall not be withheld. At present *jacta est alea*, the fate of this country is now at the hazard of events, which force, and not reason, is to decide. I am afraid we are reasoning here about things which once were, and were most dear, but are no more.

I cannot conclude this letter without saying, that as I have impressed upon my mind the highest opinion of your abilities, learning, and knowledge, and think well of your fair intentions, I hope I have never deviated from the respect which is due to such. I have taken pains to comprehend fully, and have meant to state fairly, your reasoning; and to propose my own, as I ought, with diffidence. If any expression breaths the spirit of controversy, instead of what I meant, fair discussion, I disavow it; for although personally unknown to you, yet from what I learn of you by your works, I find myself in every sentiment of respect and esteem.

Sir,
Your most obedient,
And most humble Servant,
T. Pownall.

Review

[FROM REVIEW OF] AN ENQUIRY INTO THE NATURE AND CAUSES OF THE WEALTH OF NATIONS*

William Enfield

ART. VII. *An Enquiry into the Nature and Causes of the Wealth of Nations.* By Adam Smith, LL.D. and F.R.S. formerly Professor of Moral Philosophy in the University of Glasgow. 2 vols. 4to. 1 l. 16 s. Cadell. 1776.

Whatever difficulties the financier or trader may find in the practical arts of acquiring and employing public or private wealth, the philosopher meets with difficulties no less complexing, in investigating its nature and origin, and tracing back the several variations of real or apparent wealth to their true causes. The principles of commerce, the operations of money, the grounds of the rise or fall of the price of labour or provisions, the effect of public or private funds, and other topics of a similar nature, though frequently discussed, still remain subjects of dispute, and appear to be not perfectly understood. Some writers upon these subjects have been men of business, whose situations and employments have indeed given them an accurate knowledge of facts, and enabled them to communicate valuable information to the public; but whose education and manner of life have not been peculiarly adapted to qualify them for taking those comprehensive views, and pursuing those philosophical speculations, which are necessary in order to form this kind of knowledge into a regular system. Others, without being at the pains to collect and examine particular facts, on the ground of general ideas and principles alone have formed theories, which, however ingenious, have often been found to contradict experience. Few writers in this way have

* From the *Monthly Review*, vol. 54 (January–June, 1776), pp. 299–300, 302–303, 308.

united a proper attention to facts with a regular and scientific investigation of principles.

Among the most able of this latter class, we apprehend the public will agree with us in ranking the respectable Author of this work. He has taken an extensive and connected view of the several subjects in which the wealth of nations is concerned and from an happy union of fact and theory has deduced a system, which, we apprehend, is on the whole more satisfactory, and rests on better grounds, than any which had before been offered to the Public.

The style and composition of this work, though suited to the subject, and except in a few instances sufficiently correct, is by no means its principal excellence. Its merit is of an higher order, and arises chiefly from the depth and accuracy with which the Author has investigated a subject of so complex and intricate nature, from the truth of the principles which he has established, and from the importance and utility of the conclusions which he has enabled his readers to deduce.

A mere selection of particular passages would neither do justice to the Author, nor give our Readers a competent idea of the work. We shall therefore, in this and some subsequent Articles, lay before them a connected view of the general plan and most interesting particulars of this Inquiry, in the form of abstract, without confining ourselves to the words of our Author.

The design of the first Book, to which we shall confine out attention for the present, is to trace the rise and progress of labour, and its operations, as the source of wealth; and to establish clear principles and precise ideas, concerning the origin and use of money, and the causes which determine, or which vary, the price of commodities and rent of lands. . . .

The *value* of any thing, in exchange, is *its power to purchase other goods*. The real measure of the value of all commodities is *labour*. Every man is rich or poor, according to the quantity of the produce of labour which he can purchase. The exchangeable value of any commodity is therefore equal to the quantity of labour which it will enable the owner to command. Money varies in value, according to the degree of difficulty with which it is obtained, and from other causes, and cannot therefore be a certain measure of the value of other things, but equal quantities of labour must at all times be of equal value to the labourer; labour therefore will be an invariable measure of value. Labour, as well as other commodities, has a real and a nominal price; the *real*, the quantity of real goods which is given for it; the *nominal*, the sum of money paid for it. Money is an exact measure of the value of goods at the same time and place; but at different times and places it varies. Corn is a good measure of the value of commodities from century to century, because it will nearly command equal quantities of labour from century to century; but from year to year it varies on account of the fluctuation of the seasons: nothing but labour is an uniform measure of real value. The nominal value of any commodity is the quantity of gold or silver for which it is sold, without regard to the denomination of the coin. Six shillings and eight pence was the same money price in the time of Edward II, with a pound Sterling at present, containing as much pure silver.

The price of every commodity may be resolved into one or more of these three parts, the wages paid for the labour spent upon it, the profit allowed for the stock employed in carrying on the manufacture, and the rent of land. Corn, flour, flax and most other articles, resolve their price into these three parts; that of fish commonly arises only from two of them, wages and profit of stock. The price of all the commodities which compose the whole annual produce of the labour of every country taken complexly may be thus resolved. All revenue is derived from wages, profit, or rent. The revenue arising from interest, is stock lent to be employed by another, and is therefore only a division of profit between the borrower and lender. Rent and profit, and wages and profit, are sometimes confounded by those who farm their own estates.

In every society or neighbourhood there are average rates of wages, profit, and rent, which may be called the *natural rate*. The *natural price of any commodity* is that which is just sufficient to pay the rent of land, wages of labour, and profits of stock, according to the natural rates. The actual or *market price* often differs from the natural price; being regulated by the proportion of supply and demand. When the market price sinks and continues below the natural price, either rent, wages, or profit, must be lowered; when it rises, one or more of these will rise. In those articles which do not afford regular produce according to labour, as grain, &c. the market price must be subject to frequent variations. The market price is often kept up above the natural price, by concealing the increase of demand, by preserving secrets in manufactures, by monopolizing the sale, and by all laws which limit competition in particular employments. It seldom continues long below the natural price; for, in this case, the seller feeling the loss, will soon lessen the supplies and raise the demand. . . .

The variety of subjects which our Author has discussed in this first book is so great, that it is impossible for us to enter into the particular examination of his opinions and observations on each. After the general view we have given of them we shall therefore content ourselves with remarking, that though several new opinions are advanced in the course of this Inquiry, contrary to those which have been generally received, we apprehend that, upon a close examination, they will appear to be well supported, particularly the last position, that money is not, as is generally supposed, diminishing in value.

The subjects of the second and third books are, The Nature, Accumulation, and Employment of Stock; and the different Progress of Opulence in different Nations. We propose to lay before our Readers the substance of Dr Smith's observations on these topics in our next Review.

Criticism

[FROM] OBSERVATIONS ON THE MEANS OF EXCITING A SPIRIT OF NATIONAL INDUSTRY*
James Anderson

On the nature and influence of the BOUNTY ON CORN, and the other CORN-LAWS of Great Britain.

Since writing the above, I have seen the very ingenious treatise of Dr Adam Smith on the nature and causes of the wealth of nations; and am sorry to find, that I have the misfortune to differ in opinion from an author of such extensive knowledge, and liberal sentiments, on a subject of so much real importance as that which is here treated of. And as it may be supposed that the opinion of such a respectable author will have great weight on the generality of mankind, it is of much importance to examine, whether that opinion has been adopted in consequence of just reasoning, or the reverse: for the wisest of mankind may be at times misled. Let this be my excuse for here endeavouring to investigate this subject with a more than ordinary degree of precision.

The reader will easily perceive, that the applause I have bestowed above on the general system of corn-laws in England, is founded entirely on the supposition that they are peculiarly calculated to prevent the fluctuation of the price of grain:— An object that will be allowed to be of the highest importance to the well-being of almost every individual of the state. This object seems, however, to have been entirely overlooked by Dr Smith, who considers the bounty on corn only as a contrivance calculated to enhance the price of grain, and thus to give an exorbitant profit to the farmer and corn-merchant:—Considerations which, if ever they influenced the legislature, it must be acknowledged, were little deserving their favourable notice, and which were entirely disregarded by me. This may in some

---

* Edinburgh, 1777, Postscript to letter Thirteenth, pp. 309–33.

measure account for our differing in opinion. But as it appears to me that Dr Smith's reasoning on this subject is not so strictly accurate as what we usually meet with in that valuable performance, I find it necessary to examine some of these passages with particular attention; and hope, that while I mean to proceed with that candid impartiality which becomes one who is in search of truth, I shall no where forget myself so far, as to lose the deference justly due to one of such a respectable character.

"In years of plenty," says he, "it has been already observed, the bounty by occasioning an extraordinary exportation, necessarily keeps up the price of corn in the home market above what it would naturally fall to. To do so, was the avowed purpose of the institution. In years of scarcity, though the bounty is frequently suspended, yet the great exportation which it occasions in years of plenty, must frequently hinder more or less *the plenty of one year from relieving the scarcity of another.* Both in years of plenty and in years of scarcity, therefore, the bounty necessarily tends to raise the money-price of corn somewhat higher than it otherwise would be in the home market[1]."—The hurtful effects of which general rise of price, supposing it real, he afterwards points out at great length.

That the bounty has a necessary tendency to raise the price of grain, not only *somewhat*, but *a great deal*, higher than it naturally would be, in years of plenty, in the home market, will not be denied; but it has been already showed in the preceding letter, that this circumstance is attended with the most beneficial consequences; not to the farmer only, but to the state in general, and to almost every individual in it.—This circumstance, therefore, cannot be considered as disadvantageous.

If it tended, however, to raise the price of grain also in years of scarcity, it would indeed be a destructive institution, and ought to be immediately abolished: but that it tends as much to *lower* the price of grain in times of scarcity, as to *raise* it in times of plenty, will, I hope, appear from the following considerations.

If the bounty were withdrawn, it would of necessity follow,

---

[1] Inquiry into the nature and causes of the wealth of nations, vol. 2. p. 96.

that in years of plenty, the market being overstocked, prices would naturally fall;—not in exact proportion to the amount of the surplus quantity, but a great deal below it. For where there are many sellers and few buyers, it is well known, that in all cases, but more especially with regard to those goods that are of a perishable nature, as grain, the price will fall extremely below the ordinary rate.

When this should happen,—not to mention the general stagnation to the industry of the whole nation that would ensue, the farmer in particular would find himself thrown into the most disagreeable embarrassment. A part of his corn would remain on hand; and the low price he would receive for what he could sell, would be so far from replacing to him the whole of his outlay, with the ordinary profits of stock[2], that he would find himself unable to prosecute his ordinary employment with profit.

Let us, however, suppose, that he should be able, tho' with difficulty, to bear this shock, and that he should labour his ground for the ensuing crop with the same spirit as usual. If that year should also turn out to be a year of plenty, the savings of his former crop, together with the surplus produce of this crop, added to the necessity the farmer would be under to sell *at any rate*, would now reduce the price so very low, that he would be involved in still greater and more inevitable distress. His stock, instead of being profitably employed for producing more grain, and putting in motion a greater quantity of national industry, would be locked up in attempting to preserve a perishable commodity, which no care nor expence could possibly preserve for any considerable length of time. And no man knows better than Dr Smith, what are the inconveniencies that result from thus locking up the productive stock of any community.

It does not, however, import our present argument, to point out these inconveniencies with a scrupulous minuteness. It is sufficient for our purpose here to observe, that in a few years of moderate abundance, the farmers in these circumstances would find themselves unable to follow their employment with profit, and would therefore be obliged, either to abandon it,

[2] I here, and through the whole of this Postscript, adopt the general terms employed by Dr Smith, as I think they apply with peculiar propriety to the subject treated of.

or by a less-spirited culture to raise less grain, so as to enhance the price. Less corn, in either of these cases, would inevitably be produced; and thus the farmer, by insuring a scanty crop, would secure to himself a certain market, and a good price.

In consequence of this necessary system of conduct, scanty crops would no doubt be produced, even in favourable seasons;—but if, along with this artificial scarcity, it should so happen, that the seasons were also unfavourable, the deficiency would be so very great, that the small surplus savings of former years, diminished by the innumerable accidents to which these must ever be exposed, would afford but a very trifling supply, and would be very far from making up for the double deficiency that would arise from an unfavourable season and imperfect cultivation: and if we had already occasion to remark, that the price of grain was unreasonably lowered when a small proportion of it remained unsold, it will readily occur to every reader, that the price will be still more exorbitantly raised when the quantity of grain shall thus fall a little short of the demand there is for it.

And if a second year of scarcity should succeed the first, as there would then be no surplus savings, the price would, if possible, be raised still higher, and the people be involved in greater distress.

If it should be alledged, that an unlimited freedom of importation and exportation of grain at all times, would in some measure alleviate these evils, by taking from the farmer his surplus produce in years of plenty, and by supplying the deficiencies of a scanty crop by an importation from other countries in years of scarcity, I readily allow, that it would produce these beneficial consequences *in some measure*, although in a much less perfect degree than would naturally result from a well-regulated bounty on grain. But if Dr Smith means to insinuate, that this unlimited freedom in the commerce of grain should be substituted instead of the bounty, and would be attended with those beneficial consequences he enumerates, it would seem that he has been guilty of a small inaccuracy of reasoning on this occasion, that deserves to be pointed out, as he refers to it in several other parts of his book.

If a free commerce of corn should alleviate the distress of the farmer, by taking from him in years of plenty his surplus produce, and carrying it away to other places where it might be more needed at the time, it must follow, that, in this case, *the savings of former years of plenty,* being thus carried out of the country, could no more tend *to moderate the price in times of scarcity,* than if that superfluous produce had been carried away in consequence of the bounty; so that Dr Smith must either give up with the free commerce of grain, or strike off *the savings of former years* from his list of advantages which the country is deprived of only by the bounty, seeing it would be equally deprived of it by his favourite system of a free commerce: and setting aside this article of the savings of former years, (an article besides in every possible state of things more imaginary than real), I presume it will be impossible to show, in what manner the bounty can have a tendency to raise the price of grain in years of scarcity. Considered, therefore, merely in this view, of its tending to keep the market-price of grain more steady than it otherwise would be, the bounty would seem to be highly beneficial to the state. —That this, however, is but *one* of the *many* benefits it procures, I shall have occasion to show in answering the following heavy charge brought by Dr Smith against the corn-laws and corn-merchants of England.

"There is not" says he, "perhaps but one set of men in the whole commonwealth, to whom the bounty either was or could be really serviceable. These were the corn-merchants, the exporters and importers of corn. In years of plenty, the bounty necessarily occasions a greater exportation than would other-wise have taken place; and by hindering *the plenty of one year* from relieving *the scarcity of another,* it occasioned in years of scarcity a greater importation than otherwise would have been necessary. It encreased the business of the corn-merchant in both; and in years of scarcity it not only enabled him to import a greater quantity, but to sell it at a better price, and consequently with a greater profit, than he otherwise could have made, *if the plenty of one year* had not been more or less hindered from relieving *the scarcity of another.* It is in this set of men accordingly that I have observed the greatest zeal for the continuance or renewal of the bounty." Vol. 2, p. 99.

Nothing can be more unjust and fallacious than the reasoning in this passage; and it rests on principles so diametri-cally opposite to those by which our author is usually guided, as can hardly fail to excite some degree of astonishment in the mind of the attentive reader: yet so firmly have these hetero-geneous ideas taken possession of his mind, that he repeats the same sentiments again and again in various places of his book, and dwells upon them as if they were fundamental axioms of the highest importance, which could not be controverted. It becomes necessary in these circumstances to expose their fallacy.

No one who has read Dr Smith's performance can ever suppose he means to insinuate, that the exportation and importation of corn should be always prohibited; I shall therefore omit taking any notice of the consequences that would result from that arrangement.

But if exportation of corn is allowed of in years of plenty, and importation is not prohibited in years of scarcity, the corn-merchants would have at least *as much* business without the bounty as with it, and it would be in their power to have *much higher* profits: for if, in years of plenty, the quantity of grain should be more than sufficient to supply the home market, the price, it is evident, would sink so low as to enable the merchant to have a profit on exporting it, as well as at present. The exportation, I am indeed sensible, would in this case be soon very much diminished;—but neither the employment nor the profits of the merchant would be diminished by that circumstance. For nothing can be more certain, (and Dr Smith will readily allow it), than that the quantity of grain raised in any country, will always be exactly proportioned to the ordinary and steady demand for it. When the quantity of grain produced shall exceed that ordinary demand, the farmer, finding no vent for it, will be obliged to abandon that unprofitable trade, and betake himself to some other, in which he can get more certain returns. If, on the contrary, the quantity produced should fall short of that demand, the price of grain would be raised so much by that circumstance, as to encrease the farmer's profit beyond that of other trades; which would tempt so many to go to that business, as would by their competition with one another soon reduce the profits on agriculture to the same general medium of profit as in other trades.

Now, if the farmers in Great Britain had only a demand for as much grain as the inhabitants of this island alone could annually consume, they would raise no more than was just sufficient for that purpose *in ordinary years*. But if, besides that, there were a certain and steady demand for a considerable quantity for exportation, *that* quantity also would be raised in ordinary years. But if the bounty were discontinued, there would be no certain and steady demand for exportation, so that no more grain would be reared in Britain in a year of scarcity, than would have been barely sufficient to have supported the inhabitants if it had been an ordinary crop; in which case the deficiency of that scanty crop would fall to be made up by an importation from other countries. In these circumstances, therefore, the corn-merchant would have abundant employment *in years of scarcity*; and as the inhabitants would be under the necessity of depending entirely upon him for their subsistence, he would have a better opportunity of enhancing the price, and of *grinding the faces* of the poor, than he can have according to the present system, as will by and by more clearly appear. For, on the other hand,—while the farmers continue to be employed in rearing corn for exportation as well as for the home market, in a year of scarcity, the quantity that was destined for exportation, comes to be naturally applied to make up the deficiency of that part of the crop which was originally destined for the home market; so that, instead of being obliged to import the whole of that deficiency from abroad, which otherwise must of necessity have been done, the inhabitants are supplied chiefly, perhaps entirely, with their own home produce; and are thus saved the whole amount of the price of freight, insurance, and merchants profits:—A saving of no trifling moment to them. And as the home market would be thus more abundantly supplied than it otherwise would have been, the inhabitants do not lie so much at the mercy of the corn-merchants, who are thus deprived of the possibility of demanding or of obtaining such extravagant profits as they otherwise could have easily exacted.

If, therefore, in the present system, the corn-merchants do really *export* more than they otherwise would do, they *import* less; so that they have nearly the same *quantum* of employment in the one case as in the other: but with this very important difference, that their profits are paid with infinitely greater ease to the subject, and benefit to the state, by the help of the bounty, than they could have been without it.

So far is the extraordinary exportation that may be occasioned by the bounty in years of plenty, from occasioning an extraordinary importation in years of scarcity, according to Dr Smith's hypothesis, that it produces an effect directly the reverse. For it will appear that the greater the quantity that is exported in years of plenty, the quantity imported in years of scarcity will necessarily be small in proportion to it.

An example will make this plain to the meanest capacity.

Let us suppose, that the greatest variation, in the total amount of the crop between a year of the greatest plenty and one of the greatest scarcity, amounts to one fourth of the whole crop.

Let us again suppose, that the ordinary and constant export, did, in years of medium plenty, amount to one eighth of the whole produce, the farmer would in this case be in the constant practice of rearing one eighth more grain than supplied the inhabitants *in ordinary years*; so that when the crop, through the unfavourableness of the seasons, fell short of its ordinary quantity one eighth part, there would still be enough in the country to supply the internal demand; as the eighth part of it that was destined for exportation would exactly supply the deficiency. No importation, therefore, would be needed in this case.

But if the ordinary demand for exportation should have amounted to no more than one sixteenth; although, in the case above supposed, this sixteenth part which was allotted for exportation should be kept at home, there would still remain a deficiency of another sixteenth; to make up for which deficiency, recourse must be had to importation. Nor will it be possible to obtain it from abroad till the price in the home market shall rise to such a rate as to pay for freight, insurance, and merchants profits, to enable them to bring it from foreign countries.—It is plain, however, that if the deficiency of the crop had in this case amounted to no more than one sixteenth of the medium years, there would have been no occasion for any importation; so that, according to this arrangement also, it would be but seldom that corn could be imported, and then in small quantities only.

But if, instead of one eighth, or one sixteenth, the usual quantity exported should have amounted to one fourth of the whole crop in ordinary years, it would follow, that in the greatest scarcity that could ever happen from bad seasons, there would still remain one eighth for exportation after the deficiency occasioned by the bad crop was fully supplied. According to this arrangement, the inhabitants would enjoy an universal abundance in spite of the greatest variation of seasons: nor could their markets ever experience any fluctuations of price but those that should depend on foreign markets; which might be easily so regulated by the bounty as to be scarce ever felt.

So far, therefore, is an extraordinary exportation in years of plenty from giving the merchant importers extraordinary employment in years of scarcity, that if our ordinary exports were sufficiently abundant, they would annihilate entirely the business of the merchant importer: and the importation in years of scarcity must always be diminished exactly in the same proportion as the ordinary quantity of corn exported in years of plenty shall encrease.

It is equally true, that so far is the exportation occasioned by the bounty from hindering the plenty of one year from relieving the scarcity of another, as Dr Smith supposes, that it is perhaps the only method that can be devised for effecting that purpose with any degree of laudable œconomy.

As to the supposition that farmers would ever be induced to rear more grain than was necessary for supplying the demand in years of tolerable plenty, and that they should make a constant practice of retaining the surplus quantity in their own possession till a year of scarcity should come, I frankly own, that the idea of it appears to me so extravagantly absurd, when examined even with a slight degree of attention, that I should suspect I did not understand Dr Smith's meaning in the passages above quoted, and many others where he mentions the *surplus of one crop relieving the deficiencies of another*; yet if it is not this he means, I own myself at a loss to know what it is. If I am thus induced to give answers to an opinion that he never meant to maintain, I hope he will not attribute it to any desire of misrepresenting his arguments, but purely to misconception. It would have been well if he had expressed himself a little more clearly on this head. A few observations will suffice to shew the impracticability of such a plan as that above alluded to.

Were a year of plenty to be succeeded immediately by a year of scarcity, and were that scarcity to be foreseen beforehand, like that which happened to Joseph in Egypt, such a thing as this might sometimes be done. But should seven years of plenty be succeeded by seven years of scarcity, can any one imagine, that the surplus produce of the plentiful years would be accumulated to supply a scarcity that might never perhaps be experienced? The history of Joseph's dearth gives a sufficient answer to the question.—No:—the farmer has not granaries to preserve his grain,—he has not stock to carry on his ordinary operations without regular annual returns:—and Dr Smith himself will tell us, that he would not have power to protect it from the mob, in a country like ours, were he possessed of every other convenience. Even if the internal dealer in corn should come, like Joseph, to the farmer's assistance, the immense accumulation of stock that would here be locked up, would deaden the general industry of the nation exceedingly, as all that stock must be withdrawn from some other productive employment.—The waste that would be sustained by attempting to preserve such a perishable commodity, and the risk the merchant would run of fire, of mobs, and of other disasters, would necessarily raise the price so much as could afford the merchant no sort of reasonable profit but in years of absolute famine, like that which heretofore enslaved Egypt. In short, let us view this undertaking in every possible light, and we shall find it so closely environed with difficulties on every side, as to show that it is altogether impracticable. Impracticable, however, as it is, it has been often attempted to be realised; and there are not wanting many instances of rich misers in every corner of the country, who have endeavoured to augment their stores, by refusing to sell their grain in ordinary years, and attempting to keep it till times of scarcity: but they have suffered so much for their temerity, as clearly demonstrates that such a plan can hardly be followed in any case with safety, far less with profit; and sufficiently authorises the wisdom of the general maxim, *That the farmer's best profit is the first*; and that it is always wise in him to take the current price of the year, however low that price may be. A prudent man, therefore, will have no savings of consequence, even in the most plentiful year:—a fool, if he attempts it, will not have them long.—

But, in consequence of the great exportation occasioned by the bounty, it has been showed, that a great surplus may be reared in plentiful years; which, instead of being preserved a dead and decaying stock, is immediately sent abroad. And in years of scarcity, the quantity which has been raised for suc- ceeding that which was sent abroad, by being directly applied to the use of the inhabitants, supplies, with the most judicious œconomy, the deficiency of the home market. In this manner the farmer, by never finding that he can have too great a surplus produce in years of plenty, exerts himself as much as he can to raise more; and in this manner, and in this alone, can the surplus produce of a plentiful crop be made instrumental with the strictest œconomy in diminishing the deficiency of one that is more scanty. If this method had been adopted in Egypt, the *people* might have been all abundantly fed, and still have retained their freedom during the seven years of famine, instead of becoming slaves to the cruel policy of Joseph.

Thus it appears, that Dr Smith's reasoning, as to the particulars here investigated, is entirely fallacious; and that the conclusions he draws from every position, are not only erroneous, but even directly the reverse of what they ought to have been. I would therefore apply to the merchant importer and exporter of grain, the observations he makes upon the importance of the internal corn-merchant, as they are equally applicable to both: For in this enlarged sense I perfectly agree with him in thinking, that "after the business of the farmer, that of the corn-merchant is in reality the trade, which, if properly protected and encouraged, would contribute the most to the raising of corn. It would support the trade of the farmer in the same manner as the trade of the wholesale dealer supports the manufacturer." After what has been said, it is unnecessary to add, that he has been induced to make a distinction between these two classes of corn-merchants in consequence of pursuing a train of fallacious argumentation.

It is not, therefore, because the bounty upon corn has a tendency to encrease the price of grain, and thus apparently to enrich the proprietor and farmer, or because it encreases the business and profits of the merchant exporter and importer of corn, that I have bestowed such praises upon this system of legislation. No political system that should aim at giving one class of citizens an undue preference to other classes, could be justly entitled to any degree of praise from a well-informed member of the state. But it is because that at the same time that it has a natural tendency to moderate the price of grain upon the whole, it affords a constant market to the farmer, (which is the surest way of promoting alike the interests of agriculture and of national industry); but more especially, because it tends in the most direct manner to prevent the price of grain from ever rising to an extravagant rate, or falling to an unreasonable abasement, which I consider as a benefit of the highest and most general importance; as it more effectually promotes the general industry of all ranks of people, and thus augments the vigour and internal felicity of the state, than any other circumstance that could be named.

And that the bounty has a natural tendency to produce all these salutary effects, in a higher degree than would be produced by an unlimited freedom as to the commerce of grain; and, in particular, that it necessarily moderates the price of grain in years of scarcity, instead of raising it higher than it otherwise would be, as Dr Smith asserts, will appear to the reader, I hope, very plain, not only from what has been already said, but also from the following parallel between the consequences that would be the result of a free trade in corn, compared with that which is regulated by the bounty.

First, Without the help of the bounty, no corn could ever have been exported till the price fell so low in our own market as to be the whole amount of freight, insurance, commission, and merchants profit, below the then selling price of grain in some foreign market to which it could be carried. In which case it must have been at *least* the whole amount of the bounty below the lowest price it can possibly ever fall to where that is allowed.

Secondly, There never could have been any corn imported till the price in Britain should have exceeded that in some foreign state from whence it could be brought, by the full amount of the freight, insurance, and merchants profits, for transporting it: which articles in time of war, or other disastrous occurrences, must have been on some occasions extremely high. Whereas it has been shewed, that were exportation duly encouraged by a well-regulated bounty, the home market would at all times be abundantly supplied, merely by detaining at home our own surplus produce in years of scarcity; and thus the whole freight and other charges be saved to the consumer; which alone would be an article of very great national advantage. But if it be likewise considered, that in consequence of this plenty at home, the market-price may not perhaps rise *nearly* to that height which would have admitted of importation, the national benefit procured by it will appear to be still more considerable.

Thirdly, Were we thus obliged to depend on foreign markets for a supply to our deficiencies in years of scarcity, instead of relying on our own surplus produce obtained by the aid of the bounty; in times of *general* scarcity in other countries (and such disasters do sometimes occur, from a very general failure of crop) we might be reduced to the greatest distress for want of food, and the price of grain be raised to the most extravagant height; as was frequently the case with our fore-fathers, to the utter ruin of all the poor in the kingdom. But,

Fourthly, We would in this case not only be in danger of suffering from the inclemency of seasons, but would be obliged to rely in some measure on the caprice of foreign nations for our daily bread. In consequence of wars, political alliances, or other unlooked-for circumstances that often influence the rulers of kingdoms, the only ports from which we could be supplied on a particular emergency, might be shut up from us, and we be obliged to suffer all the miseries of famine. Is it prudent in any nation which has it in its power to ward off such dreadful calamities, not to adopt that plan of conduct that would effect it, if it should even be attended with very great expence? But it is plain, that if by means of a well-regulated bounty, the general exportation of grain should ever become so considerable, as, in years of moderate plenty, always to exceed the greatest deficiency of crop that should ever be known to happen from unfavourable seasons, these very bene-ficial effects would be with certainty insured to Britain, and her inhabitants might remain in perfect security against the fear of dearth, much more against the fear of that most dreadful of all scourges, a famine.

Dr Smith asserts, that the price of grain regulates the price of every other commodity in a state; and although I may not be disposed to admit of this position in its full extent, yet upon his own principles it would seem to follow, that that state will be least liable to internal convulsions, where this universal regulator is permitted to vary as little as possible, and that he ought to have been happy at discovering an easy and effectual means of rendering that regulator as steady as the nature of things will admit of; especially if this corrector should likewise tend to make the price of that universal standard lower upon the whole than it could have been without it; (for however much I may be convinced, that an accidental depression of the price of grain below the medium price is always attended with hurtful consequences to the state; yet I presume we will both agree in thinking, that it is at all times an advantage to a state to have that general price of corn as low as the nature of things will properly admit of); and as the bounty on corn naturally tends to produce both of these good effects, we would have expected that it would have met with his approbation instead of censure. For although the bounty deprives the farmer of the profits he might reap by the great rise of price that would ensue in consequence of a scanty crop,—yet this small loss is much more than made up to him by the greater price he receives for his corn in years of plenty, and the certainty it gives him of a ready market for his grain at all times; which, however abundant, he is thus assured will never be allowed to remain unsold. He therefore goes on with spirit in his undertakings, and produces much more grain with the same expence of stock and labour than he otherwise could have done; and, like every other manufacturer in similar circumstances, can thus afford to sell his goods cheaper upon the whole than formerly, although he himself has perhaps better profit, and lives better, than he would have done in other circumstances.

Considered in this light, the bounty might with propriety be compared to a premium for insurance in any other hazardous undertaking. Agriculture is a trade necessarily subjected to very hazardous variations, owing to the unavoidable difference of seasons, and consequent encrease and decrease of crop, added to the very perishable nature of grain of all sorts. This very hazardous employment, however, must, from the nature of things, be carried on by a number of individuals, the mediocrity of whose capital stock renders them incapable of bearing these great fluctuations without the most sensible inconveniencies to themselves and families. Like every other hazardous employment, therefore, the profits must be upon the whole higher than in other less hazardous trades, otherwise it would be abandoned; and even with these high profits the risk and outlay is so great, as frequently to reduce those of moderate stock to beggary, whose ruin deranges the whole internal œconomy of the state. It is moderate profits in trade, and quick returns of stock, that most effectually contribute towards enriching the seller and accommodating the buyer; on both which accounts it would be highly beneficial to the state to devise a proper method of diminishing the risks of the farmer.

In similar circumstances with this, it has been found, that the community has derived very high advantages from insurances in every other branch of trade. By the help of this most useful invention of modern times, a man may safely venture his whole stock in the most hazardous undertaking, without the smallest risk of ruining his family. In consequence of this security, such hazardous trades are no longer abandoned to those in desperate circumstances, who in hopes of obtaining a lucky chance, venture their little all, and are ruined by its failure. They then come to be viewed as respectable employments, and are followed by men of knowledge and abilities, who by strenuous efforts strive to bring them to the utmost degree of perfection they are capable of attaining. The competition which this necessarily occasions between the numerous dealers who are thus induced to pursue these trades, soon reduces the profits upon them much lower than formerly. The market will be of course more abundantly supplied with that particular commodity in which they deal, and the price will be also more moderate than before. In every case, however, the buyers must at any rate pay the insurance-price;—and the only question that in this case remains to be determined is, Whether it will be more beneficial to the community at large to have this insurance-money advanced by some rich society, who find their profit upon such a trade; or if every individual shall still be left to bear his own private losses, and to indemnify himself for them in the best manner he can?—No man who is in the least acquainted with trade, will be at a loss to determine this question in favour of the public insurance.

But the bounty on grain gives the farmer that security he stood in need of, and is by consequence similar in its effects to an insurance-premium in every other hazardous branch of trade.

Or, if it should please another rather to consider the bounty on corn as a premium advanced by the community, for insurance against the loss they might sustain from a variation of seasons, the reasoning would be equally just, and would only differ from the former in the terms.

For in whatever manner it may be advanced, it will not admit of a doubt, that the community must pay in one way or other more money for an equal quantity of grain, the produce of a scanty crop, than of one that is more abundant, not only to make up to the grower the inlack he feels in the quantity, but also to make up for the loss he sustained by the unreasonable lowness of price in a year of too much plenty. If the farmer is left to himself, and this deficiency of crop comes to be supplied by importation, the consumers must, in the first place, pay a high premium to the farmer in the great advance on the price of grain, which must be at least so high, as to be the whole price of freight, merchants profits, &c. above some foreign accessible market at the time, and then another premium to the merchant-importer, to enable him to bring it from abroad. In this case the premium given to the farmer alone, must be altogether sufficient to indemnify *him* for his deficiency of crop and former losses, otherwise he cannot continue his employment; but besides this, there still remains to be paid another premium to the merchant-importer, which is entirely a superfluous expence to the state, as it has already paid the farmer his full insurance-profit: and what aggravates the misfortune in this case is, that both of these high premiums come to be paid at once entirely by the lower orders of the people; so that this is the most destructive method of levying it that could possibly be invented.

By contriving, however, to pay the farmer for the loss he might sustain in a year of plenty from the disproportionate lowness of price, or, in other words, by granting the bounty, they enable him to dispense with the extraordinary price he would have been obliged to exact in years of scarcity, and, by tempting him to rear as much grain as possible, they put it in his power to apply a part, or the whole, of his ordinary surplus produce to the use of the home market, instead of sending it abroad, as it was originally intended. In this manner the market is kept low; and the inhabitants are at this time saved, not only the farmer's extraordinary premium, but also the high charge of freight and merchants profits on importation, which they would otherwise have been obliged to advance. In this case also the premium is paid, viz. by the advance of the bounty-money, and the rise of price which that occasions in plentiful years; but it is paid in such a manner as not to be sensibly burdensome to the state.

Where such a political arrangement takes place, the community at large may be said to become the insurer of every individual against the inconvenience that may arise from unfavourable seasons and a scanty crop. Like the Edinburgh Friendly Insurance company, the whole society become bound to make up the loss that shall be sustained by any individual among them from fire; which enables every one of its members to live in perfect security at all times, instead of running the risk of being totally ruined by any unforeseen accident.

And as it is not in the power of man entirely to prevent

accidental fires in the one case, or accidental bad seasons in the other; so in neither case is it possible to prevent entirely the loss that may thus be sustained by those individuals that may be most exposed to danger. It ought, however, to be the study of the politician, to make these unavoidable losses be as little hurtful to the state as possible; which can be in no manner so well effected as by making that loss be borne by the community at large, as equally as possible, instead of allowing it to continue to rest entirely upon the individuals on whom the principal loss should first fall.

The bounty on corn is even perhaps more highly beneficial than the insurance on any other hazardous stock; because, in most other cases, it is those who have most property that are most exposed to danger; whereas here it is the poor, and those who have least to lose, who are the principal, and almost only sufferers, when danger comes: but as the bounty is paid out of the aggregate funds of the whole community, the rich members of the state contribute their proportion of the premium; which insures the poor a certainty of enjoying the necessaries of life at all times at a moderate price.

The bounty has a natural tendency to over-rule even the influence of bad seasons themselves, and prevent them from varying the total amount of the crop so much as they otherwise would do: for as it gives the farmer perfect security, and enables him to apply his whole capital to the improvement of his trade, it necessarily occasions a more perfect culture of the soil; and every sensible farmer knows, that a rich soil in a high degree of cultivation, is far less liable to be affected by a variation of seasons, than one that is in worse order at the time. Like a man of a robust temperament and healthy constitution, who can bear, without any sensible inconvenience, such great variations as to diet, air, exercise, &c. as would totally destroy a man of a weakly habit, the produce of an improved soil will hardly be in the least affected by a variation of season, that would entirely destroy the crop of one that was in a poor and exhausted condition. In this manner the inconveniencies of bad seasons come to be less sensibly felt, and the consequent necessity of high prices proportionally abated.

The corn-laws of England, therefore, as tending to produce all these beneficial effects, I think we need not hesitate to call extremely wise: and although it should be allowed, that in some respects they are much less perfect than they might be, we ought not to endeavour to vilify them, and cause them to be rejected on account of these defects; but rather endeavour to point out such defects as need to be corrected, so as to improve them more and more, and render them still more beneficial to posterity than they have been to ourselves. With this view I shall suggest the following hints, relating to the corn-laws, to the consideration of the judicious reader.

It would seem reasonable, that instead of one invariable bounty to be paid upon the exportation of grain equally at all times, when the grain in our home market was below one specified price, it would be more equitable, and better adapted to the end in view, (the preventing as much as possible all variations in the price of grain in the home market), to make the bounty vary with the price of grain in the home market, so as that it should encrease as the price of grain decreased.

With the same intention it would be proper, not only to permit the importation of corn when the price at home exceeded a certain rate, but even to give a premium on importation when it should rise above another limited price; and which premium should also encrease as the price in the home market encreased. . . .

[FROM] ACCOUNT OF THE LIFE AND WRITINGS OF ADAM SMITH*

Dugald Stewart

IV 7 To direct the policy of nations with respect to one most important class of its laws, those which form its system of political economy, is the great aim of Mr Smith's *Inquiry*:[1] And he has unquestionably had the merit of presenting to the world, the most comprehensive and perfect work that has yet appeared, on the general principles of any branch of legislation. The example which he has set will be followed, it is to be hoped, in due time, by other writers, for whom the internal policy of states furnishes many other subjects of discussion no less curious and interesting; and may accelerate the progress of that science which Lord Bacon has so well described in the following passage: 'Finis et scopus quem leges intueri, atque ad quem jussiones et sanctiones suas dirigere debent, non alius est, quam ut cives feliciter degant; id fiet, si pietate et religione recte instituti; moribus honesti; armis adversus hostes externos tuti; legum auxilio adversus seditiones et privatas injurias muniti; imperio et magistratibus obsequentes; copiis et opibus locupletes et florentes fuerint.—Certe cognitio ista ad viros civiles proprie spectat; qui optime nôrunt, quid ferat societas humana, quid salus populi, quid aequitas naturalis, quid

---

* From Adam Smith, *Essays on Philosophical Subjects*, ed. W. P. D. Wightman, J. C. Bryce and Ian S. Ross, general editors D. D. Raphael and A. S. Skinner (Oxford, 1980), sect. 4, pp. 311–24. Unbracketed numbered notes are by Dugald Stewart, notes in round brackets are by Ian S. Ross, and notes in square brackets are the general editor's. Superscript letters refer the reader to textual notes preserving readings from other editions of the *Account*: in *Transactions of the Royal Society of Edinburgh*, 1794 (identified as 1); in the 1795 edition of *Essays on Philosophical Subjects* (identified as 2); and in William Hamilton's *Collected Works of Dugald Stewart*, 11 vols. (Edinburgh, 1854–60) (identified as 3).

[1] [While not neglecting Smith's analytical achievement, e.g. §27 below, Stewart's preoccupation with policy may explain his defence of Smith's originality in terms of the doctrine of natural liberty at §23 and §25.]

gentium mores, quid rerumpublicarum formae diversae: ideoque possint de legibus, ex principiis et praeceptis tam aequitatis naturalis, quam politices decernere. Quamobrem id nunc agatur, ut fontes justitiae et utilitatis publicae petantur, et in singulis juris partibus character quidam et idea justi exhibeatur, ad quam particularium regnorum et rerumpublicarum leges probare, atque inde emendationem moliri, quisque, cui hoc cordi erit et curae, possit.'[2] The enumeration contained in the foregoing passage, of the different objects of law, coincides very nearly with that given by Mr Smith in the conclusion of his Theory of Moral Sentiments; and the precise aim of the political speculations which he then announced, and of which he afterwards published so valuable a part in his Wealth of Nations, was to ascertain the general principles of justice and of expediency, which ought to guide the institutions of legislators on these important articles;—in the words of Lord Bacon, to ascertain those *leges legum*, 'ex quibus informatio peti possit, quid in singulis legibus bene aut perperam positum aut constitutum sit.'[3]

8 The branch of legislation which Mr Smith has made choice

---

[2] (*Exemplum Tractatus de Fontibus Juris*, Aphor. 5: 'The ultimate object which legislators ought to have in view, and to which all their enactments and sanctions ought to be subservient, is, *that the citizens may live happily*. For this purpose, it is necessary that they should receive a religious and pious education; that they should be trained to good morals: that they should be secured from foreign enemies by proper military arrangements; that they should be guarded by an effectual policy against seditions and private injuries; that they should be loyal to government, and obedient to magistrates; and finally, that they should abound in wealth, and in other national resources.' *De Augmentis Scientiarum*, lib. viii. cap. iii: 'The science of such matters certainly belongs more particularly to the province of men who, by habits of public business, have been led to take a comprehensive survey of the social order; of the interests of the community at large; of the rules of natural equity; of the manners of nations; of the different forms of government; and who are thus prepared to reason concerning the wisdom of laws, both from considerations of justice and of policy. The great desideratum, accordingly, is, by investigating the principles of *natural justice*, and those of *political expediency*, to exhibit a theoretical model of legislation, which, while it serves as a standard for estimating the comparative excellence of municipal codes, may suggest hints for their correction and improvement, to such as have at heart the welfare of mankind.' Stewart's translation, from *Works*, i. 71–2.)

[3] (*De Fontibus Juris*, Aphor. 6: 'Laws of Laws from which we can determine what is right or wrong in the appointments of each individual law.' Stewart, *Works*, xi.2.)

of as the subject of his work, naturally leads me to remark a very striking contrast between the spirit of ancient and of modern policy in respect to the Wealth of Nations.[4] The great object of the former was to counteract the love of money and a taste for luxury, by positive institutions; and to maintain in the great body of the people, habits of frugality, and a severity of manners. The decline of states is uniformly ascribed by the philosophers and historians, both of Greece and Rome, to the influence of riches on national character; and the laws of Lycurgus, which, during a course of ages, banished the precious metals from Sparta, are proposed by many of them as the most perfect model of legislation devised by human wisdom.—How opposite to this is the doctrine of modern politicians! Far from considering poverty as an advantage to a state, their great aim is to open new sources of national opulence, and to animate the activity of all classes of the people, by a taste for the comforts and accommodations of life.

9 One principal cause of this difference between the spirit of ancient and of modern policy, may be found in the difference between the sources of national wealth in ancient and in modern times. In ages when commerce and manufactures were yet in their infancy, and among states constituted like most of the ancient republics, a sudden influx of riches from abroad was justly dreaded as an evil, alarming to the morals, to the industry, and to the freedom of a people. So different, however, is the case at present, that the most wealthy nations are those where the people are the most laborious, and where they enjoy the greatest degree of liberty. Nay, it was the general diffusion of wealth among the lower orders of men, which first gave birth to the spirit of independence in modern Europe, and which has produced under some of its governments, and especially under our own, a more equal diffusion of freedom and of happiness than took place under the most celebrated constitutions of antiquity.[5]

10 Without this diffusion of wealth among the lower orders,

---

[4] Science de la Legislation, par le Chev. Filangieri, Liv.i. chap. 13.

[5] [See, for example, WN III and especially III, iv together with the notes to the Glasgow edition. For comment, see A. Skinner. 'Adam Smith: An Economic Interpretation of History', and D. Forbes, 'Sceptical Whiggism, Commerce, and Liberty', in *Essays on Adam Smith*. The point made in the text was repeated by John Millar, *Historical View*, iv. 124.]

the important effects resulting from the invention of printing would have been extremely limited; for a certain degree of ease and independence is necessary to inspire men with the desire of knowledge, and to afford them the leisure which is requisite for acquiring it; and it is only by the rewards which such a state of society holds up to industry and ambition, that the selfish passions of the multitude can be interested in the intellectual improvement of their children. The extensive propagation of light and refinement arising from the influence of the press, aided by the spirit of commerce, seems to be the remedy provided by nature, against the fatal effects which would otherwise by produced, by the subdivision of labour accompanying the progress of the mechanical arts: Nor is any thing wanting to make the remedy effectual, but wise institutions to facilitate general instruction, and to adapt the education of individuals to the stations they are to occupy. The mind of the artist, which, from the limited sphere of his activity,[6] would sink below the level of the peasant or the savage, might receive in infancy the means of intellectual enjoyment, and the seeds of moral improvement; and even the insipid uniformity of his professional engagements, by presenting no object to awaken his ingenuity or to distract his attention, might leave him at liberty to employ his faculties, on subjects more interesting to himself, and more extensively useful to others.

11 These effects, notwithstanding a variety of opposing causes which still exist, have already resulted, in a very sensible degree, from the liberal policy of modern times. Mr Hume, in his Essay on Commerce, after taking notice of the numerous armies raised and maintained by the small republics in the ancient world, ascribes the military power of these states to their want of commerce and luxury. 'Few artisans were maintained by the labour of the farmers, and therefore more soldiers might live upon it.' He adds, however, that 'the policy of ancient times was VIOLENT, and contrary to the NATURAL course of things;'[7]—by which, I presume, he means, that it

---

[6] [See WN V.i.f.51 and this section generally, i.e. 'Of the Expence of the Institutions for the Education of Youth'.]

[7] [*Essays Moral, Political and Literary*, ed. Green and Grose (1882), i.291. The quotation reads: 'contrary to the more natural and usual course of things'.]

aimed too much at modifying, by the force of positive institutions, the order of society, according to some preconceived
idea of expediency; without trusting sufficiently to those principles of the human constitution, which, wherever they are
allowed free scope, not only conduct mankind to happiness,
but lay the foundation of a progressive improvement in their
condition and in their character. The advantages which modern
policy possesses over the ancient, arise principally from its
conformity, in some of the most important articles of political
economy, to an order of things recommended by nature; and
it would not be difficult to shew, that, where it remains imperfect, its errors may be traced to the restraints it imposes on
the natural course of human affairs. Indeed, in these restraints
may be discovered the latent seeds of many of the prejudices
and follies which infect modern manners, and which have so
long bid defiance to the reasonings of the philosopher and the
ridicule of the satirist.

12 The foregoing very imperfect hints appeared to me to
form, not only a proper, but in some measure a necessary
introduction to the few remarks I have to offer on Mr Smith's
Inquiry; as they tend to illustrate a connection between his
system of commercial politics, and those speculations of his
earlier years, in which he aimed more professedly at the
advancement of human improvement and happiness. It is this
view of political economy that can alone render it interesting
to the moralist, and can dignify calculations of profit and loss
in the eye of the philosopher.[8] Mr Smith has alluded to it in
various passages of his work, but he has nowhere explained
himself fully on the subject; and the great stress he has laid on
the effects of the division of labour in increasing its productive
powers, seems, at first sight, to point to a different and very
melancholy conclusion;—that the same causes which promote
the progress of the arts, tend to degrade the mind of the artist;
and, of consequence, that the growth of national wealth implies
a sacrifice of the character of the people.[9]

13 The fundamental doctrines of Mr Smith's system are now
so generally known, that it would have been tedious to offer

[8] [This statement, together with the broadly liberal sentiments of the preceding
paragraphs, may bear upon Stewart's own experience. See for example,
Works x. xlvi–liv.]

[9] [See, for example, WN V.i.f.50.]

any recapitulation of them in this place; even if I could have hoped to do justice to the subject, within the limits which I have prescribed to myself at present.[10] I shall content myself, therefore, with remarking, in general terms, that the great and leading object of his speculations is, to illustrate the provision made by nature in the principles of the human mind, and in the circumstances of man's external situation, for a gradual and progressive augmentation in the means of national wealth; and to demonstrate, that the most effectual plan for advancing a people to greatness, is to maintain that order of things which nature has pointed out; by allowing every man, as long as he observes the rules of justice, to pursue his own interest in his own way, and to bring both his industry and his capital into the freest competition with those of his fellow-citizens.[11] Every system of policy which endeavours, either by extraordinary encouragements to draw towards a particular species of industry a greater share of the capital of the society than what would naturally go to it, or, by extraordinary restraints, to force from a particular species of industry some share of the capital which would otherwise be employed in it, is, in reality, subversive of the great purpose which it means to promote.[12]

14 What the circumstances are, which, in modern Europe, have contributed to disturb this order of nature, and, in particular, to encourage the industry of towns, at the expence of that of the country, Mr Smith has investigated with great ingenuity,[13] and in such a manner, as to throw much new light on the history of that state of society which prevails in this quarter of the globe. His observations on this subject tend to shew, that these circumstances were, in their first origin, the

[10] A distinct analysis of his work might indeed be useful to many readers; but it would itself form a volume of considerable magnitude. I may perhaps, at some future period, present to the Society, an attempt towards such an analysis, which I began long ago, for my own satisfaction, and which I lately made considerable progress in preparing for the press, before I was aware of the impossibility of connecting it, with the general plan of this paper. In the mean time *1–2* (See the article *Smith, Adam*, in the Index to Stewart, *Works*, xi, for references to analysis of parts of WN.)

[11] [WN IV.ix.51.]

[12] [WN IV.ix.50.]

[13] [Smith makes this point in WN II.v.37, drawing attention to the two following books.]

natural and the unavoidable result of the peculiar situation of mankind during a certain period; and that they took their rise, not from any general scheme of policy, but from the private interests and prejudices of particular orders of men.

15 The state of society, however, which at first arose from a singular combination of accidents, has been prolonged much beyond its natural period, by a false system of political economy, propagated by merchants and manufacturers; a class of individuals, whose interest is not always the same with that of the public, and whose professional knowledge gave them many advantages, more particularly in the infancy of this branch of science, in defending those opinions which they wished to encourage. By means of this system, a new set of obstacles to the progress of national prosperity has been created. Those which arose from the disorders of the feudal ages, tended directly to disturb the internal arrangements of society, by obstructing the free circulation of labour and of stock, from employment to employment, and from place to place. The false system of political economy which has been hitherto prevalent, as its professed object has been to regulate the commercial intercourse between different nations, has produced its effect in a way less direct and less manifest, but equally prejudicial to the states that have adopted it.

16 On this system, as it took its rise from the prejudices, or rather from the interested views of mercantile speculators, Mr Smith bestows the title of the Commercial or Mercantile System;[14] and he has considered at great length its two principal expedients for enriching a nation; restraints upon importation, and encouragements to exportation.[15] Part of these expedients, he observes, have been dictated by the spirit of monopoly, and part by a spirit of jealousy against those countries with which the balance of trade is supposed to be disadvantageous.[16] All of them appear clearly, from his reasonings, to have a tendency unfavourable to the wealth of the nation which imposes them.—His remarks with respect to the jealousy of commerce

[14] [The title of WN IV.i. In the introduction to this book, the commercial system is described as 'the modern system, and is best understood in our own country and in our own times'.]

[15] [WN IV.i.35.]

[16] [See, for example, the conclusion of WN IV.iii.a.1.]

are expressed in a tone of indignation, which he seldom assumes in his political writings.

17 'In this manner (says he) the sneaking arts of underling tradesmen are erected into political maxims for the conduct of a great empire.[17] By such maxims as these,[18] nations have been taught that their interest consisted in beggaring all their neighbours. Each nation has been made to look with an invidious eye upon the prosperity of all the nations with which it trades, and to consider their gain as its own loss. Commerce, which ought naturally to be among nations as among individuals, a bond of union and friendship, has become the most fertile source of discord and animosity. The capricious ambition of Kings and Ministers has not, during the present and the preceding century, been more fatal to the repose of Europe, than the impertinent jealousy of merchants and manufacturers. The violence and injustice of the rulers of mankind is an ancient evil, for which[19] perhaps the nature of human affairs can scarce admit of a remedy. But the mean rapacity, the monopolizing spirit of merchants and manufacturers, who neither are nor ought to be the rulers of mankind, though it cannot perhaps be corrected, may very easily be prevented from disturbing the tranquillity of any body but themselves.'[20]

18 Such are the liberal principles which, according to Mr Smith, ought to direct the commercial policy of nations; and of which it ought to be the great object of legislators to facilitate the establishment. In what manner the execution of the theory should be conducted in particular instances, is a question of a very different nature, and to which the answer must vary, in different countries, according to the different circumstances of the case. In a speculative work, such as Mr Smith's, the consideration of this question did not fall properly under his general plan; but that he was abundantly aware of the danger to be apprehended from a rash application of political theories, appears not only from the general strain of his writings, but from some incidental observations which he has

[17] [WN IV.iii.c.8. The quotation occurs at the end of the paragraph and reads 'are thus erected'.]

[18] [The original reads 'By such maxims as these, however, . . .'.]

[19] [The original text reads 'for which, I am afraid, the nature. . . '.]

[20] (WN IV.iii.c.9.)

expressly made upon the subject. 'So unfortunate (says he, in one passage) are the effects of all the regulations of the mercantile system, that they not only[21] introduce very dangerous disorders into the state of the body politic, but disorders which it is often difficult to remedy, without occasioning, for a time at least, still greater disorders.—In what manner, therefore,[22] the natural system of perfect liberty and justice ought gradually to be restored, we must leave to the wisdom of future statesmen and legislators to determine.'[23] In the last edition of his Theory of Moral Sentiments, he has introduced some remarks, which have an obvious reference to the same important doctrine. The following passage seems to refer more particularly to those derangements of the social order which derived their origin from the feudal institutions:

19 'The man whose public spirit is prompted altogether by humanity and benevolence, will respect the established powers and privileges even of individuals, and still more[24] of the great orders and societies into which the state is divided. Though he should consider some of them as in some measure abusive, he will content himself with moderating, what he often cannot annihilate without great violence. When he cannot conquer the rooted prejudices of the people by reason and persuasion, he will not attempt to subdue them by force; but will religiously observe what, by Cicero, is justly called the divine maxim of Plato, never to use violence to his country no more than to his parents. He will accommodate, as well as he can, his public arrangements to the confirmed habits and prejudices of the people; and will remedy, as well as he can, the inconveniencies which may flow from the want of those regulations which the people are averse to submit to. When he cannot establish the right, he will not disdain to ameliorate the wrong; but, like Solon, when he cannot establish the best system of laws, he

---

[21] [The original reads 'Such are the unfortunate effects of all the regulations of the mercantile system! They not only. . . '.]

[22] [The original continues 'the colony trade ought gradually to be opened; what are the restraints which ought first, and what are those which ought last to be taken away; or in what manner'.]

[23] (WN IV.vii.c.44.)

[24] [The original reads 'still more those. . . '.]

will endeavour to establish the best that the people can bear.'[25]

20 These cautions with respect to the practical application of general principles were peculiarly necessary from the Author of 'The Wealth of Nations;' as the unlimited freedom of trade, which it is the chief aim of his work to recommend, is extremely apt, by flattering the indolence of the statesman, to suggest to those who are invested with absolute power, the idea of carrying it into immediate execution. 'Nothing is more adverse to the tranquillity of a statesman (says the author of an Eloge on the Administration of Colbert) than a spirit of moderation; because it condemns him to perpetual observation, shews him every moment the insufficiency of his wisdom, and leaves him the melancholy sense of his own imperfection; while, under the shelter of a few general principles, a systematical politician enjoys a perpetual calm. By the help of one alone, that of a perfect liberty of trade, he would govern the world, and would leave human affairs to arrange themselves at pleasure, under the operation of the prejudices and the self-interests of individuals. If these run counter to each other, he gives himself no anxiety about the consequence; he insists that the result cannot be judged of till after a century or two shall have elapsed. If his contemporaries, in consequence of the disorder into which he has thrown public affairs, are scrupulous about submitting quietly to the experiment, he accuses them of impatience. They alone, and not he, are to blame for what they have suffered; and the principle continues to be inculcated with the same zeal and the same confidence as before.' These are the words of the ingenious and eloquent author of the Eloge on Colbert, which obtained the prize from the French Academy in the year 1763; a performance which, although confined and erroneous in its speculative views, abounds with just and important reflections of a practical nature. How far his remarks apply to that particular class of politicians whom he had evidently in his eye in the foregoing passage, I shall not presume to decide.

21 It is hardly necessary for me to add to these observations, that they do not detract in the least from the value of those political theories which attempt to delineate the principles of a perfect legislation. Such theories (as I have elsewhere

[25] [TMS VI.ii.2.16.]

observed[26]) ought to be considered merely as descriptions of the *ultimate* objects at which the statesman ought to aim. The tranquillity of his administration, and the immediate success of his measures, depend on his good sense and his practical skill; and his theoretical principles only enable him to direct his measures steadily and wisely, to promote the improvement and happiness of mankind, and prevent him from being ever led astray from these important ends, by more limited views of temporary expedience. 'In all cases (says Mr Hume) it must be advantageous to know what is most perfect in the kind, that we may be able to bring any real constitution or form of government as near it as possible, by such gentle alterations and innovations as may not give too great disturbance to society.'[27]

22 The limits of this Memoir make it impossible for me to examine particularly the merit of Mr Smith's work in point of originality. That his doctrine concerning the freedom of trade and of industry coincides remarkably with that which we find in the writings of the French Economists, appears from the slight view of their system which he himself has given.[28] But it surely cannot be pretended by the warmest admirers of that system, that any one of its numerous expositors has approached to Mr Smith in the precision and perspicuity with which he has stated it, or in the scientific and luminous manner in which he has deduced it from elementary principles. The awkwardness of their technical language, and the paradoxical form in which they have chosen to present some of their opinions, are acknowledged even by those who are most willing to do justice to their merits; whereas it may be doubted, with respect to Mr Smith's Inquiry, if there exists any book beyond the circle of the mathematical and physical sciences, which is at once so agreeable in its arrangement to the rules of a sound logic, and so accessible to the examination of ordinary readers. Abstracting entirely from the author's

---

[26] Elements of the Philosophy of the Human Mind, p. 261. (Stewart, *Works*, ii.240.)

[27] ['Idea of a Perfect Commonwealth', *Essays Moral, Political and Literary*, ed. Green and Grose, i.481.]

[28] [Not perhaps a wholly fair assessment of WN. ix: cf. A. Skinner, 'Adam Smith: The Development of a System', *Scottish Journal of Political Economy*, xxiii (1976).]

peculiar and original speculations, I do not know that, upon any subject whatever, a work has been produced in our times, containing so methodical, so comprehensive, and so judicious a digest of all the most profound and enlightened philosophy of the age.

23 In justice also to Mr Smith, it must be observed, that although some of the economical writers had the start of him in publishing their doctrines to the world, these doctrines appear, with respect to him, to have been altogether original, and the result of his own reflections.[29] Of this, I think, every person must be convinced, who reads the Inquiry with due attention, and is at pains to examine the gradual and beautiful progress of the author's ideas: But in case any doubt should remain on this head, it may be proper to mention, that Mr Smith's political lectures, comprehending the fundamental principles of his Inquiry, were delivered at Glasgow as early as the year 1752 or 1753; at a period, surely, when there existed no French performance on the subject, that could be of much use to him in guiding his researches.[30] In the year 1756, indeed, M. Turgot (who is said to have imbibed his first notions concerning the unlimited freedom of commerce from an old merchant, M. Gournay), published in the *Encyclopédie*, an article which sufficiently shews how completely his mind was emancipated from the old prejudices in favour of commercial regulations: But that even then, these opinions were confined to a few speculative men in France, appears from a passage in the *Mémoires sur la Vie et les Ouvrages de M. Turgot*; in which, after a short quotation from the article just mentioned, the author adds: 'These ideas were *then* considered as paradoxical; they are since become common, and they will one day be adopted universally.'

24 The Political Discourses of Mr Hume were evidently of greater use to Mr Smith, than any other book that had

---

[29] [It is pointed out above (III.5), however, that contact with the physiocrats 'could not fail to assist him in methodizing and digesting his speculations'.]

[30] In proof of this, it is sufficient for me to appeal to a short history of the progress of political economy in France, published in one of the volumes of *Ephémérides du Citoyen*. See the first part of the volume for the year 1769. The paper is entitled, *Notice abrégée des différens Ecrits modernes, qui ont concouru en France à former la science de l'économie politique.*—Stewart's note.

appeared prior to his lectures. Even Mr Hume's theories, however, though always plausible and ingenious, and in most instances profound and just, involve some fundamental mistakes; and, when compared with Mr Smith's, afford a striking proof, that, in considering a subject so extensive and so complicated, the most penetrating sagacity, if directed only to particular questions, is apt to be led astray by first appearances;[31] and that nothing can guard us effectually against error, but a comprehensive survey of the whole field of discussion, assisted by an accurate and patient analysis of the ideas about which our reasonings are employed.—It may be worth while to add, that Mr Hume's Essay 'on the Jealousy of Trade,' with some other of his Political Discourses, received a very flattering proof of M. Turgot's approbation, by his undertaking the task of translating them into the French language.

25 I am aware that the evidence I have hitherto produced of Mr Smith's originality may be objected to as not perfectly decisive, as it rests entirely on the recollection of those students who attended his first courses of moral philosophy at Glasgow; a recollection which, at the distance of forty years, cannot be supposed to be very accurate. There exists, however, fortunately, a short manuscript drawn up by Mr Smith in the year 1755, and presented by him to a society of which he was then a member; in which paper, a pretty long enumeration is given of certain leading principles, both political and literary, to which he was anxious to establish his exclusive right; in order to prevent the possibility of some rival claims which he thought he had reason to apprehend, and to which his situation as a Professor, added to his unreserved communications in private companies, rendered him peculiarly liable. This paper is at present in my possession. It is expressed with a good deal of that honest and indignant warmth, which is perhaps unavoidable by a man who is conscious of the purity of his own intentions, when he suspects that advantages have been taken of the frankness of his temper. On such occasions, due

---

[31] [Possibly a reference to sentiments which Smith was known to have expressed. In LJ(B) 253 (ed. Cannan, 197), for example, Smith refers to the ingenuity of Hume's reasoning on the subject of money, while noting that: 'He seems however to have gone a little into the notion that public opulence consists in money.']

allowances are not always made for those plagiarisms,[32] which, however cruel in their effects, do not necessarily imply bad faith in those who are guilty of them; for the bulk of mankind, incapable themselves of original thought, are perfectly unable to form a conception of the nature of the injury done to a man of inventive genius, by encroaching on a favourite speculation. For reasons known to some members of this Society, it would be improper, by the publication of this manuscript, to revive the memory of private differences; and I should not have even alluded to it, if I did not think it a valuable document of the progress of Mr Smith's political ideas at a very early period. Many of the most important opinions in *The Wealth of Nations* are there detailed; but I shall quote only the following sentences: 'Man is generally considered by statesmen and projectors as the materials of a sort of political mechanics. Projectors disturb nature in the course of her operations in human affairs; and it requires no more than to let her alone, and give her fair play in the pursuit of her ends, that she may establish her own designs.'—And in another passage: 'Little else is requisite to carry a state to the highest degree of opulence from the lowest barbarism, but peace, easy taxes, and a tolerable administration of justice; all the rest being brought about by the natural course of things. All governments which thwart this natural course, which force things into another channel, or which endeavour to arrest the progress of society at a particular point, are unnatural, and to support themselves are obliged to be oppressive and tyrannical.—A great part of the opinions (he observes) enumerated in this paper is treated of at length in some lectures which I have still by me, and which were written in the hand of a clerk who left my service six years ago. They have all of them been the constant subjects of my lectures since I first taught Mr Craigie's class, the first winter I spent in Glasgow, down to this day, without any considerable variation. They had all of them been the subjects of lectures which I read at Edinburgh the winter before I left

---

[32] [Smith writes briefly of plagiarism, but with no especial warmth of feeling, in TMS III.2.15: 'A weak man ... pretends to have done what he never did, to have written what another wrote, to have invented what another discovered; and is led into all the miserable vices of plagiarism and common lying.' See also TMS VII.ii.4.8: 'the foolish plagiary who gives himself out for the author of what he has no pretensions to' is 'properly accused' of vanity.]

it, and I can adduce innumerable witnesses, both from that place and from this, who will ascertain them sufficiently to be mine.'

26 After all, perhaps the merit of such a work as Mr Smith's is to be estimated less from the novelty of the principles it contains, than from the reasonings employed to support these principles, and from the scientific manner in which they are unfolded in their proper order and connection.[33] General assertions with respect to the advantages of a free commerce, may be collected from various writers of an early date. But in questions of so complicated a nature as occur in political economy, the credit of such opinions belongs of right to the author who first established their solidity, and followed them out to their remote consequences; not to him who, by a fortunate accident, first stumbled on the truth.

27 Besides the principles which Mr Smith considered as more peculiarly his own, his Inquiry exhibits a systematical view of the most important articles of political economy, so as to serve the purpose of an elementary treatise on that very extensive and difficult science. The skill and the comprehensiveness of mind displayed in his arrangement, can be judged of by those alone who have compared it with that adopted by his immediate predecessors. And perhaps, in point of utility, the labour he has employed in connecting and methodizing their scattered ideas, is not less valuable than the results of his own original speculations: For it is only when digested in a clear and natural order, that truths make their proper impression on the mind, and that erroneous opinions can be combated with success.

28 It does not belong to my present undertaking (even if I were qualified for such a task) to attempt a separation of the solid and important doctrines of Mr Smith's book from those opinions which appear exceptionable or doubtful. I acknowledge, that there are some of his conclusions to which I would not be understood to subscribe implicitly; more particularly in that chapter, where he treats of the principles of taxation[c];—a subject, which he has certainly examined in a manner more

---

[33] [A rather similar judgement of TMS is given in Note C, §4.]

[c]–[c] and which is certainly executed in a manner more loose and unsatisfactory than the other parts of his system. *1–2.*

loose and unsatisfactory than most of the others which have fallen under his review.^c

29 It would be improper for me to conclude this section without taking notice of the manly and dignified freedom with which the author uniformly delivers his opinions, and of the superiority which he discovers throughout, to all the little passions connected with the factions of the times in which he wrote. Whoever takes the trouble to compare the general tone of his composition with the period of its first publication, cannot fail to feel and acknowledge the force of this remark.— It is not often that a disinterested zeal for truth has so soon met with its just reward. Philosophers (to use an expression of Lord Bacon's) are 'the servants of posterity;' and most of those who have devoted their talents to the best interests of mankind, have been obliged, like Bacon, to 'bequeath their fame' to a race yet unborn, and to console themselves with the idea of sowing what another generation was to reap:

Insere Daphni pyros, carpent tua poma nepotes.[34]

Mr Smith was more fortunate; or rather, in this respect, his fortune was singular. He survived the publication of his work only fifteen years; and yet, during that short period, he had not only the satisfaction of seeing the opposition it at first excited, gradually subside, but to witness the practical influence of his writings on the commercial policy of his country.

---

[34] [Virgil, *Eclogues*, ix.50: 'Graft your pears, Daphnis, your descendants will gather your fruits'.]

[FROM] AN INQUIRY INTO THE NATURE AND ORIGIN OF PUBLIC WEALTH*

James Maitland, Lord Lauderdale

Of Value

The Author of the Inquiry into the Wealth of Nations, is, however, the person who has struggled most to establish the opinion, that labour may be considered as an accurate measure of value.

. . .After all, it is the effect that this opinion has, in destroying all just idea of the nature of value, and the authority of those who have held it, rather than the ingenuity or even plausibility of the manner in which it is supported, that makes it worthy of consideration.

To those who understand any thing of the nature of value, or on what its variations depend, the existence of a perfect measure of value must at once appear impossible: for as nothing can be a real measure of length and quantity, which is subject to variations in its own dimensions, so nothing can be a real measure of the value of other commodities, which is constantly varying in its own value. But as there is nothing which is not subject to variations, both in its quantity and in the demand for it, there can be nothing which is not subject to alteration in value.

In the learned work, however, alluded to, the author, without descending to any reasoning, qualifies labour for sustaining the character of a measure of value, by declaring, that 'labour alone never varies in its own value[1].' And this appears more extraordinary, because labour is the thing most subject to variation in its value, and is of course, of all others that could

* Edinburgh, 1804, pp. 26–29, 38, 208–29.

[1] Wealth of Nations, vol. 1. p. 38. 4to edit [I.V.7].

have been selected, the worst calculated to perform that duty.

As, however, nothing else has ever been held out as constituting an accurate measure of value; and as the opinion still has its advocates, that labour is such, though completely destructive of every correct view of the nature of value, it is perhaps worth while, in order to extinguish the idea of the possibility of its forming an accurate measure of value, shortly to prove that, of all things, it is the least qualified for this task, by references to what seems the least suspicious authority,—opinions delivered in that very work, which declares labour to possess fixed and invariable value; and which has been affirmed to contain substantial proof that labour is a real measure of value.

Things may alter in their value:

1. At periods not remote; as for example, of the same year.

2. At remote periods of time.

3. In different countries.

4. In different parts of the same country.

These may be generally considered as the four cases which give rise to alterations in the value of all commodities; for, generally speaking, there is nothing subject to variation of value at the same time, and in the same place. Labour, however, it will appear, in the opinion of the learned author, who styles it the sole thing invariable in its value, is subject not only to all the usual sources of variation, but possesses exclusively the characteristic of varying at the same time and place.

. . .Great, therefore, as the authorities are who have regarded labour as a measure of value, and who by so doing have contradicted that view of the nature of value which has been given, it does not appear that labour forms any exception to the general rule, that nothing possess real, fixed or intrinsic value; or that there is any solid reason for doubting the two general principles we have endeavoured to establish:—

1. That things are alone valuable in consequence of their uniting qualities, which make them the objects of man's desire, with the circumstance of existing in a certain degree of scarcity.

2. That the degree of value which every commodity

possesses, depends upon the proportion betwixt the quantity of it and the demand for it.

Of Public Wealth and Individual Riches

...But popular prejudice, which has regarded the sum-total of individual riches to be synonymous with public wealth, and which has conceived every means of increasing the riches of individuals to be a means of increasing public wealth, has pointed out parsimony or accumulation by a man's depriving himself of the objects of desire, to which his fortune entitles him, (the usual means of increasing private fortune), as the most active means of increasing public wealth.

When we reflect that this abstinence from expenditure, and consequent accumulation, neither tends to increase the produce of land, to augment the exertions of labour, nor to perform a portion of labour that must otherwise be executed by the hand of man; it seems that we might be entitled at once to pronounce, that accumulation may be a method of transferring wealth from A, B and C, to D; but that it cannot be a method of increasing public wealth, because wealth can alone be increased by the same means by which it is produced.

But when the public prejudice is confirmed by men most admired for talents; when we are told by the most esteemed authority, that every prodigal is a public enemy, and every frugal man a public benefactor[2]; that parsimony, and not industry, increases capital, (meaning wealth[3]); and that, as frugality increases, and prodigality diminishes, the public capital; so the conduct of those whose expence just equals their revenue, neither increases nor diminishes it[4]; it becomes necessary to enter into a more minute examination of this opinion[5]; and the more so, as it has given birth to an erroneous system of legislation, which, if persisted in, must infallibly ruin the country that adopts or perseveres in it.

---

[2] Wealth of Nations, vol. 1. p. 414. 4to edit [II.iii.25].

[3] Ibid. vol. 1. p. 410 [II.iii.16].

[4] Ibid. p. 421 [II.iii.37].

[5] This opinion concerning the salutary effects of parsimony, is held by many other writers on political œconomy; more particularly by TURGOT, in his Treatise on the Formation and Distribution of Riches. See from paragraph 49. to paragraph 83.

The means by which stock or capital acquires a profit, have been already investigated. It has been shewn, that it is uniformly profitable to man, by supplanting the necessity of a portion of labour he must otherwise perform, or by performing a portion of labour beyond the reach of his powers; and it does not require much consideration to discover what it is that executes this labour: for it is obviously a part of the produce of the earth, or a part of the earth itself, to which either nature or art has given a form that adapts it for the purpose of supplanting labour.

If capital, however, in all its varieties, is neither more nor less than a part of the produce of the earth, or a part of the earth itself, to which either nature or art has given a form that adapts it for supplanting or performing a portion of labour; let us consider, whether there are not bounds to the quantity of its revenue, which a country can, consistent with its welfare, bestow in this sort of expenditure, that is appropriate to the execution of this duty.

For the sake of perspicuity, we shall begin by considering the effects of accumulation in a simple state of society, where capital has not yet assumed all that variety of form, which man, in the progress of society, gives it, for the purpose of performing labour; though the same observations will afterwards be found applicable to societies such as modern Europe presents to our view, where capital floats in all the variety of channels to which extended commerce destines it, and where even the natural channels, in which all property would fluctuate, are deranged by overgrown financial arrangements.

When society exists in that state where man is chiefly occupied in agriculture, or the cultivation of the land, his property can alone consist in the land he possesses,—in the grain he annually produces, and the breeding stock whose produce is reared for consumption,—and, lastly, in the animals and utensils he employs, to enable him to produce and consume his wealth with less labour; that is, in a more satisfactory and comfortable manner to himself. In such a state, his property, therefore, divides itself into three different branches.

1. The land he cultivates.

2. The stock he reserves for immediate and remote consumption; under which is comprehended the produce of his farm, whether vegetable or animal.

3. His capital, consisting of the animals or machines he employs to supplant labour in the cultivation of his farm, or in the convenient consumption of its produce.

That this last part of his wealth is highly beneficial to himself, as well as to the society in which he lives, is undoubted; it supplants a portion of labour which must otherwise be executed by the hand of man, and may even execute a portion of labour beyond the reach of the personal exertions of man to accomplish. If therefore, he is not possessed of a sufficiency of those animals, instruments and machines, which form his capital, it will most clearly be commendable, and in the highest degree advantageous to society, that he should augment the exertions of his industry, for the purpose of procuring them; and if he cannot otherwise effect this augmentation, it may even be prudent and beneficial that he should abridge a portion of his immediate consumption, for the sake of increasing his capital; that is, that he should allot a part of the live stock and grain he otherwise would immediately consume and enjoy, to purchase what would enable him, at a future period, to produce and consume more with greater ease and satisfaction to himself.

If, on the other hand, however, he is already in possession of as much capital, as, in the existing state of his knowledge, he can use for the purpose of supplanting labour in cultivating the quantity of land he possesses, it can neither be advantageous for himself nor for the public that he should abridge his consumption of food, clothing, and the other objects of his desire, for the purpose of accumulating a much greater quantity of capital, (that is of live and dead stock, for performing labour), than can by possibility be employed in supplanting labour. The extension of his lands, or the invention of new means of supplanting labour, would justify a desire for increasing his capital; but, otherwise, accumulation, by deprivation of expenditure, must be detrimental to himself as well as to the public.

To the farmer it must be disadvantageous, because he deprives himself and his family of what they naturally desire, and would otherwise enjoy, for the purpose either of acquiring a larger quantity of labouring cattle than he could usefully employ, (the maintenance of which demands farther sacrifices of what his family would wish to enjoy), or of accumulating a hoard of spades, ploughs, and other utensils of husbandry, with which he was acquainted, infinitely greater than he could use;—thus depriving himself of substantial enjoyments, for the purpose of acquiring an additional quantity of that of which an increase, after a certain portion is obtained, can be of no further utility.

To the public it is still more disadvantageous, because it diverts the channel of its industry from a path, in which it must be useful, to a path in which, unless there is either an acquisition of territory, or a discovery of new means of supplanting or performing labour by capital, it is useless to mankind.

It creates, indeed, a demand for the labour of the blacksmith, of the carpenter, and of other mechanics who are employed in giving to raw materials the form that adapts them for supplanting labour; and it will thus alter the proportion betwixt the demand for, and quantity of, this sort of labour, in such a manner as, by increasing the value of it, to encourage its augmentation. But as this increase of value, and consequent encouragement given to this species of labour, must occasion a diminution of expenditure, in things that would be immediately consumed, it must reduce their value by the portion of demand it abstracts from them, (as has been already shewn[6]), in a greater degree than it increases the value of that labour, or of those commodities, to the acquisition of which it is perverted; that is, it must produce a greater diminution of encouragement to the providing of food, clothing, and those other articles which would have been consumed, had it not been for this avidity of accumulating capital, than it gives augmentation of encouragement to the forming of those things, which, if they could all be used, would tend to supplant labour.

But further, to display the full extent of the evil that must arise from indulging this baneful passion for accumulation, that has been falsely denominated a virtue, it is necessary here to explain the singular effect which the demand it creates must have on individual riches.

It has already been made evident, that a sudden demand for any consumeable commodity, by increasing its value, encourages an augmented production, and tends, therefore, to increase wealth, though its effect is always counteracted by the

---

[6] See Lauderdale's *Inquiry* (1804), p. 86, 87.

more important diminution of the value of other commodities, (from which the sudden rise of the value of any one commodity abstracts a portion of demand); because the check given to production, by the abstraction of demand, has a more powerful effect in diminishing wealth, than the encouragement arising from an extension of demand has in augmenting it. This was illustrated, by shewing the effect which doubling the demand for sugar would have, where the means of satisfying that increased demand were to be found by abstracting a part of the expenditure of the society in butchers-meat, wine and mustard[7].

In considering that subject, it appeared, that, though the diminution of individual riches, in the articles of wine, mustard and butchers-meat, would be great, this would, in some degree, though inadequately, be compensated by an increase in the value of sugar, and the consequent augmentation of the riches of individuals in that article.

But if this abstraction of demand from the articles of butchers-meat, wine and mustard, had been occasioned by the desire of the farmer to accumulate capital; that is, to hoard up a quantity of ploughs and other instruments of agriculture, greater than could be used; then, as the quantity of these articles would be increased in proportion to the demand for them, their value must be diminished, as well as that of the butchers-meat, wine and mustard, from whence the demand is abstracted. Thus a diminution of value must be produced, not only in the articles for which parsimony occasions an abstraction of demand, but even in the article for which it creates a demand; and public wealth must severely feel the effects of the discouragement by this means given to the production of both.

The public must, therefore, suffer by this love of accumulation, if pushed beyond its due bounds;—1. By the creation of a quantity of capital more than is requisite;—and, 2. By abstracting a portion of encouragement to future reproduction.—

1. *By the creation of a quantity of capital more than is requisite* for the moment, a thing, however much esteemed, is produced in such a quantity, that the whole cannot be employed,—a part

---

[7] See Lauderdale's *Inquiry* (1804), p. 87.

ceases to be an object of desire; and as things, when no longer scarce, can form no part of individual riches, so, when no longer objects of desire, they form neither a portion of individual riches nor of wealth.—The finest palaces in the world stand empty at Delhi, unoccupied and undesired; and the spacious warehouses at Antwerp, serve only as monuments of her departed commerce.

2. *By abstracting a portion of encouragement to future reproduction*, a diminution must be occasioned in the wealth to be produced; for, as long as the nature of men remains unchanged, the knowledge of what has been consumed, and of the degree of avidity displayed in the market for the different articles of consumption, must imperiously regulate the nature of what is subsequently produced. This, indeed, may be assumed as a proposition universally admitted; inasmuch as even those who hold deprivation of expenditure, and consequent accumulation, to be a mode of increasing wealth, acknowledge (with unaccountable inconsistency) that the whole quantity of industry annually employed to bring any commodity to market, suits itself to the effectual demand[8].

If, however, deprivation of expenditure, and consequent accumulation, far from being a means of increasing the wealth of the nation, must, in this simple state of society, by discouraging production, inevitably tend to its diminution, it seems difficult to discover what alteration the circumstances of a country undergo in the progress of wealth, which can so far change the nature of things, as to make accumulation a means of increasing wealth.

It has been observed, that the property man possesses in that state of society to which allusion has been made, naturally classes itself under three different heads.

1. The land he cultivates.

2. The stock he reserves for immediate and remote consumption; under which is comprehended the produce of his farm, whether vegetable or animal.

3. His capital, consisting of the animals or machines he

---

[8] Wealth of Nations, vol. 1. p. 70. 4to edit [I.vii.12].

employs to supplant labour in the cultivation of his farm, or in the convenient consumption of its produce.

In the progress of wealth, the first article of the society's property, the land the farmer cultivates, becomes, from improvement, more productive; the improved system of cultivation requires more capital, but there can be no system of culture that can benefit by an unlimited application of capital:—*As much has been done for that field as possible*, is an expression that subsists in the phraseology of the farmer in all states of society; and, in every state of society alike, means, that as much capital has been employed in the improvement of that field as the present state of the knowledge of mankind enables him to lay out with advantage; that is, with any prospect of increasing its produce.

The increased produce of land, occasioned by the wise application of labour and capital, of course increases in a great degree the vegetable and animal substances reserved for immediate or remote consumption, which forms the second branch of the property of a society; and it is this branch of the property of mankind that alone appears capable of unlimited increase; the more man augments it, the more must the human species abound in opulence, or in numbers. The affluent member of an opulent society, consumes more by reducing his nourishment into a form suitable to his palate, by selecting, to compose his clothing, the parts of the productions of nature most kindly to his feeling, and pleasing to his eye; and by disposing of a part of what is produced, in exchange for commodities of a distant country, which affluence enables him, and habit teaches him to enjoy. If, even by all these various methods, the increased produce is not consumed, experience shews that abundance of the necessaries of life has a direct tendency to increase population, and by this means to restore the proportion betwixt the demand and the quantity of the increased commodities; thus maintaining their value notwithstanding their abundance, and perpetuating the encouragement to reproduction.

The third class or description of the property of a society, its Capital, consisting of all the various means of supplanting labour, and of performing labour which could not be accomplished by the personal exertions of man, is, in the progress of wealth and knowledge, also subject to wonderful increase; as the shipping, the navigable canals, the roads, the machines for transporting and for fabricating, and the warehouses for preserving commodities, as well as the capital employed in circulating them, sufficiently denote.

But this description of property has its limits, beyond which it cannot, with advantage, be increased. In every state of society, a certain quantity of capital, proportioned to the existing state of the knowledge of mankind, may be usefully and profitably employed in supplanting and performing labour in the course of rearing, giving form to, and circulating the raw materials produced. Man's invention, in the means of supplanting labour, may give scope, in the progress of society, for the employment of an increased quantity; but there must be, at all times, a point determined by the existing state of knowledge in the art of supplanting and performing labour with capital, beyond which capital cannot profitably be increased, and beyond which it will not naturally increase; because the quantity, when it exceeds that point, must increase in proportion to the demand for it, and its value must of consequence diminish in such a manner, as effectually to check its augmentation. It is wonderful how the Author of the Wealth of Nations, who successfully ridicules the indefinite accumulation of circulating capital, by comparing it to the amassing of an unlimited number of pots and pans[9], did not perceive that the same ridicule is applicable to the unlimited increase of every branch of that description of the property of a country which constitutes its capital.

Fortunately, however, for mankind, the mechanism of society is so arranged, that the mischief done by the parsimony and disposition to accumulation of one individual is almost uniformly counteracted by the prodigality of some other; so that in practice nothing is found more nearly commensurate than the expenditure and revenue of every society. This inquiry, therefore, if mankind were left to regulate their conduct by their inclinations, would be rather a matter of curiosity than utility; for if the effects of parsimony are uniformly counteracted by prodigality, the public wealth can be neither increased nor diminished by it.

[9] Wealth of Nations, vol. II. p. 15. 4to edit [IV.i.19].

[FROM] OBSERVATIONS ON THE SUBJECTS TREATED OF IN DR SMITH'S INQUIRY INTO THE NATURE AND CAUSES OF THE WEALTH OF NATIONS*

David Buchanan

The great change effected by Dr Smith's work, in the state of political science, affords the most decisive evidence of its originality and value. Before its publication, no work had appeared in this country, to command the conviction of mankind, on the subjects to which it relates; and, with the exception of Sir James Steuart's treatise on political economy [1767], which, though not devoid of merit, abounds too much in confused and erroneous statements to attract much attention, no attempt was even made to explain the relations of society with a view to legislation and government. All the knowledge which existed of these matters was either too obvious and familiar to merit the praise of originality, or it was comprehended in detached maxims, occasionally thrown out by speculative writers, but neither strictly demonstrated, nor followed out to solid practical conclusions. The consequence was, that the science was either left open to prejudice, or to opposite theories, all equally uninteresting, and equally remote from the truth.

In France, the subject was more studied; and, on many important questions, the doctrines of the French writers [physiocrats] are in the highest degree liberal and enlightened. They were undoubtedly the first to perceive that human laws, in order to be useful, must necessarily conform to those more general laws, on which society is founded; and that the true object of the legislator, is to uphold the social system as it is already constituted, in place of interfering to regulate or to

* 2nd edition (Edinburgh, 1817), vol. 4, pp. i–xvi, 33–41.

alter the natural course of things, according to his own limited
notions of expediency. In pursuance of these views, they are
clear and consistent in disapproving of all commercial
restraints. Commerce they maintain to be placed wholly
without the sphere of legislative control; and even the trade in
corn, which has been sometimes stated as an exception to the
general doctrine, they hold to be equally entitled to the
common privilege of entire toleration. The laws for regulating
the interest of money, and, generally, all the exclusive prefer-
ences held out for the encouragement of domestic industry,
they also condemn, on the clear principle, that every man has
a right to dispose of what belongs to him, to the best advantage; that commercial transactions are so many voluntary
contracts, with which third parties have no concern; and that
the purpose of the law is to protect, and not to disturb individuals, in their peaceable efforts for the improvement of their
condition. But, with these just and enlightened doctrines, the
French system connects various dogmas, of which the truth
and utility are more questionable. The most remarkable of
these is the notion, that agriculture is the original source of all
income; that all taxes, out of whatever revenue they are paid
in the first instance, fall ultimately on the rent of land; and
that, in place of raising the public revenue by the expensive
and vexatious process of duties on consumable commodities,
the simple expedient of a direct land tax should be at once
resorted to. That this theory is founded on error, I have elsewhere endeavoured to shew[1]; while the arguments by which it
is supported, turn frequently on points fitter for the metaphys-
ician than for the statesman; and it is indeed the great defect
of this class of writers, that though, by the boldness and originality of their speculations, they may be said to have pointed
out the path of true science, they are continually led astray
from their main object, by a propensity to subtlety and conceit.
Hence it is that their reasonings, though frequently ingenious,
are also obscure, desultory, and inconclusive; and it is seldom
that they are pursued, with brevity and vigour, to any just or
striking conclusion. This tendency to abstract and metaphysical
discussion, which distinguishes the productions of the economical school, has considerably detracted from their popularity

[1] See observations on Productive and Unproductive Labour.

and value; and it will accordingly be found, that the theories of those writers, though they have excited some speculative controversy, have never been much felt in the affairs of the world; while in other respects they have been injurious, by giving the character of verbal disputation, to a science replete with practical truth.

It may be also remarked of the French authors, that however consistently they maintain the doctrine of the freedom of trade, they seem to deduce it from the principles rather of abstract right, than of general expediency. In this strain, Turgot remarks, in a letter to Dr Price[2], in which he blames the newly established government of America for regulating trade, for authorising exclusive corporations, and for prohibiting the exportation of certain commodities, 'que la loi de la liberté entière de tout commerce est un corrollaire du droit de proprieté[3].' It was to justice, rather than to policy, that they looked for the perfection of civil society: and they generally reason in reference to this principle; not reflecting, how much more powerfully men feel the operation of self interest than of justice, and how useless it is, therefore, to build schemes of practical improvement on the vain chimeras of moral perfectibility. In proving their doctrines to be just, rather than expedient, the French writers are also excluded from all those instructive and practical views of society and of manners, which render science so much more certain and interesting, by bringing it home to the business of life.

The Inquiry into the Nature and Causes of the Wealth of Nations stands in decided contrast to all abstract theory. It is a great display of reason on the business of the world; touching society in all its essential relations, containing lessons for government as well as for common life, and embracing subjects formerly placed without the limits of philosophy. It has been followed by suitable effects; having laid the foundation of a new science, and effected a permanent change in the opinions of mankind, and the policy of states.

But, with all the high qualities of commanding reason, Dr Smith has not published a perfect work. In fixing on the wealth of nations as the object and limit of his inquiries, he has

---

[2] Œuvres de Turgot [1808–11], tom. ix. p. 383.

[3] That the law of complete commercial freedom follows as a corollary from the right of property.

adopted a narrow view of his subject; since the science of which he treats is evidently a higher branch of legislation, and must, therefore, embrace many interesting questions wholly unconnected with wealth. Human society is a great scheme of policy and justice; and as buying and selling must, under every form of it, make a great part of the business of mankind, it is highly important so far to explain the nature of trade, as to secure it against unjust and impolitic restraints. Political economy will therefore embrace the consideration of trade as part of its subject; and the effect of good government will also be to protect trade, and to enable the people to acquire wealth. But wealth is not the direct object of government, nor is it of political economy, which is a speculation founded on the principles of justice and policy, of which government is the practical result, and of which the object is to explain those fundamental laws of society to which all human regulations must necessarily be subordinate; that legislation may be confined within its proper province, and that the statesman, knowing the limits of his power, may no longer rashly interfere with the natural course of things, nor seek to introduce, on his own partial views of expediency, schemes of improvement which are at variance with the general good. In this view of the science, it must comprehend many interesting questions, which, as they have no relation to wealth, Dr Smith is precluded from considering by the terms of his plan; and, though he deviates, in the course of his inquiries, from his own rule, the subject is, in consequence of the restraint which he has imposed on himself, occasionally presented to the reader in rather an aukward and uninteresting form. In examining, for instance, in what manner a state can be best defended, he converts the question of policy into one of economy; considering, not what is the best, but what is the cheapest, system of defence. It is in this way that he finds it necessary to reconcile the discussion of his subject with the plan of his inquiry; although, in the course of his remarks, he throws off this restraint, and discusses the question on views, not of economy, but of policy, Dr Smith has also erred occasionally from too great a fondness for system. On some subjects his views are hasty, partial, and inaccurate; while on others, the truth and value of his doctrines seem to justify, and even to require farther explanation.

Since the publication of Dr Smith's work, Mr [Robert]

Malthus is the only author, who can be said to have extended the boundaries of political science. In his original and instructive essay [on population, 1798, 1803], he has traced, with discrimination and accuracy, the great law by which population and subsistence respectively increase; and his views are demonstrated with such variety of illustration, that they are no longer questioned. Some imperfect anticipations occur in former works, of the same doctrine. Sir James Steuart, in particular, expresses himself very clearly on this subject, when he compares the progress of population to the movements of a spring loaded with a variable weight. The want of subsistence he considers as the weight which depresses the elastic principle of population; and, in proportion as it is withdrawn, mankind, according to his notion, increase until they advance beyond the limits of their food, within which they are again quickly brought back by poverty and want: and in this alternate course of discouragement and increase, varying with the supply of subsistence, Sir James Steuart describes the human race as gradually multiplying. There are some original remarks on the same subject by the author of L'Ami des Hommes, who pointedly states, that while agriculture keeps its ground, neither disease nor war will cause any permanent decrease of people. He has a chapter entitled, 'Subsistence the Measure of Population;' and the commonly supposed causes of depopulation, such as the celibacy of monks, war, navigation, emigration to the New World, he considers as roots from which new branches of population gradually spring. The world he compares to a garden, planted in all its parts; and without an increase of subsistence, he observes, not a single new plant can grow up but by displacing some other. By war and disease the void spaces are made, which the power of population fills up; and, if the agriculture of a country is not injured, its inhabitants, he finally insists, can neither be permanently diminished by disease nor by war[4]. But these remarks, however striking or just, are incidentally introduced; and, far from pursuing this train of reasoning to its fair results, the ingenious author turns aside to details comparatively frivolous and inconclusive. The great merit of Mr Malthus consists in clearly discerning the value of the principle thus carelessly cast aside by former

[4] [Marquis de Miraseau,] L'Ami des Hommes [1756–60], vol. i, chap. ii. p. 15, 16, 23.

writers, and in tracing it to all its legitimate conclusions; demonstrating, in the clearest manner, that the want of subsistence is the great obstacle to the population of the world; that the tendency of mankind to multiply faster than food can be provided for their support, is the root of many of the evils which afflict society; and that without a previous increase of subsistence, laws for the encouragement of marriage are not only useless, but pernicious, as they necessarily lead to an excess of population, and to misery and want among the labouring classes, which all the artificial devices of legislation will neither relieve nor palliate. On those various points the reasonings of Mr Malthus are interesting and original; and though former writers may have incidentally suggested similar doctrines, to him unquestionably belongs the merit, of having improved scattered hints into a solid system of science, and of having made a valuable addition to the stock of practical truth.

The object of the present work is, to rectify what is amiss in Dr Smith; to supply omissions; to give his reasonings an application to modern times; and to exhibit, as far as the author is qualified, a complete system of political economy. In considering the subsequent history of the world, it is obvious that additions have now become necessary to Dr Smith's work; and the subjects of Paper Currency, Finance, Taxation, the East India Company, have only to be mentioned, to suggest the materials of important discussion. There is another subject which he has considered, namely, the military policy of states, and the power of armies; and here it is scarcely necessary to remark, what a fruitful theme modern history affords for new and interesting speculation.

The three volumes of Dr Smith's original work [WN 1814 ed.] contain incidental remarks on the text, with notes of reference; while dissertations of a general nature are reserved for this additional volume, to which the notes of the preceding volumes of course refer.

EDINBURGH,
Sept. 14. 1814.

ON THE PRICE OF SUCH COMMODITIES
AS YIELD A RENT

The price of those commodities which are produced by labour and capital, cannot for any length of time be either higher or lower than what is sufficient to pay the common rate of wages and profit. Where it is higher, capital will be attracted from other trades by the temptation of extraordinary profit, until the supply be increased and the price reduced; and where it is lower, capital will be withdrawn from the unprofitable trade until the price rise in consequence of the diminished supply. This result seems to be self-evident, because no commodity will be produced unless it can be sold for a price sufficient to repay the labour and the stock, with its ordinary profit, employed in producing it.

But this principle does not apply to the produce of land, which is generally sold for a price sufficient not only to repay the wages of labour and the profits of stock, but to yield a surplus or rent for the benefit of the proprietor. This high price is evidently not necessary to insure production, for although land yielded no rent it would still be cultivated. As long as its produce is sufficient to pay the wages of labour and the profits of stock, the labourer and the farmer will have all the inducement which they ever had to continue their industry. There will be no proprietor indeed to receive a return from their labour and capital; but that labour and capital will be still as well paid as before, and the same motives to exertion will consequently remain. The whole produce of a mine or of a coal pit is frequently no more than sufficient to pay wages and profit; in which case nothing remains for the landlord's rent; but we do not find that the mine is less diligently worked on this account.

The high price which leaves a surplus or rent to the landlord, after paying wages and profit, being no way necessary to production, must be accounted for on a different principle; and it seems accordingly to arise from the comparative scarcity in which articles that yield a rent are generally produced. It is clear that the quantity of a commodity consumed, can never for any length of time exceed the quantity produced; and it is by a rise of price that the consumption is confined within the limits of the supply; while, in the case of a more abundant supply, the consumption is accelerated by a fall of price. The price is, in this manner, the great regulator of consumption; and where a commodity is sold at such a price as to leave a surplus after paying all the necessary expences of its production, it will always be found that this high price is required to proportion the consumption to the supply. It is necessary, for example, that the yearly supply of corn should last until the produce of the succeeding season reach the market; and the price, by which the daily and weekly consumption is regulated, according to the supply of the year, is always such as to leave a rent or surplus above wages and profit. The price of every commodity which affords a rent is regulated in the same manner. A certain price is necessary to proportion the consumption to the supply; and rent is the consequence of this high price. 'High or low wages,' Dr Smith justly observes, 'are the causes of high or low price; high or low rent is the effect of it. It is because high or low wages or profit must be paid, in order to bring a particular commodity to market, that its price is high or low. But it is because its price is high or low, a great deal more or very little more, or no more than what is sufficient to pay those wages and profit, that it affords a high rent, or a low rent, or no rent at all[5].'

The price of such commodities as yield a rent being fixed with a view to regulate consumption, is in this manner wholly independent of their original cost; and though it may cost more or less to bring them to market, they will not on this account be sold for a higher or a lower price; for while the price answers its great purpose of suiting the consumption to the supply, it will not be affected by other causes. The corn of improved and fertile districts; the corn of lands recently brought under tillage at a great expence; the corn brought from a distance subject to all the charges of conveyance; and the corn produced in the immediate vicinity of the market, are all sold for the same price. There is but one market price for corn of equal quality whatever may have been its original cost; and indeed the very existence of rent, or of a surplus independent of the expences of production, is of itself a sufficient proof that those expences neither limit nor determine the price.

The price which exactly proportions the consumption of corn to the supply may be called its natural price. It is the centre point to which the market price continually tends; and while it may finally settle there, it is evident that it cannot long remain either above or below it; because a higher or a lower price implies an excess either of consumption or of supply, and

---

[5] Vol. I. Book I. Chap. XI.—Of the Rent of Land (I.xi.a.8].

it is for the express purpose of correcting such irregularities that the price is fixed.

The price of corn, which always affords a rent, being in no respect influenced by the expences of its production, those expences must be defrayed out of the rent; and when they rise or fall, therefore, the consequence is not a higher or a lower price, but a higher or a lower rent. In this view, all taxes on farm servants, horses, or the implements of agriculture, are in reality land taxes; the burden falling on the farmer during the currency of his lease, and on the landlord when the lease comes to be renewed. In like manner, all those improved implements of husbandry which save expence to the farmer, such as machines for threshing and reaping; whatever gives him easier access to the market, such as good roads, canals, and bridges, though they lessen the original cost of corn, do not lessen its market price. Whatever is saved by those improvements, therefore, belongs to the landlord as part of his rent.

A writer in the Edinburgh Review, in reasoning against a bounty on the exportation of corn, supposes, by way of illustration, a bounty granted on production, which he concludes would occasion a fall of price. 'Its immediate effect,' he observes, 'would evidently be to lower both the money price and the real price to all purchasers in the home market. Part of the old price, instead of being paid by the purchaser himself, would now be paid for him by the public, and while he paid so much less, the farmer would receive altogether the same sum as before. The farmer would no doubt be willing enough to keep up the market price to its original rate, that he might thus increase his receipts by the whole of the bounty; but the same power of competition which had before adjusted his profits would continue to adjust them to the same rate, by reducing his receipts from the private purchaser, in proportion to his new receipts from the public. Notwithstanding this bounty, therefore, the profits of the farmer would, by the operation of the principle of competition, subside towards their former level[6].'

The writer here evidently mistakes the nature of rent, which is really a bounty on the production of corn. It is a surplus paid by the consumer over and above the profits of the farmer,

---

[6] Edinburgh Review, Vol. V. p. 194.

and is in substance, therefore, the same as the bounty proposed to be paid by the public. Such a bounty, were it actually paid, would increase the rent. It would not reduce the price of corn, which depends on its plenty or scarcity; and a bounty on production, which would not increase the supply, would not therefore reduce the price.

Rent being a surplus above wages and profit, whatever yields this surplus may be said to pay a rent. The inventor of a machine for abridging labour, were he to keep his secret, might sell his goods for such a price as would yield a rent or surplus above wages and profit; but when the secret is known, and others come to abridge labour in the same way, the competition reduces the price, and his advantage is lost. In this manner improvements in manufactures benefit society by a fall of price on the goods manufactured; but improvements in agriculture, which occasion no fall of price, benefit only the landlord by an increase of rent. Manufacturing industry increases its produce in proportion to the demand, and the price falls; but the produce of land cannot be so increased; and a high price is still necessary to prevent the consumption from exceeding the supply.

When Dr Smith considers the extraordinary profit derived from secrets in manufactures as the high price of the manufacturer's private labour[7], he clearly mistakes the nature of this profit, which is in no respect different from the rent of land. It is a surplus above wages and profit, which the consumers are content to pay rather than want the commodity. And wherein does it then differ from the surplus paid for the produce of land? The produce of some fine vineyards can be sold, it appears, at a price which leaves even a greater surplus than the price of corn[8]. Now, supposing the quality for which this price is paid were derived, not from the soil or situation, but from some secret process of manufacture, in what respect would the gain in either case differ, unless that it would be called profit or rent according as it arose from the manufacture or from the land?

[7] See Vol. I. Chap. VII [I.vii.22].
[8] Ibid.

Entry of the Wealth of Nations into British Politics

[FROM] LETTER FROM JOHN MACPHERSON*[1]
28 November 1778

Kensington Gore, 28 Nov. 1778

My dear Sir.

I meant to have written you long since, and wished to have communicated some public news. . . . I had a most ample Discussion with Lord North at Bushy Park on my Return from Scotland. . . . We went over all India America Scotland and England. . . . It seems you have awaked some new Ideas about improving the Revenue. . . .

---

* From *Corr.*, no. 197, pp. 236–7. The note of the original editors has been retained.

[1] The letter has no signature, but the hand was identified by Sir Lewis Namier as that of John Macpherson (c. 1745–1821), Bt. 1786; MP 1779–82, 1796–1802. Macpherson was deeply involved in Indian affairs for much of his career. He became Acting Governor of Bengal when Warren Hastings resigned, and his successor in 1786 described Macpherson's administration as a 'system of the dirtiest jobbing'.

TAX ON MALT*
Adam Smith

Fermented liquors brewed, and spirituous liquors distilled, not for sale, but for private use, are not in Great Britain liable to any duties of excise. This exemption, of which the object is to save private families from the odious visit and examination of the tax-gatherer, occasions the burden of those duties to fall frequently much lighter upon the rich than upon the poor. It is not, indeed, very common to distil for private use, though it is done sometimes. But in the country, many middling and almost all rich and great families brew their own beer. Their strong beer, therefore, costs them eight shillings a barrel less than it costs the common brewer, who must have his profit upon the tax, as well as upon all the other expence which he advances. Such families, therefore, must drink their beer at least nine or ten shillings a barrel cheaper than any liquor of the same quality can be drunk by the common people, to whom it is every where more convenient to buy their beer, by little and little, from the brewery or the ale-house. Malt, in the same manner, that is made for the use of a private family, is not liable to the visit or examination of the tax-gatherer; but in this case the family must compound at seven shillings and sixpence a head for the tax. Seven shillings and sixpence are equal to the excise upon ten bushels of malt; a quantity fully equal to what all the different members of any sober family, men, women, and children, are at an average likely to consume. But in rich and great families, where country hospitality is much practised, the malt liquors consumed by the members of the family make but a small part of the consumption of the house. Either on account of this composition, however, or for other reasons, it is not near so common to malt as to brew for private use. It is difficult to imagine any equitable reason

* From *An Inquiry into the Nature and Causes of the Wealth of Nations* (London, 1776), vol. 2, pp. 361–3: V.ii.k.45–6. The note is the present editor's.

why those who either brew or distil for private use, should not
be subject to a composition of the same kind.

A greater revenue than what is at present drawn from all
the heavy taxes upon malt, beer, and ale, might be raised, it
has frequently been said, by a much lighter tax upon malt; the
opportunities of defrauding the revenue being much greater in
a brewery than in a malt-house; and those who brew for
private use being exempted from all duties or composition
for duties, which is not the case with those who malt for
private use.[1]

---

[1] A malt tax adjustment was duly made: see Stephen Dowell, *History of
Taxation and Taxes in England* (London, 1884–8), vol. 2, p. 169.

TAX ON INHABITED HOUSES*
Adam Smith

The rent of houses might easily be ascertained with sufficient accuracy, by a policy of the same kind with that which would be necessary for ascertaining the ordinary rent of land. Houses not inhabited ought to pay no tax. A tax upon them would fall altogether upon the proprietor, who would thus be taxed for a subject which afforded him neither conveniency nor revenue. Houses inhabited by the proprietor ought to be rated, not according to the expence which they might have cost in building, but according to the rent which an equitable arbitration might judge them likely to bring, if leased to a tenant. If rated according to the expence which they may have cost in building, a tax of three or four shillings in the pound, joined with other taxes, would ruin almost all the rich and great families of this, and, I believe, of every other civilized country. Whoever will examine, with attention, the different town and country houses of some of the richest and greatest families in this country, will find that, at the rate of only six and a half, or seven per cent upon the original expence of building, their house-rent is nearly equal to the whole neat rent of their estates. It is the accumulated expence of several successive generations, laid out upon objects of great beauty and magnificence, indeed; but, in proportion to what they cost, of very small exchangeable value[1].

---

* From *An Inquiry into the Nature and Causes of the Wealth of Nations* (London, 1776), vol. 2, pp. 285–6: V.ii.e.8. The note is the present editor's.

[1] [Smith's note in the 2nd ed., 1778 reads] 'Since the first publication of this book, a tax nearly upon the above-mentioned principles has been imposed.' See *The Statutes at Large* (London, 1811), vol. 7, p. 589, 18 Geo. III, c. 26 (1778). It reads:

C A P. XXVI.
An Act for granting to His Majesty certain Duties upon all inhabited Houses within the Kingdom of *Great Britain*.
[*Repealed*, 43 G. 3. c. 161. § 84.]

[FROM] LETTER TO DUGALD STEWART, 1795 *
William Petty-Fitzmaurice, Lord Shelburne

I owe to a journey I made with Mr Smith from Edinburgh to London, the difference between light and darkness through the best part of my life. The novelty of his principles, added to my youth and prejudices, made me unable to comprehend them at the time, but he urged them with so much benevolence, as well as eloquence, that they took a certain hold, which, though it did not develope itself so as to arrive at full conviction for some few years after, I can fairly say, has constituted, ever since, the happiness of my life, as well as any little consideration I may have enjoyed in it.

* From 'Account of the Life and Writings of Adam Smith' (1794/1811), in Adam Smith, *Essays on Philosophical Subjects* (Oxford, 1980), p. 347.

[FROM] GEORGE III'S SPEECH*
5 December 1782

[King's speech opening 3rd session of 15th Parliament of Great Britain:] The liberal principles adopted by you concerning the rights and commerce of Ireland, have done you the highest honour, and will, I trust, increase that harmony, which ought always to subsist between the two kingdoms. I am persuaded that a general increase of commerce throughout the empire, will prove the wisdom of your measures with regard to that object. I would recommend to you a revision of our whole trading system, upon the same comprehensive principles, with a view to its utmost possible extension.

* From William Cobbett et al., *The Parliamentary History of England from the Earliest Period to the Year 1803* (London, 1814), vol. 23.

SPEECH ON PRELIMINARY ARTICLES OF PEACE*
17 February 1783
William Petty-Fitzmaurice, Lord Shelburne

The Earl of *Shelburne* then rose. The lateness of the hour, my lords, said his lordship, will not suffer me to take the liberty of trespassing so far on your patience, as my feelings would prompt me to on the present occasion. I shall not address your passions—that candid province I will leave to those who have shewn such ability for its government to-night. As my conduct has been founded upon integrity—facts, and plain reasoning, will form its best support. I shall necessarily wave the consideration of the critical moment at which I stepped into the administration of the affairs of this country—a moment when, if there be any credit due to the solemn, public declarations of men, who seemed then, and seem now, to have the welfare of the state nearest to their hearts—every hope of renovated lustre was gone, and nothing but dreary despondency remained to the well-wishers of Great Britain. I am now speaking within memory, and consequently within proof. It is not for me to boast of my motives for standing forward at a period so alarming. My circumstances are not so obscure as to render my conduct a matter of dubiety; and my own explanation of my feelings would, I flatter myself, fall far short of that credit which sympathy would give me in the minds of men, whose patriotism is not that of words: the ambition of advancing to the service of our country in an hour when even brave men shrink from the danger, is honourable, and I shall not be catechized for entertaining such an impulse. I make no merit of my hardihood, and when I speak of mine, I wish your lordships to understand me as speaking of the generous enterprize of my noble and honourable colleagues in

---

* From William Cobbett et al., *The Parliamentary History of England from the Earliest Period to the Year 1803* (London, 1814), vol. 24.

administration. It was our duty as good citizens, when the state was in danger, that all selfish apprehensions should be banished. I shall not, therefore, expatiate on my reasons for coming into office, but openly and candidly tell your lordships how I have conducted myself in it. A peace was the declared wish of the nation at that time. How was that to be procured best for the advantage of the country? Certainly by gaining the most accurate knowledge of the relative condition of the powers at war. Here a field of knowledge was required to be beaten to which no one man, vast and profound as it is possible to picture human capacity, would by any means be supposed equal. Then if one man was inadequate to the whole task, the next question naturally is, what set of men are best qualified as auxiliaries in it? What is the skill required? A knowledge of trade and commerce, with all its relations, and an intimate acquaintance with military affairs, and all its concomitants. Were men of this description consulted previous to, and during the progress of the treaty now before your lordships? I answer, they were. And with this sanction administration need assume no false brow of bravery, in combatting the glittering expressions of that hasty opposition that had been set up to the present terms.

Let us examine them, my lords, let us take the several assertions in their turn and without wishing to intrude too much on your lordships time, I shall be pardoned for giving a distinct answer to each head of objection. Ministry, in the first place, is blamed for drawing the boundary they have done between the territories of the United States and those of our sovereign in Canada. I wish to examine every part of the treaties on the fair rule of the value of the district ceded—to examine it on the amount of the exports and imports, by which alone we could judge of its importance. The exports of this country to Canada, then, were only 140,000l. and the imports were no more than 50,000l. Suppose the entire fur trade sunk into the sea, where is the detriment to this country? Is 50,000l. a year imported in that article any object for Great Britain to continue a war of which the people of England, by their representatives, have declared their abhorrence? Surely it is not. But much less must this appear in our sight, when I tell parliament, and the whole kingdom, that for many years past, one year with another, the preservation of this annual import of 50,000l. has cost this country, on an average, 800,000l. I have the vouchers in my pocket, should your lordships be inclined to examine the fact. But the trade is not given up, it is only divided, and divided for our benefit. I appeal to all men conversant with the nature of that trade, whether its best resources in Canada do not lie to the northward. What, then, is the result of this part of the treaty, so wisely, and with so much sincere love on the part of England clamoured against by noble lords? Why this. You have generously given America, with whom every call under Heaven urges you to stand on the footing of brethren, a share in a trade, the monopoly of which you sordidly preserved to yourselves, at the loss of the enormous sum of 750,000l. Monopolies, some way or other, are ever justly punished. They forbid rivalry, and rivalry is of the very essence of the well-being of trade. This seems to be the æra of protestantism in trade. All Europe appear enlightened, and eager to throw off the vile shackles of oppressive ignorant monopoly; that unmanly and illiberal principle, which is at once ungenerous and deceitful. A few interested Canadian merchants might complain; for merchants would always love monopoly, without taking a moment's time to think whether it was for their interest or not. I avow that monopoly is always unwise; but if there is any nation under heaven, who ought to be the first to reject monopoly, it is the English. Situated as we are between the old world and the new, and between the southern and northern Europe, all that we ought to covet upon earth is free trade, and fair equality. With more industry, with more enterprize, with more capital than any trading nation upon earth, it ought to be our constant cry, let every market be open, let us meet our rivals fairly, and we ask no more. It is a principle on which we have had the wisdom to act with respect to our brethren of Ireland; and, if conciliation be our view, why should we not reach it out also to America? Our generosity is not much, but, little as it is, let us give it with a grace. Indeed, to speak properly, it is not generosity to them, but œconomy to ourselves; and in the boundaries which are established we have saved ourselves the immense sum of 800,000l. a-year, and shewed to the Americans our sincere love and fair intentions, in dividing the little bit of trade which nature had laid at their doors; and telling them that we desired to live with them in communion of benefits, and in the sincerity of friendship.

[FROM] REVIEW OF THE PARLIAMENT OF 1784*
Henry Mackenzie

Another measure adopted by the late Parliament, founded on the same liberal principle, but of a more fortunate issue than the preceding, was the commercial treaty with France.

National prejudices, in conjunction with those of commerce, had hitherto shut the markets of France and England respectively against many of the commodities of the other. Between those countries there was a war of prohibitions and high duties, which, in most articles of their mutual consumption, threw the trade into the hands of smugglers. The publications of an author, in whose mind, beyond that of any writer of his time, was genius chastened by wisdom, and wisdom enlightened by knowledge, had changed in a great measure the opinions of mankind on the subject of commercial restrictions, and shown how much was to be gained by restoring to trade its natural freedom, by which the surplus commodities of one country could be fairly exchanged for those of another. France and England felt in a particular manner the justice of his doctrines; and it was an article in the peace of 1783, that the two countries should take measures for setting a commercial treaty between them.

In pursuance of this agreement, Mr [William] Eden was dispatched to Paris in the beginning of the year 1786, to negotiate a treaty of navigation and commerce with France. That treaty was concluded on the 20th of September in that year. Particular notice was taken of it in his Majesty's speech on opening the session in January 1787; and it was soon after laid before Parliament, for the purpose of their taking such measures as might be necessary for carrying it into effect.

The provisions of this treaty were calculated to take off those restraints which the two countries had heretofore mutually

* From *The Works of Henry Mackenzie* (Edinburgh, 1808), vol. 7, pp. 256–9.

imposed on their commercial intercourse with each other—to give to the subjects of either country that protection for their persons and properties which is dictated by the liberal humanity of modern times—to establish a tariff to fix the rate of duties, which for the most part was not higher than 12 per cent., on the importation of those articles of the produce or manufacture of the respective kingdoms, which were most likely to be the leading objects of their commerce—to put on the footing of the most favoured nations the goods not particularised in that tariff—and to avoid, by stipulations of a friendly sort, the occasions of misunderstanding and quarrel, which might chance to arise in the navigation or commerce of either power with other countries.

SPEECH ON THE EDEN TREATY*
12 February 1787
William Pitt

He thus confined himself to the commercial part of the treaty;
nor was even all, which belonged to that part, comprehended
in the scope of these resolutions. It would be necessary for the
committee to take into their consideration the relative state of
the two kingdoms. On the first blush of the matter, he believed
he might venture to assert it, as a fact generally admitted, that
France had the advantage in the gift of soil and climate, and
in the amount of her natural produce; that, on the contrary,
Great Britain was, on her part, as confessedly superior in her
manufactures and artificial productions. Undoubtedly, in point
of natural produce, France had greatly the advantage in this
treaty. Her wines, brandies, oils, and vinegars, particularly the
two former articles, were matters of such important value in
her produce, as greatly and completely to destroy all idea of
reciprocity as to natural produce—we perhaps having nothing
of that kind to put in competition, but simply the article of
beer. But, on the contrary, was it not a fact as demonstrably
clear, that Britain, in its turn, possessed some manufactures
exclusively her own, and that in others she had so completely
the advantage of her neighbour, as to put competition to
defiance? This then was the relative condition, and this the
precise ground, on which it was imagined that a valuable
correspondence and connection between the two might be
established. Having each its own and distinct staple—having
each that which the other wanted; and not clashing in the great
and leading lines of their respective riches, they were like two
great traders in different branches, they might enter into a
traffic which would prove mutually beneficial to them.
Granting that a large quantity of their natural produce would
be brought into this country, would any man say, that we

* From *Speeches of William Pitt* (London, 1817), vol. 1, pp. 241–5.

should not send more cottons by the direct course now settled, than by the circuitous passages formerly used—more of our woollens, than while restricted in their importation to particular ports, and burthened under heavy duties? Would not more of our earthen ware, and other articles, which, under all the disadvantages that they formerly suffered, still, from their intrinsic superiority, force their way regularly into France, now be sent hither? and would not the aggregate of our manufactures be greatly and eminently benefited in going to this market loaded only with duties from twelve to ten, and in one instance with only five per cent? If the advantages in this respect were not so palpable and apparent as to strike and satisfy every mind interested in the business, would not the House have had very different petitions on their table than that presented this day? The fact was apparent. The article (sadlery) charged the most highly in the tariff, gave no sort of alarm. The traders in this article, though charged with a duty of fifteen per cent. knew their superiority so well, that they cheerfully embraced the condition, and conceived that the liberty would be highly advantageous to them. A market of so many millions of people—a market so near and prompt—a market of expeditions and certain return—of necessary and extensive consumption, thus added to the manufactures and commerce of Britain, was an object which we ought to look up to with eager and satisfied ambition. To procure this, we certainly ought not to scruple to give liberal conditions. We ought not to hesitate, because this which must be so greatly advantageous to us must also have its benefit for them. It was a great boon procured on easy terms, and as such we ought to view it. It was not merely a consoling, but an exhilarating speculation to the mind of an Englishman, that, after the empire had been engaged in a competition the most arduous and imminent of any that ever threatened a nation—after struggling for its existence, still it maintained its rank and efficacy so firmly, that France, finding they could not shake her, now opened its arms, and offered a beneficial connection with her on easy, liberal, and advantageous terms.

We had agreed by this treaty to take from France, on small duties, the luxuries of her soil, which, however, the refinements of ourselves had converted into necessaries. The wines of France were already so much in the possession of our markets, that, with all the high duties paid by us, they found their way to our tables. Was it then a serious injury to admit these luxuries on easier terms? The admission of them would not supplant the wines of Portugal, nor of Spain, but would supplant only an useless and pernicious manufacture in this country. He stated the enormous increase of the import of French wines lately, and instanced the months of July and August, the two most unlikely months in the year, to shew the increase of this trade. The committee would not then perceive any great evil in admitting this article on easy terms. The next was brandy; and here it would be inquired whether the diminution of duty was an eligible measure. He believed they would also agree with him on this article, when they viewed it with regard to smuggling. The reduction of the duties would have a material effect on the contraband in this article; it was certain that the legal importation bore no proportion to the quantity clandestinely imported; for the legal importation of brandy was no more than 600,000 gallons, and the supposed amount of the smuggled, at the most rational and best-founded estimate, was between three and four hundred thousand gallons. Seeing then that this article had taken such complete possession of the taste of the nation, it might be right to procure to the state a greater advantage from the article than heretofore, and to crush the contraband by legalizing the market.

The oil and vinegar of France were comparatively small objects, but, like the former, they were luxuries which had taken the shape of necessaries, and which we could suffer nothing from accepting on easy terms. These were the natural produce of France to be admitted under this treaty. Their next inquiry should be to see if France had any manufactures peculiar to herself, or in which she so greatly excelled as to give us alarm on account of the treaty, viewing it in that aspect. Cambric was the first which stared him in the face, but which, when he looked around him, and observed the general countenance of the committee, he could hardly think it necessary to detain them a moment upon. The fact was, it was an article in which our competition with France had ceased, and there was no injury in granting an easy importation to that which we would have at any rate. In no other article was there any thing very formidable in the rivalry of France. Glass would not be imported to any amount. In particular kinds of lace, indeed, they might have the advantage, but none which they would not enjoy independent of the treaty; and the clamours about millinery were vague and unmeaning, when, in addition to all these benefits, we included the richness of the country with which we were to trade: with its superior population of twenty millions to eight, and of course a proportionate consumption, together with its vicinity to us, and the advantages of quick and regular returns, who could hesitate for a moment to applaud the system, and look forward with ardour and impatience to its speedy ratification? The possession of so extensive and safe a market must improve our commerce, while the duties transferred from the hands of smugglers to their proper channel would benefit our revenue—the two sources of British opulence and British power.

Viewing the relative circumstances of the two countries then in this way, he saw no objection to the principle of the exchange of their respective commodities. He saw no objection to this, because he perceived and felt that our superiority in the tariff was manifest. The excellence of our manufactures was unrivalled, and in the operation must give the balance to England. But it was said, that the manufacturers dreaded the continuance of this superiority. They were alarmed at the idea of a competition with Ireland, and consequently they must be more under apprehensions at the idea of a rivalry with France. He always did think, and he must still continue to think, that the opinions of the manufacturers on this point were erroneous. They raised the clamour in respect to Ireland chiefly, he imagined, because they perceived no certain and positive advantage by the intercourse to counterbalance this precarious and uncertain evil. In this instance, their consent to the treaty did not proceed from a blind acquiescence, for they never would be blind to their interest; but now that they saw so certain and so valuable an advantage to be reaped, the benefits being no longer doubtful, they were willing to hazard the probability of the injury.

TRIBUTE TO SMITH*
17 February 1792
William Pitt

Having gone thus far, having stated the increase of revenue, and shewn that it has been accompanied by a proportionate increase of the national wealth, commerce, and manufactures, I feel that it is natural to ask, what have been the peculiar circumstances to which these effects are to be ascribed?

The first and most obvious answer which every man's mind will suggest to this question, is, that it arises from the natural industry and energy of the country: but what is it which has enabled that industry and energy to act with such peculiar vigour, and so far beyond the example of former periods?— The improvement which has been made in the mode of carrying on almost every branch of manufacture, and the degree to which labour has been abridged, by the invention and application of machinery, have undoubtedly had a considerable share in producing such important effects. We have besides seen, during these periods, more than at any former time, the effect of one circumstance which has principally tended to raise this country to its mercantile pre-eminence—I mean that peculiar degree of credit, which, by a twofold operation, at once gives additional facility and extent to the transactions of our merchants at home, and enables them to obtain a proportional superiority in markets abroad. This advantage has been most conspicuous during the latter part of the period to which I have referred; and it is constantly increasing, in proportion to the prosperity which it contributes to create.

In addition to all this, the exploring and enterprising spirit of our merchants has been seen in the extension of our navigation and our fisheries, and the acquisition of new markets in different parts of the world; and undoubtedly those efforts have been not a little assisted by the additional intercourse with

* From *Speeches of William Pitt* (London, 1817), vol. 1, pp. 357–9.

France, in consequence of the commercial treaty; an intercourse which, though probably checked and abated by the distractions now prevailing in that kingdom, has furnished a great additional incitement to industry and exertion.

But there is still another cause, even more satisfactory than these, because it is of a still more extensive and permanent nature; that constant accumulation of capital, that continual tendency to increase, the operation of which is universally seen in a greater or less proportion, whenever it is not obstructed by some public calamity, or by some mistaken and mischievous policy, but which must be conspicuous and rapid indeed in any country which has once arrived at an advanced state of commercial prosperity. Simple and obvious as this principle is, and felt and observed as it must have been in a greater or less degree, even from the earliest periods, I doubt whether it has ever been fully developed and sufficiently explained, but in the writings of an author of our own times, now unfortunately no more, (I mean the author of a celebrated treatise on the Wealth of Nations,) whose extensive knowledge of detail, and depth of philosophical research, will, I believe, furnish the best solution to every question connected with the history of commerce, or with the systems of political economy. This accumulation of capital arises from the continual application, of a part at least, of the profit obtained in each year, to increase the total amount of capital to be employed in a similar manner, and with continued profit in the year following. The great mass of the property of the nation is thus constantly increasing at compound interest; the progress of which, in any considerable period, is what at first view would appear incredible. Great as have been the effects of this cause already, they must be greater in future; for its powers are augmented in proportion as they are exerted. It acts with a velocity continually accelerated, with a force continually increased—

Mobilitate viget, viresque acquirit eundo.

['(It) increases by motion, and acquires strength by advancing': Virgil, *AEn.* iv. 175.]

It may indeed, as we have ourselves experienced, be checked or retarded by particular circumstances—it may for a time be interrupted, or even overpowered; but, where there is a fund of productive labour and active industry, it can never be totally extinguished. In the season of the severest calamity and distress, its operations will still counteract and diminish their effects;—in the first returning interval of prosperity, it will be active to repair them. If we look to a period like the present of continued tranquillity, the difficulty will be to imagine limits to its operation. None can be found, while there exists at home any one object of skill or industry short of its utmost possible perfection;—one spot of ground in the country capable of higher cultivation and improvement; or while there remains abroad any new market that can be explored, or any existing market that can be extended. From the intercourse of commerce, it will in some measure participate in the growth of other nations in all the possible varieties of their situations. The rude wants of countries emerging from barbarism, and the artificial and increasing demands of luxury and refinement, will equally open new sources of treasure, and new fields of exertion, in every state of society, and in the remotest quarters of the globe. It is this principle which, I believe, according to the uniform result of history and experience, maintains on the whole, in spite of the vicissitudes of fortune and the disasters of empires, a continued course of successive improvement in the general order of the world.

LETTER TO WILLIAM PITT*
24 October 1800
William Wyndham Grenville, Lord Grenville

[MS. Dacres Adams Papers 30/58/3/85 (unpublished)]
Dropmore [Buckinghamshire], 24 Oct. 1800
My Dear Pitt

Lord Buckingham's[1] letter is nothing more than an exaggerated statement of my fixed and, I am sure, immutable opinion on the subject of all Laws for lowering the price of provisions, either directly, *or by contrivance*. That opinion you know so well that it is idle for me to trouble you with long discourses or long letters of mine about it. We in truth formed our opinions on the subject together,[2] and I was not more convinced than you were of the soundness of Adam Smith's principles of political economy till Lord Liverpool[3] lured you from our arms into all the mazes of the old system.

I am confident that Provisions like every other article of commerce, if left to themselves, will and must find their own level, and that every attempt to disturb that level by artificial contrivances has a necessary tendency to increase the evil it seeks to remedy.[4]

In all the discussions with which we are overwhelmed on this subject one view of it is wholly overlooked. Every one takes it for granted that the present price of Corn is in itself undue, and such as ought not to exist: and then they dispute whether it is to be ascribed to combinations, which they wish to remedy by such means as will destroy all commerce, or to

---

* A previously unpublished MS. The notes are by the present editor.

[1] The writer's older brother and mentor, George Nugent-Temple (1753–1813), cr. 1st Marquess of Buckingham, 1784.

[2] c.1784.

[3] Charles Jenkinson (1727–1802), President of the Board of Trade under Pitt; cr. Earl of Liverpool, 1796.

[4] Cf. WN IV.ii.2 and IV.ix.50.

an unusual scarcity which they propose to supply by obliging the grower to contend in the home market not with the natural rivalship of such importations as the demand might and would produce of itself, but with an artificial supply poured in at the expense of I know not how many Millions to the State.

Both these parties assume that the price is undue—that is, I presume, that it is more than would be produced by the natural operation of demand and supply counteracting each other. For I know no other standard of Price than this. But if the Price be really so much higher as is supposed, what prevents the increase of supply at home? Or what bounty could operate so effectually to increase the quantity of wheat produced in the Country, as the experience of the farmer teaching him that by the increased growth of the article he can make two or three times as great a profit as he can by any other[?]

No man with the least knowledge of the subject will say that the Country now produces all the Wheat it could, if it answered to apply more capital to the produce.—Give me my own price for it, and I will engage to produce more Wheat in my Kitchen Garden than any farmer in this neighbourhood now does in his whole farm. But the Wheat so produced will have cost so much in labour and manure that unless it were sold at two or three times more than even the present price, I should receive no return for my Capital—perhaps not even recover the capital itself.

It has never been proved to me that the price of Wheat in these last two years has been more than sufficient to afford a reasonable profit on the Capital of the Farmer who has produced it: considering the increased expence of every article which he must consume in producing it, and the very scanty crop of last Year, which gave so much smaller a quantity while it left the expence the same as before or rather indeed much increased by some of the unfortunate circumstances of the Season.

It is for this reason that I detest and abhor as imperious and heretical the whole system on which we are now acting on the subject.

First a forced price of bread fixed in London by a Lord Mayor who can know nothing of the matter, aided by fictitious averages which do not even profess to give the information which this system supposes to be necesary in order to fix the price, and which if they did give it would still supply a very small part of that knowledge, which would in truth be necessary for such a purpose.

2dly. Bounties on importation which have a direct tendency to discourage the domestic produce of an article the domestic produce of which is so necessary to the Plan of the Community that perhaps a Legislative provision which gave the Farmer the monopoly of the home market would, tho' absurd, be less absurd than a similar provision as to any other article.

3d. and most of all a perpetual reference to Laws, and Magistrates, and Government, on a matter respecting which every interposition of any one of these except for the mere purpose of protecting an unrestrained liberty of trade, is injurious to the very object which it seeks to promote.

The real reason of my speaking with so much confidence of the effect to be produced by an increase in Wages to the labourer in Husbandry is because I conceive such increase is nothing else than the natural consequence which, if things were left to [?find] their own level, must result from an increase in the price of their food. I by no means wish to give to the Magistrate the power (ultimately) of regulating the price of labour, any more than of provisions. But I wish to remove the artificial system which deranges the natural operation of the two causes on each other, and in the mean time to do that by authority, or better still if it could be done by example only, which I think it demonstrable would be done in the common course of things by those natural causes if operating unrestrained.

If I am right in my opinion that the price of provisions is not undue, but the necessary result of many concurring causes the more you succeed in lowering it (and succeed for a time you unquestionably may) the more you discourage the production of the Article.

If the price ought now, and ultimately must, continue to be principally governed by those circumstances which have caused the rise, and if that price be confessedly such as will not, at the present rate if wages allow the labourer to live, it follows that one of three things must happen.

You must artificially keep the price of provisions below that amount at which the grower can make an adequate profit of his labour and capital, and recompense him in some other way.

Or you must enable the labourer to purchase provisions at that price by raising his Wages.

Or you must continue a system of expedients which has the advantage of neither, and the disadvantage of both.

Dixi—dogmatically enough you will say—but so as a man ought to speak on such a subject when he thinks he has arrived at almost mathematical certainty upon it.

As to tithes—when we begin to rob and confiscate I imagine we shall not stop at Corn rents, nor will the *tithes* of the Parish of Stowe be all that will fall a prey to that system.

How can any man of sense who looks at this Country and sees what has been done in it in the last 100 years pretend or believe that there exists in it an obstacle which will let no man employ Capital in the improvement of land?—Has no land been improved in that period? Or has it been employed but by the application of Capital to it? The Chancellor's[5] plan on that subject I look at with great satisfaction because it increases instead of diminishes the Power of the life tenant over his own property, and tho' by this individuals sometimes lose, the Public I am confident always gains by it.

Considering that I began by saying that it was useless to trouble you with a long letter I have not been very forbearing—but my mind is full of the subject, and I cannot restrain myself till the moment comes when I may vent myself upon it and by endeavouring to convince all the world of their ignorance, satisfy them of my folly—

[?Ever] most affectionately
G[renville]

---

[5] Alexander Wedderburn (1733–1805), cr. Baron Loughborough, 1795; (then Earl of Rosslyn, 1801); Lord Chancellor, 1793–1801.

Early Reception of the Wealth of Nations Abroad

[FROM] UNTERSUCHUNG DER NATUR UND URSACHEN VON NATIONAL REICHTHÜMERN VON ADAM SMITH*

J. F. Schiller

VORBERICHT

Ohnerachtet der Verfasser und der deutsche Uebersetzer dieses Werks es ohne einige Vorrede dem Urtheile der Leser und Kenner überließen, muß doch letzterer hier noch die Ursachen erwähnen, weswegen er die Ausgabe dieses zweyten Bandes in Einer Rücksicht so lange verzögert hat, und nun, in einer Andern, beschleunigt.

Die günstige Aufnahme des Originals in England lies dessen Verleger bald an eine zwote Auflage denken, bey deren Veranstaltung aber sein Verfasser die freundschaftlichen Erinnerungen scharfsinniger Engländer und Deutschen gegen einige seiner Sätze erwägen und benutzen wollte; und um die etwanigen Verbesserungen in der zwoten Auflage des Originals abzuwarten und dem zweyten Bande der deutschen Uebersetzung noch beyzufügen, verzögerte der Uebersetzer dessen Ausgabe verschiedene Monate lang, nachdem derselbe vollendet und abgedruckt war.

Immittelst reiste Herr D[r]. Smith nach Edinburgh zurück, und wurde bald darauf zum Obercommissar der Zölle in Schottland ernannt; und der hieraus entstehende nochmalige Aufschub [bewog] den Uebersetzer endlich, den zweyten Band dem Verlangen deutscher Leser nicht länger vorzuenthalten.

Sobald aber die zwote englische Auflage vollendet seyn wird, will er sie mit der Ersten sorgfältig vergleichen, und die etwanigen Verbesserungen in derselben den deutschen Lesern in einem Nachtrage liefern. Ein so originales Werk zum eilften und zwölftenmale durchzulesen, wird ihm keine Ueberwindung kosten: er hält es für ein lehrreiches und wahres Vergnügen,

---

* Leipzig, 1778, vol. 2, pp. iii-vi.

ihm auf jeder Annäherung zur Vollkommenheit nachzuspüren. Auch ist er diese Aufmerksamkeit dem deutschen Publikum, den billigen und sachkundigen göttingischen Kunstrichtern, die den Ersten Band der Uebersetzung mit dem Originale verglichen haben, und dem verehrungswürdigen Verfasser der Theorie moralischer Empfindungen schuldig, dessen persönliche Achtung und Freundschaft er unter die glücklichsten Umstände seines Lebens zählt.

[REVIEW OF] THE WEALTH OF NATIONS*
29 November 1794
Georg Friedrich Sartorius

Breslau

Bey Korn: Untersuchung über die Natur und die Ursachen des Nationalreichthums, von Adam Smith. Aus dem Engl. der vierten Ausgabe neu übersetzt. B.I. 1794. XX und 476 S. in Octav.

Hr. Garve bestimmte die Uebersetzung dieses classischen Werks zu einer Beschäftigung in seinen Nebenstunden, da er aber fand, daß er auf diese Art nur sehr langsam fortrücken würde; so wählte er sich einen Gehülfen bey dieser Arbeit, Hrn. Ober-Postcommissär Dörrien zu Leipzig; weil er diesem seinem Freund hinlängliche Kenntniß der Sprachen und Sachen zutrauen konnte, und von dessen Schreibart vermuthete, daß sie der seinigen ähnlich wäre. In der That scheint dieß vollkommen der Fall gewesen zu seyn, da man nicht gewahr werden wird, daß zwey verschiedene Hände daran gearbeitet haben, wenn an diesem ersten Theile beyde theilweis übersetzten, was man jedoch so eigentlich nicht weiß, indem Hr. Garve erst am Ende des Werks Auskunft zu geben verspricht, in wie fern sie beyde sich in die Arbeit getheilt haben; dorthin will er auch die bekannt gewordenen Lebensumstände Smith's und einen doppelten Anhang versparen, worin er theils die neuern Sätze Smith's, als die eigentliche Ausbeute, womit er den Schatz menschlicher Kenntnisse bereichert habe, zusammen zu stellen gedenkt; und theils einige der von Smith aufgestellten allgemeinen staatswirthschaftlichen Grundsätze einer neuen Prüfung unterwerfen wird. Dieß Versprechen zeigt jedem, daß diese Uebersetzung vor der frühern einen beträchtlichen Vorzug haben werde, wenn sie beendigt ist, und die Versprechungen

---

* From *Göttingische Anzeigen von Gelehrten Sachen*, 190 Stück, 1901–4.

erfüllt werden; doch, schon in dem Theil, der vor uns liegt, ist ein beträchtlicher Vorzug unverkennbar. Dieser zweyten Uebersetzung ist die vierte Englische Ausgabe zum Grund gelegt worden, zu der ältern Uebersetzung nach der ersten Ausgabe des Originals sind zwar die neueren Zusätze besonders abgedruckt erschienen; man wird indeß freylich lieber diese vorziehen, wo man alles beysammen findet. Was aber den innern Werth der Uebersetzung selbst betrifft, so kann man sich durch das Aufschlagen und Vergleichen auf den ersten Blick überzeugen, daß diese neuere Arbeit in Hinsicht auf Correctheit, Deutlichkeit, Treue und Sprache den Vorzug hat. Es würde sich nicht der Mühe lohnen, die kleinen Bemerkungen auszuzeichnen, welche sich bey sorgfältiger Vergleichung beyder Uebersetzungen ergaben; oder einige kleine Sprachfehler zu rügen, die sich etwa finden möchten, denn die meisten lassen sich ohnehin noch als Druckfehler entschuldigen, obschon sie nicht unter dem beträchtlichen Verzeichnitz derselben angegeben sind. Der große Vorzug dieser Uebersetzung vor der ältern liegt am Tag. Allein dieß ist es dennoch vielleicht nicht, warum man so viel Dank Hrn. G. schuldig ist. Wem die Verbreitung der Wahrheit am Herzen liegt, und wer seine Wissenschaften aus anderer Hinsicht treibt, als bloß um sein tägliches Brod zu gewinnen, den wird es herzlich freuen, daß Garve's Name der Uebersetzung dieses Werks vorsteht, und die Verbreitung desselben gewissermaßen garantirt; es wird ihn freuen, daß Hr. G. in der Vorrede erklärt, daß nicht leicht ein Buch an Kenntnissen ihn so bereichert und ihm so viele neue Aufschlüsse gewährt habe, als dieß. Smith's Grundsätze müssen mehr verbreitet, und wenn sie falsch sind, so müssen sie gründlich widerlegt werden; dieß ist bis jetzt nicht geschehen, und bey uns auch nicht einmal versucht worden; und wenn man sein Buch hier und da citirt findet, so scheint es doch fürwahr, die leichten Capitel abgerechnet, als habe man ihn nie gelesen, als habe er nie gesprochen. Auf Veränderung der Doctrin der Staatswirthschaft in unserm Vaterlande hat er noch gar keinen Einfluß gehabt; gelobt und citirt ist er worden, aber die Compendien sind nach wie vor geblieben; man betet lieber andern nach, weil man sie mit mehr Gemächlichkeit verstehen kann. Dieß ist die Seite, von welcher dem Verf. dieser Anzeige das Verdienst dieser neuen Uebersetzung recht groß erscheint, und er hofft, daß er sich nicht täuschen werde. Es bleibt nichts zu wünschen übrig, als daß diese Uebersetzung bald gefördert und beendigt werden möge.

[FROM] GRUNDSÄTZE DER NATIONAL–OEKONOMIE ODER NATIONAL–WIRTHSCHAFTSLEHRE*
Ludwig Heinrich von Jakob

Vorrede
zur ersten Auflage

Daß die Polizey- und Finanz-Wissenschaft öfters zu Untersuchungen über die Entstehung und Vermehrung des National-Reichthums leiten mußten, war natürlich und nothwendig, da beyde ihre Maßregeln zum Theil darauf bauen, und dadurch rechtfertigen müssen. Allein vollständig und gründlich konnte auf diesem Wege diese wichtige Materie nicht abgehandelt werden.

Zwar hat man schon längst den einzelnen Zweigen der National-Industrie besondere Wissenschaften gewidmet; und den Landbau, das Manufacturwesen und die Handlung zum Gegenstande derselben gemacht. Aber diese beschäftigen sich ihrer Natur nach mehr mit den mechanischen Handgriffen und den Details der Operationen jener nützlichen Gewerbe, als mit den allgemeinen Grundsätzen der Entstehung des Reichthums; sie geben mehr Anleitung, wie die Unternehmer dieser verschiedenen Gewerbe ihren Privat-Vortheil zu bewirken haben, als daß sie die Art und Weise betrachten sollten, wie dieselben auf Vermehrung des National-Reichthums einfließen. Wer einen Staat im Ganzen beurtheilen will, muß sein Augenmerk mehr auf das Zusammenwirken der allgemeinen Ursachen richten, welche das National-Vermögen ursprünglich erzeugen, und die entgegen strebenden Hindernisse, so wie die Gesetze beyder, vollständig kennen. Diese zu zergliedern, die Elemente des Reichthums vollständig zu bestimmen, und die Regeln ihrer Zusammensetzung und Scheidung zu entwickeln, war dem berühmten Verfasser des Werkes: Ueber die Natur

* 3rd ed., Vienna, 1814, pp. ii–xii, 1–11.

und die Ursachen des National-Reichthums vorbehalten, der hierdurch eine Wissenschaft gegründet hat, welche nicht nur aller Polizey- und Finanz-Lehre voran gehen muß, sondern deren Studium auch für alle, welche sich ein Urtheil über National-Wohl anmaßen wollen, nothwendig ist.

Ich habe seit etwa sechs Jahren auf hiesiger Akademie jedes halbe Jahr über Herrn Sartorius sehr zweckmäßigen Auszug aus Smith Vorlesungen gehalten. Mein eigener Ideen-Gang und die Ueberzeugung, daß in der Smithschen Anordnung der Begriffe etwas liege, was die Leichtigkeit der Darstellung und die Faßlichkeit seines Systemes erschwert[1], da auch selbst in den Auszug vieles aufgenommen ist, was zur Staats- und Finanz-Lehre gehört, und dessen vollständige Erörterung der akademische Vortrag nicht zuläßt, wenn man nicht allzu viel aus dem Gebiethe solcher Wissenschaften, deren Principien der Wirthschaftslehre fremd sind, hinein ziehen will, haben mich vermocht, dieses Lehrbuch zu schreiben und heraus zu geben.

Mein Vorsatz dabey war, alle staatsrechtlichen, alle polizey- und finanzwissenschaftlichen Untersuchungen davon gänzlich auszuschließen, und das reine Problem aufzulösen: Wie entsteht der Reichthum bey einer Nation, wie wird die Vermehrung desselben befördert und gehindert, wie vertheilen sich die Elemente desselben unter die Glieder des Volkes, und wie wird er verzehrt?—Welches sind die allgemeinen Gesetze, wornach alles dieses erfolgt? Müssen die einzelnen Ursachen eingeschränkt oder kann ihnen ein vollkommen freyes Spiel unter bloßen Gesetzen der Gerechtigkeit verstattet werden?—Daß dabey auch der Polizey und des Finanz-Wesens gedacht werden mußte, ergibt sich leicht. Denn beyde können ja einen bedeutenden Einfluß auf das National-Vermögen ausüben. Aber nicht diese Wissenschaften selbst, sondern nur der Einfluß der Polizey- und Finanz-Operationen auf den National-Reichthum wird vorgetragen. Ergibt sich aus der Natur dieser Wissenschaften, daß bey ihren Anordnungen auf den Einfluß, den sie auf das National-Vermögen äußern, Rücksicht genommen werden muß: so werden sie Lehrsätze aus den Untersuchungen über den National-Reichthum entlehnen müssen.

Meine Absicht war daher nicht, ein Handbuch der Staatswirthschaft zu schreiben. Der Ausdruck Staat kann nur

---

[1] Wie auch alle Uebersetzer und Commentatoren des Smithschen Werkes einmüthig klagen, als Garve, Garnier, Say u. s. w.

gebraucht werden, um öffentliche Angelegenheiten zu bezeichnen; das Staatsvermögen ist ein Theil des Volksvermögens, das die Nation von dem Privat-Vermögen abgesondert, und zu öffent-lichen gemeinsamen Zwecken bestimmt hat; die regierenden Personen sind die Verwalter, oder die Wirthe dieses Vermögens, das National-Vermögen aber haben diese nicht zu bewirthschaften. Staatswirthschaftslehre kann in der That nichts seyn, als Finanz-Wissenschaft und allenfalls Polizey, in wie fern die Sorge für öffentliche Ordnung mit zu einer guten öffentlichen Wirthschaft gehört.

Zieht man die Lehre von dem National-Reichthume mit in die Finanz- und Polizey-Wissenschaft hinein, wie es in den meisten Englischen, Französischen und Deutschen Lehrbüchern bis jetzt noch fast überall geschehen ist: so kann sie nur als Einleitung oder als Corollarium in beyden erscheinen, indem freylich beyde Wissenschaften derselben öfters zu ihrer Grundlage bedürfen. Sehr leicht aber wird diese Vermischung dazu verleiten, die Lehre von dem National-Reichthume nach den Polizey- oder Finanz-Grundsätzen einzurichten, und auf jeden Fall wird die Vollständigkeit und Einheit der Untersuchung dabey leiden müssen.

Der Ausdruck National-Oekonomie, oder National-Wirthschaftslehre, scheint mir am besten zu passen, um ein System von Begriffen zu bezeichnen, worin die ganze Natur des Volksreichthums, sein Entstehen und Vergehen, also gleichsam seine Physik aus einander gesetzt werden soll.

Auf dieselbe kann sodann der Vortrag über Polizey- und Finanz-Wissenschaft in desto größerer Reinigkeit und Bestimmtheit folgen. Die National-Oekonomie enthält die einschränkenden Principien für beyde.

Was die Materien betrifft, so hat Adam Smith nicht leicht eine vergessen, welche zum vollständigen Bau einer National-Oekonomie gehört, und sie zugleich größten Theils aufs gründlichste abgehandelt. Ob die eine oder die andere durch die in meiner Schrift getroffene Anordnung mehr Licht gewonnen, und ob das Ganze sich leichter und deutlicher werde überschauen lassen, muß ich von Anderer Urtheile erwarten.

Der Smithsche Lehrsatz, daß Arbeit der allgemeine und letzte

Maßstab des Werthes der Dinge sey, ist von Baptist Say²), und von dem Grafen Lauderdale³), neuerlichst bestritten worden, und konnte es leicht, so wie der Satz von Smith dargestellt ist. Daß er aber dennoch richtig sey, glaube ich durch eine andere Darstellung desselben gezeigt zu haben.

Die Physiokraten haben einen neuen scharfsinnigen und originellen Vertheidiger an Herrn Garnier⁴) gefunden, und auch in Deutschland sind seit kurzen wieder mehrere denkende Männer aufgestanden, die sich ihres Systemes von neuen angenommen haben. Alles kommt bey ihrer Theorie darauf an, ob bloß der Landbau einen reinen Ertrag gebe. Mit diesem Satze steht und fällt das System. Daher habe ich dessen Prüfung nirgends unterlassen zu dürfen gemeint, wo meine Untersuchung mich dahin führte.

Ich habe sehr bedauert, daß mir die beyden letzten Theile des schätzbaren Werkes des Hofrathes Lüder über National-Industrie und Staatswirthschaft wegen eines seltenen Zufalles, erst in die Hände gekommen sind, als ich mit Ausarbeitung meines Buches schon fertig war; ich würde die Belehrungen, die ich daraus geschöpft habe, sonst eben so dankbar als den ersten Theil benutzt, und die Gründe für meine hier und da abweichenden Meinungen ausführlicher angedeutet haben.

Wenn Sachkenner urtheilen, daß dieser Versuch auch andere akademische Lehrer bestimmen kann, die so wichtige Lehre von der Natur und den Ursachen des National-Reichthums zu einem besondern Gegenstande ihrer Vorlesungen zu machen: so ist meine Absicht vollkommen erreicht. Von diesen Männern darf ich auch billige Nachsicht wegen der Unvollkommenheiten erwarten, die sich in der Anordnung der Begriffe finden mögen. Sie kennen die Schwierigkeiten zu gut, welche damit verbunden sind, Erfahrungsbegriffe, wo man selten einen voraus schicken kann, zu dessen Verständniß nicht einer der folgenden nöthig wäre, lichtvoll zu ordnen, und ohne Wiederhohlungen genau zu bestimmen. Was ich hierin zu leisten hatte, war mir bekannt,

---

² *Économie politique*, ein Werk, das die National-Oekonomie nach Smiths Principien populär vorträgt, und dem ich in Absicht auf Anordnung der Materie und Zergliederung einiger Begriffe viel Belehrung schuldig bin.

³ Dessen Werk ich nur aus einem Auszuge in den Englischen Miscellen (XV. 3.) kenne.

⁴ In der Vorrede zur Französischen Uebersetzung von Adam Smiths Werke, und in den Noten dazu im fünften Bande.

und ich habe es auch nicht an Mühe und öftern Umarbeitungen
fehlen lassen, um gerechte Ansprüche zu befriedigen. Aber
ich zweifle nicht, daß sich noch Vieles theils abkürzen, theils
verbessern läßt; und so wie ich mein eigenes Nachdenken stets
dazu anwenden werde, die Fehler dieses Buches, welche ich
darin entdecke, zu vermindern: so werde ich auch alle Winke
und Belehrungen, falls es eine neue Auflage erleben sollte, aufs
dankbarste benutzen.

Halle, den 1. Jänner 1805.

Vorrede
zur zweyten Auflage.

Ich habe um so weniger für nöthig erachtet, bey dieser zweyten
Auflage meines Werkes wesentliche Veränderungen darin vor-
zunehmen, da nicht nur alle öffentliche Urtheile ihm ihre
Zufriedenheit bezeigt, sondern auch mehrere akademische
Lehrer es zweckmäßig gefunden haben, darüber Vorlesungen
zu halten. Der Ausdruck ist hier und da berichtiget und verbes-
sert, einige Stellen sind abgekürzt, andere erweitert worden,
auch habe ich die neueste Literatur ergänzt, so weit sie mir,
bey der großen Entfernung vom literarischen Markte, in
welcher ich jetzt lebe, und bey den localen Schwierigkeiten,
alte und neue Bücher zu erhalten, bekannt geworden ist. Das
Fehlende wird jeder leicht ergänzen können.

Charcow, den 1. December 1808.

Einleitung.

I.

BEGRIFF VON DER NATIONAL-WIRTHSCHAFTSLEHRE.

§.1

Der Hauptendzweck, den ein jeder bey der Vereinigung zu
einer bürgerlichen Gesellschaft hat, ist: ein desto sichreres,
gemächlicheres und glücklicheres Leben zu führen.

§.2.

Die Mittel zu einem glücklichen Leben, so weit sie in die Gewalt der Menschen gegeben sind, liegen theils in den Privat-Kräften der einzelnen Glieder, theils in den öffentlichen, vereinten Kräften des Staates.

§.3.

Ein glückliches Leben hängt nähmlich zunächst davon ab, daß die gehörigen Mittel vorhanden sind, um die Bedürfnisse, welche man hat, zu stillen. Diese Mittel müssen größten Theils von den Gliedern der Nation hervor gebracht oder erworben werden; ihren Inbegriff nennt man das National–Vermögen, oder in wie fern ein Ueberfluß davon vorhanden ist, den National-Reichthum.

§.4.

Zur Erwerbung dieses Reichthums gehört Sicherheit der Personen und des Eigenthums, als die erste und wesentlichste Bedingung und da, wo die Privat-Kräfte nicht hinreichen, ihn zu erhalten, oder zu vermehren, Vereinigung Aller, oder öffentliche Macht.

§.5.

Da Sicherheit des Rechtes und Beförderung des allgemeinen Wohles, durch vereinte Kraft, von den einzelnen Gliedern des Volkes, so lange sie ihrer Willkühr überlassen bleiben, nicht zu erwarten ist: so vereiniget sich dasselbe zu einem Staate, d. h.: es überträgt einer höchsten Gewalt die Ausführung dieser Zwecke, welche wegen ihrer Macht die souvraine Gewalt, und wegen der ihr anvertrauten Ausführung der gemeinschaftlichen Zwecke die Regierung genannt wird.

§.6.

Hieraus folgt, daß alle vom Staate anzuwendenden Mittel dem höhern Zwecke der Nation (§. 1.) untergeordnet seyn, und demselben nie widersprechen müssen.

§.7

Die Wissenschaft der Mittel, wodurch der Staat oder die Regierung ihren Zweck (§. 5.) erreichen kann, heißt Staats- oder Regierungs-Politik, die entweder innere oder äußere ist, je nachdem die Mittel innerhalb oder außerhalb der Gränzen des Staates liegen.

§.8.

Die Regeln, wodurch die innere Politik ihre Mittel näher bestimmt und zur Befolgung vorschreibt, heißen Gesetze. Die innere Regierungs-Politik ist also nichts anders, als die Wissenschaft der Gesetzgebung.

§.9.

Der Gegenstand dieser Gesetze ist aber: 1) eine zweckmäßige Organisation des Staates—Staatsverfassungslehre; 2) die Bestimmung der rechtlichen Verhältnisse der Staatsglieder unter einander und der rechtlichen Folgen—Justiz-Gesetzgebung; 3) Sicherheit der Rechte und Beförderung des allgemeinen Wohles, so fern es durch isolirte Privat-Kräfte nicht so leicht erreichbar ist, durch Bestimmung gewisser Handlungen und Einrichtung öffentlicher Anstalten—Polizey Gesetzgebung; 4) Bestimmung der Art und Weise, wie das öffentliche Vermögen zusammen gebracht und zu den öffentlichen Zwecken verwandt werden solle—Finanz-Wissenschaft oder Staatswirthschaftslehre—Staats-Oekonomie.

§.10.

Die Mittel, wodurch das Volk, unter dem Schutze der Regierung, seinen Zweck, nähmlich Erwerbung, Vermehrung und Genuß seines Vermögens am besten erreichen kann, die Art, wie der National-Reichthum entstehet, vertheilt, verzehrt und wieder hervor gebracht oder immer fort erhalten wird, den Einfluß, welchen alle Umstände und Ereignisse im Staate darauf haben, untersucht die National-Oekonomie oder National-Wirthschaftslehre.

II.

UNTERSCHIED UND VERBINDUNG DER NATIONAL-WIRTHSCHAFT, DER STAATSWIRTHSCHAFT UND DER IHR VERWANDTEN WISSENSCHAFTEN.

§.11.

Die Staatswirthschaftslehre bekümmert sich bloß um einen Theil des National-Vermögens, nähmlich um denjenigen, welcher für die Regierung zur Erreichung ihres Zweckes bestimmt ist. Um diesen desto sicherer und desto dauerhafter zu erlangen, muß sie freylich öfters die National-Wirthschaftslehre befragen, und hat daher mehrere Artikel derselben an sich gezogen. Denn ein guter Staatswirth muß die Quellen der

Einnahme für die Regierung einerseits erhalten und erweitern, andererseits neue eröffnen. Um beydes sicher zu erreichen, muß er solche Finanz-Maßregeln ergreifen, welche die Quellen des National-Reichthums nicht verstopfen. Die Finanz-Wissenschaft muß sich daher natürlicher Weise oft über die Quellen des National-Reichthums ausbreiten, so lange diese nicht in einer besondern Wissenschaft zergliedert sind.

§.12.

Die Polizey hat unter andern den Zweck, die Hindernisse der nützlichen Thätigkeit aus dem Wege zu räumen, und das allgemeine Wohl durch öffentliche Mittel zu befördern, so weit solches möglich ist. Daher ist zur Beurtheilung ihrer Anordnungen freylich die Kenntniß der Art und Weise, wie durch die Gewerbe der Reichthum am besten bewirkt wird, nöthig, und dem Polizey-Gesetzgeber werden also mehrere Zweige der National-Wirthschaftslehre ganz unentbehrlich seyn.

§.13.

Dennoch darf die National-Wirthschaftslehre nicht bloß als ein Corollarium der Polizey- und Finanz-Wissenschaft (§. 9.) behandelt werden, wo sie immer nur fragmentarisch vorgetragen werden kann, und wo sich leicht irrige Grundsätze in sie einschleichen: sondern sie verdient als eine ganz eigene, für sich bestehende Wissenschaft eine Stelle, und muß die Basis, nicht einen bloßen Anhang der Finanz- und Polizey-Wissenschaft, ausmachen.

§.14.

In der National-Oekonomie muß ebenfalls gezeigt werden, wie die Staatseinrichtung und die Gesetze auf Vermehrung oder Verminderung des National-Reichthums einfließen. Hier wird aber die Wirkung der Staatsgesetze nicht in Beziehung auf den Zweck der Regierung, sondern in Beziehung auf den Zweck der Erhaltung oder Vermehrung des Reichthums beurtheilt. Beyde Wissenschaften stehen also zwar mit einander in enger Verbindung, sie sind aber ihrem Inhalte und ihrem Zwecke nach von einander verschieden. Die National-Oekonomie ist eine die Staats-Oekonomie einschränkende und leitende Wissenschaft.

§.15.

Die National-Oekonomie hat ein Interesse für jedermann, der sich mit den Triebrädern, wodurch die menschliche

Industrie in Thätigkeit gesetzt wird, wodurch Wohlstand und Reichthum zunehmen und abnehmen kann, bekannt machen will. Polizey- und Finanz-Wissenschaft hat nur ein besonderes Interesse für die, welche die Mittel, welche die Regierung zur Erreichung ihrer Zwecke anwenden kann und soll, kennen und beurtheilen wollen.

III.
GESCHICHTE UND LITERATUR DER NATIONAL-OEKONOMIE.

§.16.
Man hat vor Adam Smith nicht daran gedacht, die Lehre von den Ursachen der bürgerlichen Wohlfahrt von der Regierungs-Wissenschaft (Politik) abgesondert vorzutragen. Locke, Stewart, Rousseau, die Französischen Encyclopädisten und selbst die Physiokraten tragen unter dem Titel Économie politique, political oeconomie die Regierungswissenschaft vor, und indem sie hauptsächlich zeigen wollen, wie der Staat sich die Quellen seiner Einnahmen in dem vermehrten Reichthume des Volkes zu versichern habe, entdecken sie den Staatsmännern, wie sie durch ihre Maßregeln das National-Vermögen bald schwächen, bald vermehren können, und werden hierdurch hauptsächlich auf die Untersuchung mehrerer Materien der National-Oekonomie geleitet.

§.17.
Adam Smith ist der erste, welcher die Lehre von der Natur und den Ursachen des National-Reichthums systematisch entwickelt und als eine ganz eigene Wissenschaft gegründet hat. Zwar kommen viele Betrachtungen über die Grundsätze der Staatswirthschaft der verschiedenen Regierungen in seinem Werke vor, aber alle größten Theils nur in der Absicht, um zu zeigen, was diese mannigfaltigen Systeme für einen Einfluß auf die Vermehrung oder Verminderung des National-Reichthums haben, und er unterscheidet das National-Einkommen und die National-Ausgaben sehr sorgfältig von den Einnahmen und Ausgaben des Staates als eines politischen Körpers, die wiederum in einem eigenen Verhältnisse zum National-Vermögen stehen.

§.18.
Ob nun gleich nach Adam Smith mehrere Lehrer der Politik die Grundlehren der National-Oekonomie nicht vergessen

haben: so sind doch wenige darauf bedacht gewesen, sie als eine eigene Wissenschaft abzusondern, sondern haben sie bald mehr, bald weniger dem Vortrage der Polizey- und Finanz-Wissenschaft angehängt. Bloß einige Deutsche, welche Smith sehr genau gefolgt sind, Sartorius und Lüder, und einige Franzosen, Garnier, Canard, Say u. s. w., haben die National-Oekonomie, jene unter dem Nahmen der Staatswirthschaft, diese unter dem Nahmen der Économie politique mehr abgesondert vorgetragen.

A [nmerkung:] Staat hat allerdings eine doppelte Bedeutung: 1) die bürgerliche Gesellschaft als Nation und 2) als öffentliche Regierung, oder souvraine Gewalt betrachtet. Daher kann Staatswirthschaft so wohl National-Wirthschaft, als Regierungswirthschaft bedeuten. Alle Schriftsteller vor Adam Smith haben es im letzten Sinne genommen, und vielleicht hat jene Zweydeutigkeit bewirkt, daß man den Begriff der National-Oekonomie auch in denen Schriften, welche sie vorzüglich im Auge gehabt zu haben scheinen, öfters verlassen findet. Ich habe daher, um allen Zweydeutigkeiten zu entgehen, mich des Ausdruckes National-Wirthschaft, zum Unterschiede der Regierungs- oder Staatswirthschaft, bedient. Da alles, was die Nation im Allgemeinen betrifft, so bald es einer Regel unterworfen werden soll, vom Staate ausgehen muß: so müssen freylich auch die allgemeinen Anordnungen der National-Oekonomie von der Regierung getroffen werden.

§.19.

Die wichtigsten Schriften, welche Untersuchungen über die allgemeinsten Materien der National-Wirthschaft enthalten, ob sie dieselbe gleich nicht als eine abgesonderte Wissenschaft vortragen, sind:

James Stewart [Steuart], Inquiry into the Principles of political oeconomie. 2 Vol. London 1767; auch Basel bey Thurneisen. (Eine neue Ausgabe in London ist 1804 angekündigt.) Ins Deutsche übersetzt. Hamburg 1769 3 Bände; in Tübingen bey Cotta, 1769. 5 Bände, gr. 8.

Maximes générales de Gouvernement économique par Fr. Quesnay 1758. Auch dessen Tableau économique.

Büsch, G., Schriften über Staatswirthschaft und Handlung, 3 Theile, 2. Ausgabe. Hamburg und Kiel 1801.

Deßgleichen die Lehr- und Handbücher von Justi, Pfeifer, Genovesi, Sonnenfels, Niemann, Voß, Walter, Bensen u. s. w. Auch die politischen Schriften von David Hume, Verri, Rousseau, Vernier, Friedrich dem II., Mortimer, Necker, Herzberg, Struensee und andern, enthalten treffliche Gedanken über einzelne Materien der National-Wirthschaft.

Mehr abgesondert von der Staats-Politik findet man sie in folgenden Schriften:

Smith, A., Inquiry into the nature and causes of the Wealth of Nations. London 4. edit. 1785. Deutsch mit (wenig) Anmerkungen von Garve. Wien bey Bauer 1814. Französisch von Garnier, in 5 Bänden. Paris bey Agasse.

Sartorius Handbuch der Staatswirthschaft, zum Gebrauch bey akademischen Vorlesungen, nach Adam Smith's Grundsätzen. Berlin 1796.

Lüder, über National-Industrie und Staatswirthschaft, nach Adam Smith. 1. Theil. 1800 2. Theil.

Abrégé élémentaire des Principes de l'Économie politique, par Gamier, à Paris 1796.

Principes d'Économie politique, par B. V. F. Canard, à Paris, chez F. Buisson 1801.

Traité d'Économie politique, par Jean Baptiste de Say. Tom. I. II. à Paris, chez Deterville 1803. gr. 8. Uebersetzt mit Anmerkungen und Abhandlungen von L. H. Jakob.2 Bände, Halle 1807.

Die National-Oekonomie von Julius Gr. v. Soden. Erster Theil, Leipzig 1805. Zweyter 1806. Dritter 1808. [Other vols. iv, 1810; v, 1811; vi, 1816; vii, 1817; viii, 1821; ix, 1824].

Die vollständigen Titel der Schriften, wo hier die Nahmen der Verfasser, um der Kürze willen, bloß angeführt sind, so wie mehrere andere, findet man in: Niemanns Staatswirthschaftslehre oder auch in Rößigs neuerer Literatur der Cameralistik und Polizey. Nach alphabetischer Ordnung. 2 Theile. Leipzig 1802.

IV.

PLAN DES GANZEN.

§.20.

Die National-Oekonomie handelt:

1. Von der Entstehung und Vermehrung des National-Reichthums.
2. Von den Principien der vortheilhaftesten Vertheilung des National-Reichthums unter die Glieder der Gesellschaft.
3. Von der Consumtion des National-Vermögens und den verschiedenen Wirkungen derselben.

Erstes Hauptstück.
Von der Entstehung und Vermehrung des National-Reichthums.

Erster Abschnitt.

Vorläufige Begriffe von dem National-Vermögen und National-Reichthum.

§.21.

Man unterscheidet die Person von ihrem Vermögen sehr genau, und versteht unter letzterem sodann den Inbegriff der ihr gehörigen äußeren Sachen, welche zur Befriedigung der menschlichen Bedürfnisse dienen. Die Person ist der Zweck, das Vermögen das Mittel.

§.22.

Wenn daher auch gleich Personen theils die äußern Bedürfnißmittel erzeugen, theils selbst zur Stillung der Bedürfnisse unmittelbar beytragen: so rechnet man sie und ihre Eigenschaften dennoch gewöhnlich nicht zu dem Vermögen, im wirthschaftlichen und eigentlichen Sinne.

§.23.

Was zur Befriedigung menschlicher Bedürfnisse dient, heißt ein relatives Gut, und ist in dieser Hinsicht nützlich oder hat einen Nutzen. In der vollkommenen Befriedigung der Bedürfnisse aber besteht das absolute Gut, oder die Glückseligkeit.

A [nmerkung:]. Es ist hier nicht von dem moralischen, sondern dem physischen absoluten Gute die Rede.

§.24.

Das Vermögen besteht daher in dem Inbegriffe der äußeren

Güter der Menschen. Sind dieselben Güter für jedermann zugänglich: so heißen sie das gemeinsame oder allgemeine Vermögen; gehören sie nur Einigen oder Einem ausschließlich an: so heißen sie ein eigenthümliches, besonderes, vorzügliches Vermögen. Wenn vom Vermögen im Allgemeinen die Rede ist; so versteht man hauptsächlich das eigenthümliche Vermögen darunter.

§.25.

Die Bedürfnisse können in Bedürfnisse der Nothwendigkeit, der Bequemlichkeit oder Gemächlichkeit, und des Wohllebens eingetheilt werden; je nachdem sie zur nothdürftigen Erhaltung oder zur Zufriedenheit des Lebens, oder endlich zur Erhöhung des Vergnügens desselben dienen.

§.26.

Ein Vermögen, das eine beharrliche Quelle ist, alle Arten von Bedürfnissen zu befriedigen, heißt Reichthum; National-Vermögen oder National-Reichthum ist der Inbegriff aller, einer ganzen Nation und deren Individuen gehörigen eigenthümlichen Güter.

§.27.

Jede nützliche Sache, die irgend eines Menschen Eigenthum geworden ist, ist daher ein Bestandtheil des National-Reichthums.

§.28.

Diese Bestandtheile unterscheiden sich aber nicht bloß durch ihre Mannigfaltigkeit und durch ihren verschiedenen Gebrauch, sondern hauptsächlich durch den verschiedenen Grad ihrer Güte, d. h.: durch ihren Werth.

§.29.

Der Werth aber (§. 28.) wird entweder durch die Art ihres Bedürfnisses und durch den Grad der Nothwendigkeit eines Dinges, oder durch die Menge und Art der nützlichen Dinge, welche dafür zu erhalten sind, bestimmt. Den erstern kann man den Bedürfnißwerth, den letztern den Tauschwerth nennen.

§.30.

Alle Dinge, welche einen Tauschwerth haben, müssen auch einen Bedürfnißwerth haben, aber dieses ist nicht umgekehrt der Fall, weil viele Dinge von hohem Bedürfnißwerthe ganz umsonst zu haben sind.

§.31.

Der Reichthum besteht hauptsächlich aus dem Inbegriffe solcher Dinge, die einen Tauschwerth haben, und er ist um so größer, je mehr dafür nützliche Dinge von aller Art beliebig zu haben sind, oder je mehrere Bedürfnisse aller Art damit befriedigt werden können.

§.32.

Die Bestandtheile des Reichthums sind daher: 1) alle nützlichen Erd-Producte, die nicht in beliebiger Menge ohne alle Arbeit zu haben sind; 2) alle nützlichen Producte der menschlichen Kunst; 3) alle äußeren Quellen, woraus beyde Producte fließen.

AVERTISSEMENT DU TRADUCTEUR*
Jean-Antoine Roucher

On demandoit depuis long-tems une traduction françoise de l'ouvrage de M. Smith. On la demande sur-tout aujourd'hui, que l'ASSEMBLÉE NATIONALE s'occupe des moyens de régénérer la fortune publique, dilapidée par une longue suite de prodigalités & de malversations, autant que par un choc continuel de systêmes d'administration opposés les uns aux autres. Quiconque aspire au bonheur de vivre sous un gouvernement qui respecte les droits sacrés de la liberté & de la propriété, trouvera dans ces recherches les principes immuables qui doivent diriger les chefs des nations.

La France a produit sans doute des ouvrages qui ont jeté des lumières partielles sur les différens points de l'économie politique. Ce seroit trop d'ingratitude que d'oublier les services rendus à la patrie par les travaux des écrivains économistes. Les jours de la détraction & du ridicule sont passés; ils ont fait place à ceux de la justice; & quels que soient les écarts, les conséquences forcées où l'esprit de systême ait pu entraîner une association de citoyens honêtes & philosophes, il n'en est pas moins reconnu aujourd'hui qu'ils ont donné le signal à la recherche des vérités pratiques, sur lesquelles doit s'élever & s'asseoir la richesse des nations.

Mais l'Angleterre a sur nous l'avantage d'avoir donné au monde un systême complet de l'économie sociale. Cette partie, la plus belle & la plus utile de toutes celles qui composent l'ensemble des connoissances humaines, se trouve dans l'ouvrage de M. Smith, approfondie & développée avec une sagacité qui tient du prodige.

Mais, qu'on y prenne garde, on se tromperoit étrangement, si l'on se promettoit ici une lecture de pur agrément. L'ouvrage de M. Smith n'est pas fait pour ces hommes qui lisent uniquement pour le plaisir de lire. Il veut des têtes pensantes, des

* From *Recherches sur la Nature et les Causes de la Richesse des Nations* (Neuchâtel, 1792), pp. vii–xii.

têtes accoutumées à méditer sur les grands objets qui intéressent l'ordre & le bonheur de la société. Peut-être qu'en un tems qui n'est pas encore bien éloigné de nous, Smith n'auroit trouvé en France qu'un petit nombre de lecteurs dignes de lui & de ses pensées. Mais aujourd'hui que la sphère de nos espérances s'est agrandie, & avec elle le cercle de nos idées, j'ai cru qu'une traduction où l'on auroit tâché de réunir la fidélité à l'élégance, & cette précision modérée, qui, bien loin de nuire à la clarté, la rend, pour ainsi dire, plus visible encore, j'ai cru, dis-je, que les disciples de Smith pourroient devenir plus nombreux parmi nous. Il faut maintenant que la lumière descende des hauteurs où la forçoient à rester concentrée l'indifférence des uns & l'inquiétude des autres; il faut qu'elle se répande dans toutes les classes, qui désormais pourront fournir des membres aux prochaines législatures.

C'est dans cette vue que, renonçant à des occupations moins austères, je me suis voué à un travail qui auroit cent fois rebuté mon courage, si je n'eusse vu devant moi le grand objet de l'utilité publique. Puisque le François prétend au titre d'homme libre, il faut qu'il commence par s'occuper en homme fait. Nous habitons une maison délabrée & tombant de vétusté: des circonstances impérieuses l'ont renversée. Le moment présent doit être employé tout entier à la reconstruire sur un nouveau plan. C'est l'œuvre de la philosophie. Quand elle aura achevé sa tâche, nous pourrons appeler les arts, & leur confier le soin d'ajouter l'agrément à la solidité.

CRITICAL NOTES ON THE WEALTH OF NATIONS*
Jean-Baptiste Say

I-1 (Introduction and plan of the work. 1)
Le travail est le seul fondement de la valeur des choses (Je crois que c'est une erreur).

I-6 (I.i.1)
La division du travail est ce qui a le plus augmenté sa puissance productive. (Smith se trompe. C'est le pouvoir productif des agen[t]s naturels que l'homme force à travailler de concert avec lui qui porte si loin la somme des produits.)

I-11, en bas, (1) marqué après le texte 'because the silk manufacture' (I.i.4)
(1) Le mot anglais *manufacture* veut dire *produit manufacturé*. *Silk manufacture* ne veut pas dire *manufacture de Soyeries*, mais les *soyeries* elles-mêmes. Le français manufacture se dit en anglais *manufactory*.

I-14, à gauche, référence implicitement faite au mot '... indolent careless application' (I.i.7)
application n'a pas le même sens qu'en français; il signifie l'action de se mettre à une occupation quelconque.

I-14 (I.i.8)
(La grande puissance de la séparation des occupations vient—I-12 (I.i.6))
3° des procédés expéditifs qu'elle découvre. (Ici Smith lui attribue la puissance productive des machines. Il a tort car cette puissance existe indépendamment de la sépar[ation] des occ[upations].)

* This is a selection from Say's marginal notes (1789–1802) in a copy of the *Wealth of Nations* held at the Bibliotheque de l'Institut de France, transcribed by Hitoshi Hashimoto and published as 'Notes inédites de J.-B. Say qui couvrent les marges de la *Richesse des Nations* et qui la critiquent', *Kyoto Sangyo University Economic and Business Review*, no. 7 (1980), pp. 67–81. The volume and page references are to the 5th edition (1789), and book, section, and paragraph references are to the Glasgow edition. Nine notes identified CPE (V) or (VI), with page citations, were published in *Collection des principaux économistes* (Paris, 1843), vols. 5 and 6, devoted to WN.

I-16 (I.i.9)

Les découvertes scientifiques sont dues à la séparation des occup[ations]. (C'est vrai, mais la puissance productive des agen[t]s naturels une fois connues, leur action *produit* de son côté concur[r]emment & additionnellement au travail de l'homme qui n'est donc pas le seul producteur.)

I-44, à gauche, sur la feuille collée, (1) marqué à la fin du paragraphe 'to purchase or command' (I.v.2). . .CPE (V) 37

(1) Smith me paraît commettre en ce chapitre une double erreur. 1° Tous les biens du monde n'ont pas été achetés par le travail de l'homme. La nature a une part dans certaines productions et son travail donne une valeur additionnelle à celui de l'homme. Cela est évident dans l'industrie agricole dont les produits payent (outre le salaire de l'industrie de l'homme & les profits de son capital qui peut à la rigueur représenter du travail accumulé) un revenu foncier. 2° Il y a des travaux plus ou moins bien récompensés, suivant le plus ou le moins d'utilité de leurs produits. La quantité de travail qu'une *valeur* quelconque commande, est donc variable & si la *valeur* est égale à toutes deux, la mesure est donc variable selon les quantités auxquelles elle est appliquée. Ce n'est donc pas une mesure, qui est une grandeur invariable susceptible d'être comparée à des grandeurs variables.

I-49, en bas, sur la feuille collée, (1) marqué après le texte 'its nominal price, in the quantity of money' (I.v.9)

(1) Distinction inutile. Un prix payé en monnaye n'est pas plus nominal que lorsqu'il est payé en denrées, parce qu'il ne se règle pas suivant le *nom* de la monnaye, mais suivant la quantité de métaux précieux qu'elle contient. [Ici Say raye les mots suivants—Ainsi un travail qu'il soit payé en blé ou en monnaye] Voyez Smith lui-même; la fin de son chapitre, où il dit que par le prix en monnaye il veut toujours dire le métal contenu dans cette monnaye et non sa dénomination qui varie selon le bon plaisir des gouvernement[s].

I-50, en bas, (1) marqué après le texte 'and hardly ever augmenting' (I.v.11)

(1) Les gouvernemen[t]s sont quelquefois revenus à ce qu'ils appelaient la forte monnaye, pour tirer des contribuables de plus fortes contributions.

I-52 (I.v.15)

La valeur du blé varie moins que celle des autres denrées.

(Smith n'explique pas pourquoi. Il le dit page 292 & 293 de ce volume.)

I-61, en bas, sur la feuille collée, (1) marqué après le texte 'regulates the value of the whole coin' (I.v.29). . .CPE (V) 54

(1) Je crois que Smith se trompe. Quand la monnaye de cuivre sert seulement à faire l'appoint de ce qu'on ne peut payer en monnaye d'argent, la valeur intrinsèque du cuivre n'en est pas changée, son empreinte seule a une valeur monétaire qui représente une coupure d'argent; ce sont des billets de confiance écrits sur cuivre émis par la monnaye remboursables en argent du moment qu'on en porte à la monnaye assez pour avoir la plus petite pièce d'argent. Quand la monnaye ne les rembourse pas à vue, ils perdent sur la place contre de l'argent, donc l'argent n'en augmente pas la valeur. Quand on force à en recevoir dans les payemen[t]s pour une certaine proportion, pour 1/40ᵉ par exemple, alors c'est comme si l'on mettait pour 1/40 d'alliage de cuivre dans l'argent. Le trésor public n'y gagne rien dans les marchés qu'il fait, puisque les marchés sont faits en conséquence; quand il paye ainsi une dette contractée en argent, il fait la même banqueroute que s'il dégradait le titre. Dans ces cas là le change étranger baisse en proportion; c'est[-]à[-]dire qu'on donne moins de monnaye étrangère pour de la monnaye nationale en proportion de ce que le titre en est moins bon.

I-62, en bas, sur la feuille collée, (1) marqué après le 2ᵉ paragraphe '. . .exchanged for it' (I.v. 30)

(1) Oui; parce que les payements se font en or & qu'on ne paye en shillings d'argent [illisible] que les appoints des guinées mais si l'on venait à payer le principal des sommes en shillings, toute la monnaye baisserait de valeur relativement à tout.

I-75, en bas, sur la feuille collée, (1) marqué après le 2ᵉ paragraphe '. . .resolves itself into profit' (I. vi. 9). . .CPE(V)68

(1) Ici je ne peux être de l'avis de Smith, ou plutôt je ne sais quel est l'avis de Smith. Quel travail mesure le profit de la terre & celui du capital qui ont concouru à la création d'un produit? Ce profit est tout à fait indépendant du travail de l'homme & montre que le service rendu par la terre et par le capital, est autre chose que celui rendu par le travail. Même un capital qui est une accumulation de valeurs dues en partie au travail de l'homme, rend un service où le travail

de l'homme n'a plus de part. Le capital représente en partie un travail humain & partie de sa valeur en provient; mais la valeur du service qu'il rend ne représente plus de travail humain. Il n'en entre pas dans le service que rend le capital.

I-77, en bas, sur la feuille collée, (1) marqué à la fin du 2ᵉ paragraphe '. . .make any part of it' (I. vi. 15)

(1) Leur [=gatherers of Scotch Pebbles] entretien exige cependant un petit capital, dont il faut bien que l'avance soit faite ou par eux ou par ceux qui les employent. Leurs produits coûtent donc outre le salaire de l'industrie, un intérêt d'un petit capital.

I-81, en bas sur la feuille collée, (1) marqué après le texte qui se lit; '. . .in which the whole annual produce is employed in maintaining the industrious' (I. vi. 24)

(1) Le produit annuel ne représente donc pas le travail annuel. Il y a donc une production indépendante de celle du travail & du revenu qui ne viennent d'aucun travail de l'homme, ni ancien ni récent. Or c'est cette partie de la production qu'on doit aux services productifs de la nature & à ceux des capitaux. Donc ils sont agen[t]s de la production aussi bien que le travail humain.

I-84, en bas, sur la feuille collée, (1) marqué après le 1ᵉʳ paragraphe '. . .with its natural price' (I. vii. 7)

(1) Je n'aime pas l'expression *natural price, prix naturel,* car ce n'est pas un *prix* que le taux auquel une chose ne se vend pas. Du moment qu'elle s'y vend, ce taux devient son prix courant son *market-price.* Voilà pourquoi j'appelle dans mon ouvrage *frais de production,* ce que Smith appelle *natural price.*

I-96, sur la feuille collée, référence implicitement faite à la fin du chapitre VII (I.vii.37)

L'objet des Chapitres 8, 9, 10, et 11 du 1ᵉʳ Livre de Smith est d'examiner quel est le taux naturel des salaires, des intérêts et des fermages dans des circonstances données. Ce qui indique ce que Smith appelle le *prix naturel* de leurs produits.

J'appelle ce prix, le *prix coûtant,* car parmi les circonstances qui influent sur ce prix il y en a qu'on ne peut pas appeler naturelles. Et si on l'appelle *naturel* parce qu'il dérive de la *nature des choses,* le *prix courant* ou *marchand,* mériterait la même appellation, car il dérive aussi de la nature des choses. [Ce paragraphe est rayé par Say lui-même.] Le Chapitre 10 est rempli par de noveaux développements qui ont rapport aux chapitres 8 et 9.

Et le Chapitre 11 est grossi outre mesure par des digressions qui mériteraient seules de former des *chapitres*, et même des *livres* par elles-mêmes.

I-111, à droite, sur la feuille collée, (1) marqué à la fin du 3ᵉ paragraphe '. . .with common humanity' (I.viii.28)

(1) C'est déjà une proposition accidentelle que celle-ci: *Les salaires sont en Angleterre au dessus du taux qui suffirait pour procurer l'absolu nécessaire*. Et Smith employe pour la prouver huit pages!

I-119, en bas, sur la feuille collée, (1) marqué à la tête du dernier paragraphe, qui commence par 'Poverty, though it. . .' (I.viii.37)

(1) Voici des considérations purement relatives à la population lorsqu'il ne devrait être question que de *salaires*. Elles n'en sont pas moins fort intéressantes; mais il aurait fallu en faire l'objet de quelque traité ou de quelque chapitre particulier. On est toujours étonné qu'une si excellente tête que *Smith* mette tant de justesse et si peu d'ordre dans ses idées.

I-123, à droite, sur la feuille collée, (1) marqué à la fin du 1ᵉʳ paragraphe qui finit par '. . .so very high' (I. viii. 41)

(1) J'ai de la peine à être convaincu que le travail de l'esclave revienne plus cher que celui du serviteur. On nourrit l'esclave de l'absolu nécessaire & il est peu d'ouvrier libre qui s'en contente. On tire de l'esclave tout le travail qu'il peut supporter; or il est peu d'ouvrier libre qui ne perde une partie de son tem[p]s dans l'oisiveté ou la ribote; or il faut que le salaire paye tout cela.

I-133, en bas, sur la feuille collée, (1) marqué à la fin du titre de chapitre 'Of the Profits of Stock' (I.ix). . .CPE(V)119

(1) Smith s'est jeté dans un grand embarras faute d'avoir séparé en deux parties ce qu'il appelle *profits du fonds*. Il y a dans cette valeur deux éléments qu'il a distingués ailleurs (tome 1, p. 72) sans pousser cette distinction dans le reste de son ouvrage. Ces deux éléments sont le *profit de l'industrie* ou si l'on veut le *salaire du travail*, et *l'intérêt du capital*. Pourquoi vouloir chercher la valeur de l'un d'après la valeur de l'autre? Leur valeur se règle d'après des principes différen[t]s. Celle du profit de l'industrie se règle sur le degré d'habileté, la longueur des études, &c. Celle de l'intérêt du

capital se règle sur l'abondance des capitaux, la sureté du placement &c.....

Ce qu'il y a de singulier c'est que *Smith* lui même en traitant son sujet, a fini par s'apercevoir qu'il avait eu tort; ainsi qu'on peut le voir à la page 171 de ce tome où il dit: 'La différence *apparente* dans les profits des capitaux suivant les diverses professions, est en général *une erreur* provenant de ce que nous ne distinguons pas toujours, ce qui doit être regardé comme salaires du travail de ce qui doit passer pour profits des capitaux.'

C'est un exemple de plus de la négligence des auteurs anglais dans la formation, et la réforme de leurs plans.

I-150, en bas, sur la feuille collée, (1) marqué après le texte 'The rise of profit operates like compound interest.' (I. ix. 24)

(1) Cette remarque de Smith est ingénieuse; mais est-elle bien juste? Dans la série des producteurs, chacun rembourse les avances de son prédécesseur & se fait payer par son successeur l'intérêt de ses propres avances; par conséquent il se fait rembourser non seulement l'augmentation de main-d'oeuvre payée par son prédécesseur, mais encore l'intérêt de cette augmentation. Si à son tour il paye une augmentation de main-d'oeuvre, l'intérêt de cette avance s'est payée [*sic*] par le producteur suivant & ainsi de suite jusqu'au consommateur. On voit que quand il y a renchérissement de main-d'oeuvre dans toutes les périodes de la production, le renchérissement qui en résulte est supérieur à celui qu'indiquerait une simple progression arithmétique.

I–154, en bas, sur la feuille collée, (1) marqué après le paragraphe 'Disagreeableness. . .as the wages of labour' (I. x. b. 4)

(1) Est-ce bien sûr? Quand un entrepreneur tire un fort gros profit des désagrémen[t]s de son état, n'est-ce point le désagrément de ses travaux qui est bien payé plutôt que l'emploi de son capital, lequel n'éprouve ni désagrément ni agrément? Veux t'on [*sic*] savoir dans quels cas les capitaux sont bien payés, qu'on sépare le capitaliste, de l'entrepreneur? Je croirais que si dans telle entreprise les capitaux sont mieux payés que dans une autre, c'est parce qu'ils y courent plus de risques ou parce qu'ils y sont engagés pour plus longtem[p]s.

Cependant, il n'est pas impossible que les gros profits de l'entrepreneur, en le mettant à portée de payer un gros intérêts, le capitaliste ne participe quelquefois aux gros profits de l'industrie.

I–157, à droite, sur la feuille collée, (1) marqué après le 1ᵉʳ paragraphe '. . .more intricate business than another' (I. x. b. 10)

(1) L'intérêt des fonds ne varient pas d'une profession à l'autre, mais il n'y en a pas deux peut[-]être ou les profits de l'industrie soient pareils. En confondant les *salaires* avec les *intérêts* ou les profits du capital Smith a été conduit à un paradoxe, qui est que toutes les branches de commerce ne sont pas plus compliquées, plus difficiles les unes que les autres.

I–170, en bas, (1) marqué après le paragraphe qui finit par 'the risk or security with which it is attended.' (I. x. b. 34)

(1) Je serais tenté de croire que cette dernière est la seule qui affecte les profits des capitaux. Smith en convient presque dans la phrase suivante: son excellent esprit le ramène souvent malgré lui à la vérité.

I–277, en bas, sur la feuille collée (I. xi. e)

Smith cherche à prouver dans cette Digression (Tome 1 page 276) que depuis l'an 1350 jusque vers 1570, la valeur de l'argent a fort augmenté, doublé même relativement à la valeur du blé et par conséquent de toutes les autres denrées. Les progrès de l'industrie & de la civilisation augmentait la demande d'argent, tandis que les mines connues diminuaient de fécondité.

Que depuis 1570 jusqu'à peu près en 1640, la quantité d'argent fournie par les mines d'Amérique a été si considérable, que bien que la demande ait augmenté par les mêmes raison[s], la masse d'argent a augmenté dans une proportion encore plus grande; tellement qu'on a donné 6 ou 8 onces pour la même denrée qui auparavant se donnait pour 2 onces d'argent.

Enfin que depuis 1636 ou 1640, l'argent a haussé un peu de valeur, et qu'on en donne un peu moins à présent pour la même quantité de blé.

Il croit qu'il continue à augmenter de valeur; mais les observations plus récentes de Humboldt & l'élévation presque générale du prix nominal de toutes choses me font supposer au contraire que la valeur relative de l'argent diminue continuellement.

I-307, en bas, référence implicitement faite au mot 'quarter' (I. xi. g. 9)

le quarter de 8 Boisseaux vaut à peu près deux septiers ou plutôt 1⅞ septier.

I-371, à droite des phrases suivantes: 'The real price of this commodity [= fish], therefore, naturally rises in the progress of improvement. It has accordingly done so, I believe, more or less in every country.' (I. xi. m. 15)

Je ne sais si le fait est conforme à ce que dit ici l'auteur.

I-373 et 374 (I. xi. m. 19, 20, 21)

La découverte des plus riches mines n'affecterait que le prix nominal des métaux précieux. (Selon ma théorie Smith devait dire que de nouvelles & riches mines n'affecteraient que le prix nominal de tous les autres produits mais que le prix *réel*, les frais de production, des métaux précieux, baisserait beaucoup.)

I-394, à gauche, sur la feuille collée, (1) marqué à la fin du 1ᵉʳ paragraphe qui finit par 'the produce of the labour of other people' (I. xi. p. 6)

(1) Il me semble qu'une augmentation quelconque dans les pouvoirs productifs, une augmentation de produits pour le même travail, c'est[-]à[-]dire une baisse de prix, de valeur échangeable dans les produits, est profitable, non seulement à celui qui jouit du revenu territorial, mais encore à ceux qui vivent du revenu capital & industriel. C'est une baisse réelle dans le prix de la denrée qui équivaut à une hausse de tous les revenus quelconques. Smith a donc eu tort de la borner au revenu territorial seulement.

I-415, à droite, sur la feuille collée, (1) marqué après le texte 'The revenue, however, which is derived from such things, must always be ultimately drawn from some other source of revenue.' (II. i. 12)

Il y a ici capital productif de jouissance. Mais la thèse que Smith soutient ici rentre dans son système qui range dans la classe des travaux improductifs, ceux qui ne sont productifs que d'une utilité ou d'une jouissance incorporelle, comme le travail d'un magistrat, d'un musicien.

Ce système tient un peu de celui des Economistes; & ceux[-]ci pourraient s'en servir pour combattre Smith lorsqu'il prétend que le travail des manufactures est productif. En effet que produit-il? pas un atome; mais seulement une utilité, une valeur de plus dans la chose travaillée, & par conséquent une qualité purement immatérielle.

I-416, en bas, (1) marqué après le mot 'Thirdly, . . .' (II. i. 16)
(1) Cette 2ᵉ & 3ᵉ subdivision rentrent l'une dans l'autre &
pouvaient n'en faire qu'une.

I-418, en bas, (1) marqué après le mot 'Fourthly, . . .' (II. i. 22)
(1) La 2ᵉ & la 4ᵉ subdivision rentrent l'une dans l'autre, étant
composées l'une & l'autre des denrées prêtes à consommer.
Toutes les quatre me semblent futiles.

I-428, à gauche, sur la feuille collée, (1) marqué à la fin du 1ᵉʳ
paragraphe '. . .or of theirs' (II. ii. 10). . .CPE (V) 348
(1) Smith me paraît ici confondre le revenu consistant en
produits, avec le capital. Son capital circulant ou mobile,
disparaît pendant la production, reparaît ensuite, mais ne
fait point partie du revenu de la société. C'est le produit
sortant de toutes ces métamorphoses, qui en fait partie.
Sous ce point de vue il n'y a, quoiqu'en dise Smith, aucune
différence entre le capital mobile de la société & le capital
d'un particulier. Je sais bien que cette erreur n'entraîne
aucune fausse conséquence dans les raisonnemen[t]s de
Smith, mais elle obscurcit singulièrement son idée.

I–433, à droite, sur la feuille collée, (1) marqué à la fin du 1ᵉʳ
paragraphe '. . .from hand to hand' (II. ii. 22). . .CPE (V)
352
Toute cette explication est pénible et imparfaite dans Smith,
faute par lui d'avoir éclairci la théorie des valeurs. S'il avait
dit que le revenu c'est la valeur de ce qu'on reçoit en échange
des frais de production qu'on fait, il n'aurait pas été obligé
de distinguer le revenu net du revenu brut de la société; ce
qui est faux. Le revenu de la société est toujours un revenu
brut. Le revenu n'est jamais telle matière ou telle autre: c'est
une valeur produite quelle que soit sa forme.

I–498, à gauche, sur la feuille collée, (1) marqué à la fin du 1ᵉʳ
paragraphe '. . .any other sort of goods' (II. ii. 105). . .CPE
(V) 409
(1) Smith ne se tromperait-il point ici. La valeur d'une marchandise est en raison composée de ce qu'il en coûte pour
l'amener au marché & de la proportion entre la quantité de
cette marchandise & la demande qui en est faite dans le
même marché. Si on émet des billets de banque qui rendent
inutiles, comme monnaye, les 2/3 de l'argent qui circule, ces
deux-tiers se répandront dans tous les marchés & augmen-
teront la proportion de cette marchandise, comparée avec la
demande qui en est faite. Rien dans cette opération ne doit

augmenter la demande en même tem[p]s que la fourniture. Celle-ci étant plus grande & la demande étant la même, la valeur de l'argent doit baisser jusqu'à ce que la baisse augmente la demande au niveau de la fourniture.

Il est vrai que le marché pour l'or et l'argent étant par tout le monde ce qu'un pays peut en verser dans un si grand marché doit déranger bien peu la proportion.

II–2, à gauche, sur la feuille collée, (1) marqué après le texte '. . .a multitude of menial servants' (II. iii. 1)

Le travail des domestiques nombreux appauvrit non parce qu'il ne produit pas, mais parce que ce qu'ils produisent (c'est[-]à[-]dire les services) est consommé à mesure. Or comme ce travail ne peut être entretenu qu'au moyen d'un capital circulant qui se consomme (leur entretien) et que ce qu'ils produisent est consommé à mesure et par conséquent ne peut rétablir le capital employé, on perd chaque année une portion de son capital à entretenir des domestiques, ou du moins cette portion de son revenu qu'on aurait pu amasser en capital.

II–8, à gauche, sur la feuille collée, (1) marqué après le texte '. . .greater than the whole had been before.' (II. iii. 9)

(1) Ce produit annuel est en grande partie composé du profit des capitaux répandus sur les terres en améliorations. Ce n'est pas tant que le revenu territorial soit augmenté que les capitaux & leurs profits.

II-11, en bas, (1) marqué après le texte '. . .all the trade which it carries on' (II. iii. 12)

(1) Paris a toujours vendu hors de ses murs des gazes, des rubans, des modes, des meubles, des livres, des quincailleries fines, comme des cuivres dorés, des lampes, des objets de beaux arts comme des tableaux &c. C'est une ville très manufacturière.

II-21, en bas, (1) marqué après le texte '. . .by the produce of other men's labour' (II. iii. 30)

(1) Les guerres des Romains leur fournissaient de quoi consommer aux dépens des productions du monde entier.

II-33, en bas, (1) marqué après le texte '. . .reserved for immediate consumption' (II. iv. 1)

(1) Si c'est pour une consommation reproductive, l'emprunteur l'employe toujours comme un capital.

II-45, à droite, sur la feuille collée, (1) marqué à la fin du 1ᵉʳ paragraphe qui finit par '. . .employed with advantage' (II. iv. 15)

(1) Smith s'écarte ici de ses principes. Si la prohibition du prêt à intérêt ne fait qu'augmenter l'usure, la fixation de l'intérêt, qui est une prohibition pour tous les intérêts supérieurs au taux fixé, ne fait qu'augmenter le mal produit par l'usure, mais ne l'arrête pas. Non, il ne doit y avoir de taux légal que pour les cas ou [*sic*] le taux doit être réglé *d'office*, comme dans le cas des dommages-intérêts, des remboursements ordonnés en justice &c. Pour ce qui est des transactions libres entre particuliers, elles ne peuvent pas plus admettre une fixation légale, que les prix des choses dans les ventes et achats. Toute fixation de ce genre est contraire à la justice, produit du mal et est toujours éludée.

II-47, en bas, (1) marqué à la fin du 1ᵉʳ paragraphe qui finit par '. . .other of those four' (II. v. 2)

(1) Les deux dernières manières rentrent l'une dans l'autre; c'est le transport des marchandises pour les mettre à portée des consommateurs; que ce transport se fasse en gros ou en détail, de près ou de loin, peu importe.

II-53, à droite de la phrase qui se lit 'This rent may be considered as the produce of those powers of nature, the use of which the landlord lends to the farmer,' (II. v. 12)
aveu curieux de Smith.

II-53, en bas, (1) marqué après le texte '. . .a third of the whole produce' (II. v. 12)

(1) On peut dire avec plus d'exactitude que le revenu du propriétaire va en diminuant graduellement depuis ½ environ jusqu'à rien, puisqu'il y a des terres qui ne valent pas d'être cultivées.

II-59, en bas, (1) marqué à la fin du 1ᵉʳ paragraphe qui finit par '. . .frequently gold and silver' (II. v. 22)

(1) Cependant, Tyr, Carthage, Venise se sont enrichies principalement par le commerce extérieur: Smith méconnait trop la faculté productive de l'industrie commerçante.

II-61, en bas, sur la feuille collée, (1) marqué à la fin du 1ᵉʳ paragraphe qui finit par '. . .labour of the country' (II. v. 26)

(1) Il me semble que Smith commet ici une erreur. Quand deux négociants négocient ensemble & font des échanges, ce n'est pas au moyen d'un seul capital, il en faut deux, le capital qu'on donne & qui vous appartient et le capital qu'on reçoit et qui ne vous appartient pas encore.

Quand un de ces capitaux appartient à un pays étranger, il
ne faut pas dire que celui qui vous reste ne vous produit que
la moitié de ce qu'il vous aurait produit étant employé dans
le pays. Il produit tout ce qu'il doit produire; et si un échange
entre deux compatriotes produit le double, c'est[-]à[-]dire un
profit à deux nationaux au lieu d'un, c'est qu'il y a deux
capitaux nationaux employés au lieu d'un.

II-63, à droite, sur la feuille collée, (1) marqué à la fin du 1ᵉʳ
paragraphe qui finit par '. . .of the same kind' (II. v. 28)
(1) Cela donne moins d'encouragement à l'industrie
manu–facturière, mais cela en donne davantage à l'industrie commerçante, dont à la vérité une partie des profits est
gagnée par des étrangers.

Quant au produit des capitaux ils sont précisément les
mêmes: s'ils sont dans un commerce indirect employés trois
fois plus longtem[p]s, il y a des profits sur trois sortes de
marchandises.

II-71, à droite, sur la feuille collée, (1) marqué après le texte
'. . .sometimes from no capital' (II. v. 37)
(1) Comment cela seul n'avertit-il pas Smith qu'il n'est pas
ici question seulement d'emploi de capital, mais d'emploi
d'industrie & de capital. Il fallait dire: l'industrie manufacturière & commerçante, par suite du système commercial
moderne, donnent de plus gros profits que l'industrie agricole; c'est pourquoi elles attirent plus de capitaux.

II-89, en bas, sur la feuille collée, (1) marqué à la fin du 1ᵉʳ
paragraphe qui finit par '. . .like the plains of Babylon' (III.
ii. 9)
(1) J'avoue que je ne suis pas convaincu par ces exemples;
que le travail des esclaves anciens fut moins productif que
celui des manouvriers libres des modernes. Chez les modernes je vois une grande production opérée; mais aussi je
vois une population laborieuse toute entière, occupée à cul-
tiver tous les genres d'industrie. Chez les anciens, il y avait
tant de citoyens noblement oisifs depuis les plus pauvres qui
recevaient le pain de distribution, jusqu'aux plus riches dont
les consommations désordonnées passaient tout ce que nous
voyons de nos jours, qu'il fallait que le travail des esclaves
fût bien productif pour pourvoir à tout cela. Sans parler de
ces grands travaux publics, bains, aqueducs, ports, amphi-
théatres, chaussées qui s'opéraient couramment chez eux et
dont nous ne pouvons jamais venir à bout.

II-90, à gauche, sur la feuille collée, (1) marqué à la fin du 1ᵉʳ paragraphe qui finit par '. . .in our tobacco colonies' (III. ii. 10)

(1) Le même fait ne pourrait-il pas prouver également, exactement le contraire de l'opinion de Smith? Les profits sont considérables dans la culture du sucre et dans celle du tabac, parce que l'entretien des esclaves-travailleurs est excessivement mince & leurs travaux poussés au délà de ce que feraient volontairement des mains libres.

II-98, à gauche de la phrase 'More does. . .commonly acquired most slowly' (III. ii. 20)

Profits du fermier sont moindres de tous selon Smith.

II-101, à droite du mot 'poll-tax' (III. iii. 2)

capitation.

II-138, à gauche, sur la feuille collée, (1) marqué à la fin du 1ᵉʳ paragraphe (IV. Introduction. 1). . .CPE (VI) 1

(1) J'aimerais mieux dire que l'objet de l'économie politique est de faire connaître les moyens par lesquels les richesses se forment, se distribuent, et se détruisent. Le gouvernement n'entre qu'accessoirement dans ce système de choses, soit pour favoriser ou contrarier la production; soit pour prendre une partie des produits.

II-165, en bas, (1) marqué à la fin de la phrase 'This inability. . .more improved manufactures' (IV. i. 30)

(1) Quand les armées vivent aux dépens du pays où elles font la guerre on n'a pas besoin d'envoyer des valeurs au dehors pour les soutenir.

II-168, en bas, (1) marqué à la fin de la phrase 'These great and important services. . .it is carried on' (IV. i. 31). . .CPE (VI) 26

(1) Smith oublie le principal produit du commerce: c'est à dire l'augmentation de valeur donnée à la march[andise] indigène en l'exportant & à la marchandise étrangère en l'important.

II-209, à droite, sur la feuille collée, (1) marqué après 'Part I' (IV. iii)

(1) Le sens de cette première partie est ceci. Quand même la balance du commerce de l'Angleterre avec la France, serait contre l'Angleterre, celle-ci gagnerait: ne point prohiber, parce que la quantité de valeurs importées serait moindre, les marchandises étant à meilleur marché. Mais a[-]t'on un moyen de connaître si la balance est contre l'Angleterre.

Les déclarations des douanes sont fausses.

Le cours des changes n'est pas une annonce certaine, pour 3 raisons.

II-237, à droite des phrases qui commencent par 'The whole French capital. . .' et par 'But that part. . .' (IV. iii. c. 5)

Je crois que Smith se trompe: Sa portion du capital en France est aussi bien consommée que si elle l'était dans l'Amérique ou dans l'Indostan.

II-238, à gauche, sur la feuille collée, (1) marqué à la fin de la phrase 'The greater part of it. . .those distant countries' (IV. iii. c. 5)

(1) En définitif on achète toujours les produits étrangers en les payant avec des produits intérieurs. Smith dit que si les Anglais achètent les vins de France avec des tabacs de Virginie, la France gagne l'entière valeur des vins & l'Angleterre une partie seulement des tabacs; mais avec quoi a[-]t'elle acheté les tabacs? avec ses propres produits dont l'entière valeur a été distribuée entre ses producteurs.

II-434, à gauche de la phrase 'The effect of monopoly has been, not to augment the quantity, but to alter the quality . . .' (IV. vii. c. 55)

Voilà bien les répétitions.

II-489, à droite des deux dernières phrases de la 1ᵉʳ paragraphe qui commencement par 'It is the industry. . .' et par 'That which is carried on. . .' (IV. viii. 4)

prohibit. faites en faveur de qui.

III-2, à gauche, sur la feuille collée, (1) marqué à la fin de la phrase 'It would not. . .any part of the world' (IV. ix. 2)

Ce que Smith dit ici est vrai; cependant quoique Turgot fût trop éclairé pour marcher aveuglément sous aucune bannière, il a fait pendant son ministère des opérations qui étaient tout à fait dans le sens des Economistes; et ces opérations quoique fort bonnes, ont été blamées par les hommes à vieux préjugés, comme systématiques et économiques.

Je ne sais encore si dans quelques points l'administration chinoise, n'est pas Economiste. Le gouvernement chinois ne semble pas du moins attacher un grand prix à se procurer une balance avantageuse du commerce par le moyen des exportations.

III-41, en bas, (1) marqué après 'Those systems, therefore, . . . impose restraints upon manufactures and foreign trade' (IV. ix. 49)

(1) C'est ce que ne fesaient [*sic*] pas les Economistes: il faut être juste.

III-62, en bas, (1) marqué à la fin du 1ᵉʳ paragraphe qui finit par '. . .of those battles' (V. i. a. 31)
(1) Les premières défaites des Français en 1792 doivent être attribuées à la même cause.

III-68 et 69, en bas, (1) marqué après la phrase de la page 68 'It is the instrument which executes and maintains all his other regulations' (V. i. a. 40)
(1) Elle maintient, non les lois fondées sur l'intérêt de la nation, mais sur la volonté arbitraire du prince. C'est[a]dire que la tranqui[l]lité avec le despotisme vaut mieux que les agitations avec la liberté. Cette question ne peut pas être résolue absolument. Un certain degré d'agitation avec la liberté vaut incontestablement mieux qu'un certain degré de despotisme avec la tranqui[l]lité.

III-254, en bas, (1) marqué à la fin du 3ᵉ paragraphe qui finit par '. . .ought to belong to the crown' (V. ii. a. 20)
(1) Smith aurait dû ajouter [illisible] les fonds de terre sur lesquels sont élevés des établissemen[t]s publics ou qui fournissent immédiatement à leur entretien.

III-284, à gauche du 2ᵉ paragraphe qui commence par 'The rent of houses, . . .' (V. ii. e. 7)
Le loyer de la terre paye un service productif. Le loyer des maisons paye un service improductif; dans mes principes productif d'un produit immatériel.

III-288, en bas, (1) marqué à la fin du 1ᵉʳ paragraphe qui finit par '. . .support of that government' (V. ii. e. 11)
(1) Le bon gouvernement augmentant la production et la population augmente de même considérablement le revenu provenant des terres en culture.

III-321, en bas, (1) marqué à la fin de la 1ᵉʳ phrase du 2ᵉ paragraphe: 'Such stamp-duties. . .who use or consume such commodities' (V. ii. h. 18)
(1) Ceci ne me paraît pas exact; ces droits diminuent la consommation en fesant [*sic*] renchérir le produit, et diminuent par conséquent le revenu du producteur de tout le profit qu'il aurait fait sur une consommation plus étendue.

III-372, en bas, (1) marqué à la fin de la 3ᵉ phrase du 2ᵉ paragraphe: 'Some of the little Indian states. . .or commerce of its own' (V. ii. k. 57)
(1) Oui, quand ils sont très modérés; car lorsqu'ils détournent

le cours du commerce d'étranger à étranger, l'état perd les profits que les aubergistes et fournisseurs intérieurs font sur les marchands de passage.

A SHORT VIEW OF THE DOCTRINE OF SMITH, COMPARED WITH THAT OF THE FRENCH ECONOMISTS*

Comte Germain Garnier

The ancient philosophers were little accustomed to employ themselves in the observation of those laws which regulate the distribution of riches among the different orders of society in a nation, or in the search after the sources of the increase of its wealth. In fact, political economy is a science of very modern origin; for although, towards the end of the seventeenth century, several writers, both of France and England, had begun to discuss the comparative advantages of agriculture and commerce, yet it was not till the middle of the eighteenth, that any thing like a complete system appeared upon the growth and distribution of national wealth. At this period, the philosophical Quesnai directed his attention to this very abstract subject, and became the founder of a celebrated school, which may boast among its adherents many distinguished men of talents and extensive knowledge.

All philosophical sects owe their first origin and foundation to the discovery of some great truth; and it is the madness inspiring their members, to deduce every thing from this new discovery, that contributes most to their downfal. Thus it was with the economists. They saw that the original source of all wealth was the soil, and that the labour of its cultivation produced not only the means of subsisting the labourer, but also a neat surplus, which went to the increase of the existing stock: while, on the other hand, the labour applied to the productions of the earth, the labour of manufactures and commerce, can only add to the material a value exactly equal to that expended during the execution of the work; by which means, in the end, this species of labour operates no real change on the total sum of national riches. They perceived that

---

* From the *Wealth of Nations* (Edinburgh, 1826), pp. xvii–xxii.

the landed proprietors are the first receivers of the whole wealth of the community; and that, whatever is consumed by those who are not possessed of land, must come, directly or indirectly, from the former; and hence, that these receive wages from the proprietors, and that the circulation of national wealth, is, in fact, only a succession of exchanges between these two classes of men, the proprietors furnishing their wealth, and the non-proprietors giving as an equivalent their labour and industry. They perceived that a tax, being a portion of the national wealth applied to public use, in every instance, however levied, bears finally upon the landed proprietors inasmuch as they are the distributors of that wealth, either by retrenching their luxuries, or by loading them with an additional expense; and that, therefore, every tax which is not levied directly on the rude produce of the earth, falls in the end on the landed proprietors, with a surplus produce, from which the amount of the revenue receives no addition.

These assertions are almost all incontestible, and capable of a rigorous demonstration; and those who have attempted to shew their falsity, have, in general, opposed them only with idle sophistry. Why, then, has this doctrine met with so little success, and why does every day diminish its reputation? because it agrees in no one point with the moral condition, either of societies or of individuals; because it is continually contradicted by experience, and by the infallible instinct of self-interest; because it does not possess that indispensible sanction of all truths, utility. In fact, of what consequence is it, that the labour of agriculture produces not only what covers its own expenses, but new beings which would never have existed without it, and that it has this advantage over the labour of manufactures and commerce? Does it by any means follow from this, that the former kind of labour is more profitable to the community than the latter? The real essence of all wealth, and that which determines its value, is the necessity under which the consumer lies to purchase it; for, in truth, there is no such thing as wealth properly so called, nor absolute value; but the words wealth and value are really nothing more than the co-relatives of consumption and demand. Even the necessaries of life, in a country which is inhabited, but incapable of commercial intercourse, will not form wealth; and to whatever degree of civilization that country may have reached, still the same principle will hold without alteration.

If the sum of national wealth shall in any case have exceeded the sum of demands, then a part of the former sum will cease to bear the name of wealth, and will again be without value. In vain, then, will agriculture multiply her produce; for the instant that it exceeds the bounds of actual consumption, a part will lose its value; and self-interest, that prime director of all labour and industry, seeing herself thus deceived in her expectations, will not fail to turn her activity and efforts to another quarter.

In almost every instance, it is an idle refinement to distinguish between the labour of those employed in agriculture, and of those employed in manufactures and commerce; for wealth is necessarily the result of both descriptions of labour, and consumption can no more take place independently of the one, than it can independently of the other. It is by their simultaneous concurrence that any thing becomes consumable, and, of course, that it comes to constitute wealth. How then are we entitled to compare their respective products, since it is impossible to distinguish these in the joint product, and thus appreciate the separate value of each? The value of growing wheat results as much from the industry of the reaper who gathers it in, of the thrasher who separates it from the chaff and straw, of the miller and baker who convert it successively into flour and bread, as it does from that of the ploughman and of the sower. Without the labour of the weaver, the raw material of flax would lose all its value, and be regarded as no way superior to the most useless weed that grows. What then can we gain by any attempts to determine which of these two species of labour conduces most to the advancement of national wealth; or, are they not as idle, as if we busied ourselves in inquiring, whether the right or the left foot is the most useful in walking?

It is true, indeed, that in every species of manufacture, the workman adds to the value of the raw material a value exactly equal to that which was expended during the process of manufacture; and what is the conclusion we are to draw from this? It is merely, that a certain exchange has taken place, and that the food consumed by the manufacturer is now represented by the increase of value resulting from his manual labour. Thus wool, when converted into cloth, has gained a value precisely equal to that expended by the manufacturer during the conversion. But, if it is shown that, without this exchange, the wool would have remained without value, while, on the other hand, the food of the manufacturer would have been without a consumer; it will then appear, that this exchange has, in fact, done what is equivalent to creating these two values, and that it has proved to the society an operation infinitely more useful, than if an equal quantity of labour had been spent in the increase of that rude produce, which already existed in over-abundance. The first description of labour has been truly productive; while the last would have been altogether unproductive, since it would not have created any value.

The soil, say the economists, 'is the source of all wealth.' But, to prevent this assertion from leading us into erroneous conclusions, it will be necessary to explain it. The materials of all wealth originate primarily in the bosom of the earth; but it is only by the aid of labour that they can ever truly constitute wealth. The earth furnishes the means of wealth; but wealth itself cannot possibly have any existence, unless through that industry and labour which modifies, divides, connects, and combines the various productions of the soil, so as to render them fit for consumption. Commerce, indeed, regards those rude productions as real wealth; but it is only from the consideration, that the proprietor has it always in his power to convert them, at will, into consumable goods, by submitting them to the necessary operations of manufacture. They possess, as yet, merely the virtual value of a promissory-note, which passes current, because the bearer is assured that he can, at pleasure, convert it into cash. Many gold mines, which are well known, are not worked, because their whole produce would not cover the incidental expenses; but the gold which they contain is, in reality, the same with that of our coin; and yet no one would be foolish enough to call it wealth, for there is no probability it will ever be extracted from the mine, or purified; and, of course, it possesses no value. The wild fowl becomes wealth the moment it is in the possession of the sportsman; while those of the very same species, that have escaped his attempts, remain without any title to the term.

It is further, without question, true, that all who do not possess property in land must draw their subsistence from wages received, directly or indirectly, from the proprietors, unless they violate all rights, and become robbers. In this respect, every service is alike; the most honourable and the most disgraceful receives each its wages. It is certain, too, that if the circumstances determining the rate of the various kinds of wages remain the same, that is if the offers of service, and the demand, preserve the same proportion to each other, after as well as before the imposition of a tax; then, of course, the wages will continue at the same rate, and thus the tax, however imposed, will uniformly, in the end, fall on that class in the community who furnish the wages; so that they must suffer, either an addition to their former expenses, or a retrenchment of those luxuries they enjoyed. And according as the tax is less directly levied, the greater will be the burden they are subjected to; for besides indemnifying all the other classes who have advanced the tax-money, a further expense must be incurred, in the additional number of persons now necessary to collect it. The natural conclusion we must draw from the theory is, that a tax, directly levied on the neat revenue of the land proprietors, is that which agrees best with reason and justice, and that which bears lightest on the contributors.

If, however, this theory should be found to throw entirely out of consideration a multitude of circumstances, which possess a powerful influence over the facility of collecting a tax, as well as over its consequences; and if the general result of this influence be of far more importance than the single advantage of a less burden; then the theory, inasmuch as it neglects a part of those particulars which have their weight in the practice, is contradicted by this last. And this is exactly what happens in the question respecting the comparative advantages and inconveniencies of the two modes of levying taxes.

The habit which men have acquired, of viewing money as the representation of every thing which contributes to the support or comfort of life, makes them naturally very unwilling to part with what portion of it they possess, unless it be to procure some necessary or enjoyment. We spend money with pleasure; but it requires an effort to pay a debt, and particularly so when the value received in exchange is not very obvious to the generality, as in the case of a tax. But by levying the tax on some object of consumption, by thus confounding it with the price of the latter, and by making the payment of the duty and of the price of enjoyment become one and the same act, we render the consumer desirous to pay the impost. It is amid the profusion of entertainments, that the duties on wine, salt, &c. are paid; the public treasury thus finding a source of gain in the excitements to expense, produced by the extravagance and gaiety of feasts.

Another advantage of the same nature, possessed by the indirect mode of taxation, is its extreme divisibility into minute parts, and the facility which it affords to the individual, of paying it off day by day, or even minute by minute. Thus the mechanic, who sups on a portion of his day's wages, will sometimes in one quarter of an hour, pay part of four or five different duties.

In the plan of direct taxation, the impost appears without any disguise; it comes upon us unexpectedly, from the imprudence so common to the bulk of mankind, and never fails to carry with it constraint and discouragement.

All these considerations are overlooked by the friends of direct taxation; and yet their importance must be well known to all who have ever attended to the art of governing men.

But, perhaps, this is not all. An indirect tax, by increasing from time to time the price of the objects of general consumption, when the members of the community have contracted the habit of this consumption, renders these objects a little more costly, and thus gives birth to that increase of labour and industry which is now required to obtain them. But if this tax be so proportioned as not to discourage the consumption, will it not then operate as a universal stimulus upon the active and industrious part of the community? Will it not incite that part to redoubled efforts, by which it may still enjoy those luxuries which, by habit, have become almost necessaries, and, of course, produce a further development of the productive powers of labour, and of the resources of industry? Are we not, in such a case, to conclude, that after the imposition of a tax, there will exist not only the quantity of labour and industry which was formerly requisite to procure the necessaries and habitual enjoyments of the active class of mankind, but also such an addition to this, as will suffice for the payment of the tax? And will not this tax, or increase of produce required for the tax—as it is spent by the government that receives it—will it not serve to support a new class of consumers, requiring a variety of commodities which the impost enables them to pay? If these conjectures are well founded, it will follow, that indirect taxation, far from having any hurtful influence on wealth and population, must, when wisely regulated, tend to increase and strengthen these two great

foundations of national prosperity and power. And it will tend
to do this, inasmuch as it bears immediately on the body of
the people, and operates on the working and industrious class,
which forms the active part of the community; while, on the
other hand, direct taxation operates solely on the idle class of
landed proprietors—which furnishes us with the characteristic
difference existing between these two modes of taxation.[1]
These hints, which seem to afford an explanation of that most
extraordinary phenomenon in political economy, viz. the rapid
and prodigious increase of wealth in those nations which are
most loaded with indirect taxes, deserve to be discussed at
greater length than our limits will allow. Enough, however, has
been said to shew, that no rigorous and purely mathematical
calculation will ever enable us to appreciate the real influence
of taxes upon the prosperity of a nation. Thus, some of the
truths perceived by the economists are of little use in practice;
while others are found to be contradicted in their application,
by those accessory circumstances which were overlooked in
the calculations of the theory.

While this sect of philosophers filled all Europe with their
speculations, an observer of more depth and ability directed
his researches to the same subject, and laboured to establish,
on a true and lasting foundation, the doctrines of political
economy.

Dr Smith succeeded in discovering a great truth,—the most
fruitful in consequences, the most useful in practice, the origin
of all the principles of the science, and one which unveiled to
him all the mysteries of the growth and distribution of wealth.
This great man perceived, that the universal agent in the
creation of wealth is labour; and was thence led to analyse
the powers of this agent, and to search after the causes to
which they owe their origin and increase.

The great difference between the doctrine of Smith and of
the economists lies in the point from which they set out, in the
reduction of their consequences. The latter go back to the soil
as the primary source of all wealth while the former regards
labour as the universal agent which, in every case produces it.

---

[1] This observation, as may easily be perceived, cannot apply to certain indirect
imposts such as those for the support of the roads; which, as they cannot
be confounded with the price of any consumable commodity, combine all
the inconveniencies of indirect, with that of direct imposts.

It will appear, at first sight, how very superior the school of the Scotch professor is to that of the French philosophers, with regard to the practical utility, as well as to the application of its precepts. Labour is a power of which man is the machine; and, of course, the increase of this power can only be limited by the indefinite bounds of human intelligence and industry; and it possesses, like these faculties, a susceptibility of being directed by design, and perfected by the aid of study. The earth, on the contrary, if we set aside the influence which labour has over the nature and quantity of its productions, is totally out of our power, in every respect which can render it more or less useful—in its extent, in its situation, and in its physical properties.

Thus the science of political economy, considered according to the views of the French economists, must be classed with the natural sciences, which are purely speculative, and can have no other end than the knowledge of the laws which regulate the object of their researches; while, viewed according to the doctrine of Smith, political economy becomes connected with the other moral sciences, which tend to ameliorate the condition of their object and to carry it to the highest perfection of which it is susceptible.

A few words will suffice to explain the grounds of the doctrine of Smith. The power by which a nation creates its wealth is its labour; and the quantity of wealth created will increase in direct proportion as the power increases. But the increase of this last may take place in two ways—in energy, and in extent. Labour increases in energy, when the same quantity of labour furnishes a more abundant product; and the two great means of effecting the increase, or of perfecting the productive powers of labour, are the division of labour, and the invention of such machines as shorten and facilitate the manual operations of industry. Labour increases in extent, when the number of those engaged in it augments in proportion to the increasing number of the consumers, which can take place only in consequence of an increase of capitals, and of those branches of business in which they are employed.

Now, to accomplish the increase of labour in both these ways, and to conduct it gradually to the utmost pitch of energy and extent to which it can reach in any nation, considering the situation, the nature, and the peculiarities of its territories, what are the exertions to be made by its government? The subdivision of labour, and the invention and perfecting of machines. These two great means of augmenting the energy of labour, advance in proportion to the extent of the market, or, in other words, in proportion to the number of exchanges which can be made, and to the ease and readiness with which these can take place. Let the government, then, direct all its attention to the enlargement of the market, by forming safe and convenient roads, by the circulation of sterling coin, and by securing the faithful fulfilment of contracts; all of which are indispensible measures, at the same time that, when put in practice, they will never fail to attain the desired end. And the nearer a government approaches to perfection in each of these three points, the more certainly will it produce every possible increase of the national market. The first of the three means is, without doubt, the most essential, as no other expedient whatever can possibly supply its place.

The gradual accumulation of capitals is a necessary consequence of the increased productive powers of labour, and it becomes also a cause of still farther increase in these powers; but, in proportion as this accumulation becomes greater and greater, it serves to increase the extent of labour, inasmuch as it multiplies the number of labourers, or the sum of national industry. This increase, however, of the number of hands in the nation employed, will always be regulated by the nature of the business to which the capitals are dedicated.

Under this second head of the increase of the products of labour, the exertions of government are much more easy. In fact, it has only to refrain from doing harm. It is only required of it, that it shall protect the natural liberty of industry; that it shall leave open every channel into which, by its own tendencies, industry may be carried; that government shall abandon it to its own direction, and shall not attempt to point its efforts one way more than another; for private interest, that infallible instinct which guides the exertions of all industry, is infinitely better suited than any legislator to judge of the direction which it will with most advantage follow. Let government, then, renounce alike the system of prohibitions and of bounties; let it no longer attempt to impede the efforts of industry by regulations, or to accelerate her progress by rewards; let it leave in the most perfect freedom the exertions of labour and the employment of capital; let its protecting influence extend only to the removal of such obstacles as avarice or ignorance

have raised up to the unlimited liberty of industry and commerce;—then capitals will naturally develope themselves, by
their own movement, in those directions which are at once
most agreeable to the private interest of the capitalist, and most
favourable to the increase of the national wealth.

METHOD OF FACILITATING THE STUDY OF DR SMITH'S WORK*

Comte Germain Garnier

Such are the results of the doctrine of Smith, and the fruits we are to reap from his immortal work. The proofs of the principle upon which his opinions are grounded, and the natural and easy manner in which his deductions flow from it, give it an air of simplicity and truth, which render it no less admirable than convincing. This simplicity, however, to be fully perceived, requires much study and consideration; for it cannot be denied that the 'Wealth of Nations' exhibits a striking instance of that defect for which English authors have so often been blamed, viz. a want of method, and a neglect, in their scientific works, of those divisions and arrangements which serve to assist the memory of the reader, and to guide his understanding. The author seems to have seized the pen at the moment when he was most elevated with the importance of his subject, and with the extent of his discoveries. He begins, by displaying before the eyes of his reader the innumerable wonders effected by the division of labour; and with this magnificent and impressive picture, he opens his course of instructions. He then goes back, to consider those circumstances which give rise to or limit this division; and is led by his subject to the definition of values— to the laws which regulate them, to the analysis of their several elements, and to the relations subsisting between those of different natures and origin; all of which are preliminary ideas, which ought naturally to have been explained to the reader before exhibiting to him the complicated instrument of the multiplication of wealth, or unveiling the prodigies of the most powerful of its resources.

On the other hand, he has often introduced long digressions, which interrupt the thread of his discussion, and, in many

---

* From the *Wealth of Nations* (Edinburgh, 1826), pp. xxiii–xxx.

cases, completely destroy the connection of its several parts.
Of this description is the digression

> On the variations in the value of the precious metals during
> the four last centuries, with a critical examination of the
> opinions that their value is decreasing—book 1, chap. xi.
> Upon banks of circulation and paper money—book 2,
> chap. ii.
> Upon banks of deposit, and particularly that of
> Amsterdam—book 4, chap. iii.
> Upon the advantage of seignorage in the coining of money—
> book 4, chap. vi.
> Upon the commerce of grain, and the laws regarding this
> trade—book 4, chap. v.

These different treatises, although they are unquestionably the
best that have ever been written on the subjects to which they
relate, are, however, so introduced, as to distract the reader's
attention—to make him lose sight of the principal object of
the work—and to lessen the general effect of it as a whole.

To remedy, as far as I am able, these inconveniencies, and
to facilitate to beginners the study of the doctrine of Smith, I
have thought proper to point out the order which appears to
me most agreeable to the natural progress of ideas, and, on
this account, best calculated for the purpose of instruction.

I would begin by remarking, that the whole doctrine of
Smith, upon the origin, multiplication, and distribution of
wealth, is contained in his two first books; and that the three
others may be read separately, as so many detached treatises,
which, no doubt, confirm and develope his opinions, but do
not by any means add to them.

The third book is an historical and political discussion on
the progress which wealth would make in a country where
labour and industry were left free; and upon the different
causes which have tended, in all the countries of Europe, to
reverse this progress.

In the fourth book, the author has endeavoured to combat
the various systems of political economy which were popular
previous to his time; and, in a particular manner, that which
is denominated the mercantile system, which has exercised so
strong an influence over the financial regulations of the European governments, and particularly over those of England.

In the fifth and last book, he considers the expenses of

government; the most equitable and convenient modes of providing for these expenses; and lastly, public debts, and the influence they have over national prosperity.

The three last books may be read and studied in the same order and arrangement in which they were written, without any difficulty, by one who is completely master of the general doctrine contained in the two first.

I regard, then, the two first books, as a complete work, which I would divide into three parts.

The 1st relates to values in particular. It contains their definition; the laws which regulate them; the analysis of the elements which constitute a value, or enter into its composition; and the relations which values of different origin bear to each other.

The 2d part treats of the general mass of national wealth, which is here divided into separate classes, according to its destination or employment.

The 3d and last part explains the manner in which the growth and distribution of national wealth takes place.

PART FIRST.—OF VALUES IN PARTICULAR

The essential quality which constitutes wealth, and without which it would not be entitled to the name, is its *exchangeable value.*

Exchangeable value differs from the value of utility—book 1, end of chap. iv.

The relation existing between two exchangeable values, when expressed by a value generally agreed upon, is denominated *price.*

The value generally agreed on among civilized nations, is that of metals. Motives to this preference. Origin of money—book 1, chap. iv. Relation between money and the metal in the state of bullion—book 1, chap. v.

The price in money, or *nominal* price of a thing, differs from its *real* price, which is its valuation by the quantity of labour expended upon it, or which it represents—ibid.

Laws, according to which the price of wealth is naturally fixed; and those accidental circumstances which occasion the actual to differ from the natural price, and which gave rise to a distinction between the *natural* and the *market price*—book 1, chap. vii.

The price of a thing, in most cases, consists of three distinct elements—the wages of the labour, the profit of the master who directs the labour, and the rent of the ground that furnishes the materials on which it is erected. There are, however, some descriptions of merchandize in which the rent forms no part of the price; and others, in which the profit forms no part of it; but none, in which it is not formed principally by the wages—book 1, chap. vi.

Of *wages*. Laws, according to which the natural rate of wages is fixed; accidental circumstances which cause them to vary, during a short period, from that natural rate—book 1, chap. viii.

Of the *profit* of capitals. Laws, by which the natural rate of profit is fixed; accidental circumstances which, for a long while, increase or diminish it beyond that rate—book 1, chap. ix.

Labour and capitals tend naturally to diffuse themselves through every species of employment; and, as certain employments are, by their nature, accompanied with inconveniencies and difficulties which do not occur in others; while these, on the contrary, offer some real or imaginary advantages which are peculiar to themselves; wages and profits should rise and fall in proportion to these advantages and disadvantages; thus forming a complete equilibrium between the various kinds of employment. The arbitrary and oppressive policy of Europe, in many instances, opposes the establishment of this equilibrium, which is conformable to the order of nature—book 1, chap. x.

Of the *rent* of the ground. The nature of rent: the manner in which it enters into the price of wealth; and according to what principles it in some cases forms an integral part of that price, while in others it does not—book 1, chap. xi.

Division of the rude produce of the earth into two great classes:
1. That produce which is always necessarily disposed of in such a way as to bring a rent to the landed proprietor.
2. That which, according to circumstances, may be disposed of so as to bring, or so as not to bring, a rent.

The produce of the first description is derived from the ground appropriated to furnishing subsistence for man, or for those animals which he uses as food. The value of the produce of the ground cultivated for the support of man, determines the value of the produce of all other ground proper for this species of culture. This general rule allows of some exceptions. Causes of these exceptions.

The produce of the second class consists of the materials of clothing, lodging, fuel, and the ornaments of dress and furniture. The value of this species of produce depends on that of the first description. Some circumstances render it possible that the produce of the second kind may be disposed of in such a way as to furnish a rent to the landed proprietor. Principles which regulate the proportion of the price of these products, which is formed by the rent—book 1, chap. xi.

Relation between the respective values of the produce of the first class, and those of the produce of the second. Variations which may take place in this relation, and the causes of such variations—ibid.

Relation existing between the values of the two descriptions of rude produce above mentioned, and the values of the produce of manufacture. Variations which may occur in this relation—ibid.

Certain kinds of rude produce, procured from very different sources, are, however, intended for the same kind of consumption; and hence it happens, the value of one determines and limits that of another—ibid.

The relations between values of different natures vary according to the state of society. This state is *improving, declining,* or *stationary*; that is to say, society is either increasing in wealth, or falling into poverty, or remaining in the same unchanged state of opulence.

Of the effects of these different states of society,
Upon the price of wages—book 1, chap. viii.
Upon the rate of profit—book 1, chap. ix.
Upon the value of the rude produce of the earth, and on that of the produce of manufacture—book 1, chap. xi.

Difference, in this respect, between the various kinds of rude produce, viz. 1. Those which the industry of man cannot multiply: 2. Those which his industry can always multiply in proportion to the demand: 3. Those over which human exertions have only an uncertain or limited influence—ibid.

PART SECOND.—OF STOCK AND ITS EMPLOYMENT

Wealth, accumulated in the possession of an individual, is of two descriptions, according to its destination or employment:

1. That reserved for immediate consumption.
2. That employed as capital; for the production of a revenue—book 2, chap. i.

Capital is also of two kinds:

1. Fixed capital, which produces a revenue and still remains in the same hands
2. Circulating capital, which yields no revenue unless it be employed in trade—book 2, chap. i.

The whole accumulated wealth of any community may be divided into three parts:

1. The fund appropriated to the immediate consumption of the proprietors of wealth.
2. The fixed capital of the community.
3. Its circulating capital.

The *fixed capital* of the society consists,

1. Of all machines and instruments of labour;
2. Of all buildings and edifices erected for the purposes of industry;
3. Of every kind of agricultural improvement which can tend to render the soil more productive;
4. Of the talents and skill which certain members of the community have acquired by time and expense.

The *circulating capital* of a community consists,

1. In the money in circulation;
2. In the stock of provisions in the hands both of the producers and of the merchants, and from the sale of which they expect to derive a profit;
3. In the materials of lodging, clothing, dress, and ornament, more or less manufactured, which are in the hands of those who are employed in rendering them fit for use and consumption;
4. In the goods more completely fit for consumption, and

preserved in warehouses and shops, by merchants who propose to sell them with a profit—book 2, chap. i.

Of the relation existing between the employment of these two kinds of capital—ibid.

Of the mode in which the capital withdrawn from circulation is disposed of—ibid.

The sources which continually renew the circulating capital, as soon as it enters into the fixed capital, or the stock for immediate consumption, are,

1. Lands;
2. Mines and quarries;
3. Fisheries—ibid.

Of the purposes accomplished by circulating coin—book 2, chap. ii; and the expedients which may be resorted to, in order to attain these with less expense, and fewer of those inconveniencies to which money is subjected—ibid.

Of the stock lent at interest; and of those things which regulate the proportion that this kind of stock bears to the whole existing stock of the community. The quantity of stock which may be lent depends in no degree upon the quantity of money in circulation—book 2, chap. iv.

Of the principles which determine the rate of interest—ibid.

There exists a necessary relation between this and the price of land—ibid.

PART THIRD.—OF THE MANNER IN WHICH THE MULTIPLICATION AND DISTRIBUTION OF WEALTH TAKES PLACE

Wealth uniformly increases in proportion to the augmentation which the power producing it receives, whether that be in *energy* or in *extent*—book 1, introduction.

Labour, in which this power increases in *energy*,

1. By the division of the parts of the same work;
2. By the invention of such machines as abridge and facilitate labour—book 1, chap. i.

The division of labour adds to its energy,

1. By the skill which the workman in this way acquires;

2. By the saving of time—ibid.

The invention of machines is itself an effect of the division of labour—ibid.

The natural disposition of mankind to exchange with each other the different productions of their respective labours and talents, is the principle which has given birth to the division of labour—book 1, chap. ii.

The division of labour must of course be limited by the extent of the market; therefore, whatever tends to widen the market, facilitates the progress of a nation towards opulence—book 1, chap. iii.

Labour gains in *extent*,

1. In proportion to the accumulation of capital;
2. In proportion to the manner in which these are employed—book 1, introduction.

The accumulation of capitals is hastened by the increase of the proportion existing between the productive and unproductive consumers—book 2, chap. iii.

The proportion between these two classes of consumers is determined by the proportion existing between that part of the annual produce destined to the replacement of capital, and that destined for the purpose of revenue—ibid.

The proportion between that part of the annual produce which goes to form capital, and that which goes to form revenue, is great in a rich country, and small in a poor one—ibid.

In a wealthy country, the rent of land, taken absolutely, is much greater than in a poor country; but, taken in relation to the capital employed, it is much less—book 2, chap. iii.

In a wealthy country, the whole profits of its capital are infinitely greater than in one that is poor; although a given quantity of capital will, in a country of the latter description, produce profits much greater than in an opulent one—ibid.

It is industry that furnishes the produce; but it is economy that places in the capital that part of it which would otherwise have become revenue—ibid.

The economy of individuals arises from a principle which is universally diffused, and one that is continually in action; the desire of ameliorating their condition. This principle supports the existence and increase of national wealth, in spite of the prodigality of some individuals; and even triumphs over the profusion and errors of governments—ibid.

Of the different modes of spending money, some are more favourable than others to the increase of national wealth—ibid.

Those branches of employment which require a capital, never fail to call forth more or less labour; and thus contribute, in a greater or less degree, to increase the extent of national labour.

Capital can be employed only in four ways:

1. In cultivating and improving the earth, or, in other words, multiplying its rude produce;
2. In supporting manufactures;
3. In buying by the gross, to sell in the same manner;
4. In buying by the gross, to sell by retail.

These four modes of employing capital are equally necessary to, and serve mutually to support, each other. The first supports, beyond all comparison, the greatest number of productive hands; the second occupies more than the two remaining; and the fourth, the fewest of any.

Capital may be employed, according to the third mode, in three different ways; each contributing in a very different degree to the support and encouragement of national industry.

When capital is employed in exchanging one description of the produce of national industry for another, it then supports as great a portion of industry as can be done by any capital employed in commerce.

When it is employed in exchanging the produce of national for that of foreign industry, for the purposes of home consumption, half of it goes to the support of foreign industry; by which means, it is only of half that service to the industry of the nation which it would have been had it been employed another way.

Lastly, when it is employed in exchanging one description of the produce of foreign industry for another, or in what is termed the *carrying trade*, it then serves wholly for the support and encouragement of the industry of the two foreign nations, and adds only to the annual produce of the country the profits of the merchant—book 2, chap. v.

Self-interest, when left uncontrouled, will necessarily lead the proprietors of capitals to prefer that species of employment which is most favourable to national industry, because it is, at the same time, most profitable for themselves—ibid. For, when capitals have been employed in a way different from that suggested by the infallible instinct of self-interest, it has always been in consequence of the peculiar circumstances of the European governments, and of that influence which the vulgar prejudices of merchants have had over the system of administration which these governments have adopted.

The account of these circumstances, with the discussion of the errors of this system, form the matter of the third and fourth books.

Political Economy is, of all sciences, that which affords most room for prejudices, and in which they are most liable to become deeply rooted. The desire of improving our condition, that universal principle, which continually acts upon every member of the community, is ever directing the thoughts of each individual to the means of increasing his private fortune. But should this individual ever chance to raise his views to the management of the public money, he would naturally be led to reason from analogy, and apply to the general interest of his country those principles which reflection and experience have led him to regard as the best guides in the conduct of his own private affairs. Thus, from attending to the fact, that money constitutes a part of the productive stock in the fortune of an individual, and that his fortune increases in proportion to the increase of this article, there arises that erroneous opinion so generally received, that money is a constituent part of national wealth, and that a country becomes rich, in proportion as it receives money from those countries with which it has commercial connections.

Merchants who have been accustomed to retire each night to their desks, to count, with eagerness, the quantity of currency, or of good debts, which their day's sale has produced, calculating their profits only by this result, and confident that such a calculation has never deceived them, are naturally led to think that the affairs of the nation must follow the same rule; and they have been strengthened in this opinion by that unshaken confidence which a long and never-failing experience, that has been the source of wealth and prosperity, inspires. Hence those extravagant opinions respecting the advantages and profits of foreign commerce, and the importance of money; hence those absurd calculations that have been made regarding what is termed the balance of trade, the thermometer of public prosperity; hence those systems of regulations, and those oppressive monopolies, which are resorted to for the purpose of making one side of the balance preponderate; hence, too, those bloody and destructive wars, which have raged in both hemispheres, from the period in which the road to the Indies, and to the new world, became familiar to European nations.

When we observe, that the many bloody wars that have been waged in the different parts of the world for these two last centuries, and even the present war, in many points of view, have had, as their principal end, the maintenance of some monopoly, contrary even to the interest of the nation armed to protect it; we shall feel the full importance of those benefits which the illustrious author of the 'Wealth of Nations' has endeavoured to confer upon mankind, by victoriously combating such strong and baneful prejudices. But we cannot help deeply lamenting, to see how slowly, and with what difficulty, reason in all its strength, and truth in all its clearness, regain the possession of these territories which error and passion have so rapidly overrun.

The prejudices so successfully attacked by Dr Smith, appear again and again, with undiminished assurance, in the tribunals of legislature in the councils of administration, in the cabinets of ministry, and in the writings of politicians. They still talk of the importance of foreign and colonial commerce; they still attempt to determine the balance of trade; they renew all the reveries of political arithmetic, as if these questions had not been determined by Smith, in a way which renders them no longer capable of controversy.

It was in the midst of a country, the most deeply imbued with mercantile prejudices; the most completely subjected to its prohibitory policy, that Dr Smith sapped the foundations of this absurd and tyrannical system; it was at the very moment when England, in alarm, saw, with terror, the possibility of a separation from her American colonies: it was then that he derided the universal fear, and proudly prophesied the success of the colonists, and their approaching independence; and that he confidently announced, what experience has since completely affirmed, the happy consequences which this separation and this independence, so much dreaded, would produce upon the prosperity, both of Great Britain and her colonies—book 4, chap. vii. part 3.

The wealth of communities is so intimately connected with their civil and political existence, that the author has been drawn by his subject into numerous other discussions, which seem more or less removed from it; and in which we discover the same sagacity of observation, the same depth of research, and the same force of reasoning.

The advantages of a complete and permanent freedom in the corn trade have never been better shown; and they have been proved by Dr Smith, to arise from that fruitful source of wealth, the division of labour—book 4, chap. v.

The national defence and public education, two objects of very high importance, have also been discussed at length by our author.

He proves, that, in conformity to that desire to better our condition, by which all men are directed, and upon which the author has founded his whole doctrine, the teacher, whose wages are a fixed salary, will have no other end than to spare himself every trouble, and dedicate as little attention as possible to his pupils; while he that is paid in proportion to his labour, will naturally endeavour, by every means in his power, to increase his success, at the same time that he confers a great advantage on his scholars and on society. He confirms his theoretical opinions by incontestible examples—book 5, chap. i. part 3.

The superiority of regular troops over national militia is proved in theory, by the division of labour; and in practice, by the most remarkable facts in history—book 5, chap. i, part 1.

[FROM] IL COLBERTISMO*
Francesco Mengotti

Della vera ricchezza di una Nazione.

La vera ricchezza di una Nazione non è riposta solamente nella copia dell'argento e dell'oro, come dai più si crede; ma in una gran massa di prod otti proprj, che sempre rinascono, e sempre si riproducono, e che possono essere consumati e disposti, senza nuocere alla loro riproduzione, ed abbondanza. Anzi tal'è la felice natura di questi veri e reali beni della vita, che per riprodurli, e perpetuarli, convien che sieno consumati, diventando la consumazione, come vedremo, un eccitamento di nuova e più copiosa riproduzione; cosicchè non v'é tema di perderli mai coll'uso e col godimento, ma il godimento e l'uso ne perpetua l'abbondanza, e ne assicura il possesso.

Dove si trovano cotali vere e permanenti ricchezze, una generale prosperità si diffonde da se stessa in tutte le classi della società, cresce la popolazione a misura delle sussistenze, e crescono le sussistenze a misura della popolazione, e quindi sorge naturalmente l'industria per variare in mille modi le forme delle materie rozze, e renderle atte al comodo ed al piacere; e finalmente tutta la Nazione sempre più ricca e feconda si rivolge a versare, e a spandere, se così può dirsi, il succhio suo soprabbondante sopra le altre Nazioni, per ricevere in cambio da esse i prodotti degli altri climi e paesi, se di quelli ha bisogno; ovvero l'oro e l' argento, se di essi piuttosto ha bisogno.

Ora questi metalli non nutrono per se stessi, non estinguono la sete, non riparano dalla ingiuria delle stagioni, nè i loro amplessi hanno nulla di pruriginoso, e di caro. Il loro uffizio, siano in verghe e sbarre, o coniati in moneta, non è che di essere lo stromento delle nostre contrattazioni, e il segno delle cose. Ma il segno appoco appoco si usurpò il credito della cosa

* Florence, 1819, pp. 4–19.

rappresentata, e si arrogò nella volgar opinione i primi onori, com'è succeduto dei titoli, delle divise, e di tutti gli altri segni del merito e della virtù, che poi dispensarono dal merito e dalla virtù.

Che codesti metalli siano un segno di convenzione, non v'ha dubbio. Molti popoli non li conobbero per tali, come i Messicani, e i Peruviani avanti la scoperta dell'America; nè potevano comprendere, come da noi si pregiassero cotanto, abbenchè poi lagrimando il compresero. Altri popoli si servirono di altri segni; chi del sale, chi delle conchiglie, chi del pepe, o delle noci di cacao, o del tabacco. I Greci antichi de'tempi eroici, valutavano le cose di maggior prezzo dal numero de'buoi, come si vede in Omero. Gli Spartani non ebbero lungamente che moneta di ferro, e i Romani fino a Servio Tullio usarono il rame rozzo, che pesavasi sopra pubbliche bilancie; e dopo ancora per più di quattro secoli non conobbero che monete di rame coll'impronta di una pecora; onde vennero i nomi di peculio, di pecunia, e di pecunioso, a noi sì cari. Il rame cosi coniato si disse anche moneta, perchè battevasi nel Tempio della Dea Moneta, o del buon consiglio, onde fosse ognuno avvertito, che il segno della ricchezza non è la vera ricchezza. Ma nè i Romani profittarono del buon consiglio, nè molti dappoi[1].

Ma vano è cercare antichi e remoti esempj, quando vediamo che le più ricche e colte Nazioni di Europa fanno tuttogiorno lo stesso, e moltiplicano i lorgo segni con azioni, cedole, e simili ritrovati, di cui tanto è l'uso e l'abuso. Dunque il danaro non è che lo strumento della circolazione e del commercio, e il segno delle cose. Si dirà forse che queste sono verità semplici e triviali, e io lo desidero, perchè sieno innegabili. Dal credere appunto che il danaro sia il fondamento della ricchezza delle Nazioni, è derivata la massima che le primarie cure de'Governi

---

[1] Servius rex ovium boumque effigie [primum] aes signavit.... Pecunia ipsa a pecore adpellabatur. [King Servius stamped first the bronze coinage with the likeness of sheep and oxen.... The word for money itself was derived from 'cattle'.]

Plin Hist. Nat. Lib. 18.3: 11–12.
Periz. Disert. de aere gravi.
Salmas. de Usur. Cap. 16.
Arbuthnot. Tab. de la Pes. et. Mes. Dis. I.
Smith Riches. des Nat. Lib. I. Cap. 4.
Genov. Elem. di Commer. Tom. 2. Cap. 2.

esser debbano rivolte a chiamar tutto l'oro che non si possiede, e a ritener gelosamente tutto quello che si possiede. Da ciò pure è nato il credito e la fama dei Colbertisti, che insegnano il modo di attrarre l'oro e l'argento di tutta la terra. All'udirli parlare, si direbbe che siano quegli Adepti, che si vantano di possedere il gran segreto. Egli è gran tempo che i politici chimici promettono alle Nazioni di riempirle d'oro, e intanto la povertà, la debolezza, il disordine, e tutto continua come prima, anche la credenza ai politici chimici. Le loro magnifiche promesse furono favole, i tristi effetti furono istorie.

Ma poichè tanta, e si eminente è la considerazion per il danaro, che ha senza dubbio la sua grande utilità, giova di far conoscere che l'oro entra necessariamente e si diffonde da se stesso in un popolo che possiede le vere ricchezze; che fugge inevitabilmente da un popolo che non le possiede, nè v'ha forza che possa ritenerlo; e che da se solo, e senza leggi e discipline si conserva, e si proporziona alla massa dei prodotti in ogni Stato.

L'oro o l'argento non è un prodotto del nostro paese, non si semina, nè si miete ne' nostri campi, non entra per le grondaje, nè cade in pioggia dal cielo, ma si acquista, e si compra dagli stranieri. Ora una Nazione, che possiede le vere ricchezze, se ne procaccierà quanto ella crede, o per bisogno, come strumento di commercio, o per vanità, come oggetto di ostentazione e di lusso. Nè questa Nazione sarà mai priva di metalli, come non è mai priva dello zucchero, della cocciniglia, del pepe, della cannella, che ci vengono dall'Asia e dall'America, nello stesso modo, con le stesse navi, con gli stessi contratti, coll' opera degli stessi trafficanti, e dai popoli stessi. In ciò non v'è arcano, non v'è sottigliezza; la cosa è semplice e naturale. Le Nazioni commercianti si dividono in due classi. Altre hanno più oro ed argento che cose, come la Spagna e il Portogallo; altre hanno più cose che oro ed argento, come la Francia e l'Inghilterra. Ora gl'Inglesi e i Francesi danno le merci di cui abbondano, e ricevono l'oro di cui mancano.

Nè gli Spagnuoli e i Portoghesi ricuseranno mai di ricevere le cose a loro necessarie o piacevoli; perciocchè, permuterebbero forse l'oro e l'argento con altr' oro ed argento? Se un Italiano andasse a Londra espressamente per cambiar mille Ghinee con mille Ghinee, si direbbe ch'è pazzo. Dunque gli Spagnuoli, e i Portoghesi, e tutti i possessori di ricche miniere saranno sempre disposti a cedere l'oro e l'argento, ch'è un prodotto lor proprio e superfluo, per le derrate di cui essi hanno bisogno; e se così fecero per tre secoli dopo la scuoperta dell'America, il faranno anche in avvenire, nè certamente sara minore la loro premura in privarsene, di quello che possa esser la nostra in farne l'acquisto.

Ma chi è veramente che contribuisce per la maggior parte alle infinite spese, che si ricercano per trar l'oro dalle viscere della terra? Siamo noi cittadini dell'Europa, noi agricoltori, noi manifattori, che mandiamo in America le nostre derrate, le nostre tele di lino e di bambagia, e i panni di lana e di seta, per nutrire e vestire i lavoratori delle mine, e i loro Signori. Siamo noi dunque che stando qui ne' nostri poderi e nelle nostre officine, esercitiamo le miniere del Potosì, di Oruca, di Tarapaca, di Rirotinto, di Vega, di Buenaventura, enel mietere le nostre spighe, e nello sfrondare i nostri gelsi noi raccogliamo l'oro e l'argento: le nostre mogli e figli ne sono i lieti raccoglitori, e senza il rimorso e l'orrore di umane vittime. Gli Spagnuoli e i Portoghesi non hanno dunque che una picciola parte di codesti metalli; il più è nostro, è frutto della nostra industria, è prezzo dei nostri prodotti, e ci appartiene di buon diritto.

Ed ecco il perchè l'oro e l'argento si spargono per tutta l'Europa, per tutta l'Asia dove più, dove meno, secondo la quantità delle cose che ogni popolo vi ha dal canto proprio contribuite. Nè importa che sia immediato un tal commercio; poichè o gli Olandesi per esempio, o gl'Inglesi sieno quelli che portino in America le tele, i panni, e le stoffe, l'oro si spargerà nella Slesia e in Livonia, d'onde vennero i canapi e i lini; e in Egitto e nel Levante, dove si raccolse la bambagia; e in Puglia, e in Calabria, che vi misero gli olj e le lane; e in Piemonte, e Lombardia, da cui si trassero le sete; e in Polonia che somministrò il frumento ai tessitori; e nella Svezia e in Moscovia, da cui provennero il ferro e i legnami da costruir le navi, che portarono le merci alle miniere, e riportarono l'oro e l'argento; e così con una gradazion meravigliosa, e con una proporzione invariabile e necessaria, quest' oro ed argento si vedra dividersi e diramarsi in tutte le Nazioni a misura delle cose che furono da ognuno conferite, cosicchè le Nazioni più ricche di prodotti, e più industriose beveranno copiosamente al fiume, altre ai ruscelli, altre ai rigagnoli; nè alle più povere mancherà qualche filo, nè alle più inerti qualche goccia di questo umor aureo ed argenteo, che tende per sua natura a seguir le cose, e a livellarsi con esse quando sia libero, come le acque scorrono in abbondanza per i canali larghi e profondi, e vanno a rilento, o retrocedono pèr i canali angusti ed ostrutti.

Ma senz' anche andar dietro all' immenso giro del Commercio Europeo, noi abbiamo sott' occhio un fenomeno, che da tutti si vede, che si conosce da tutti, che si ripete ogni giorno, e che ci mostra visibilmente l'attrazione imperiosa e fortissima delle cose sul danaro. Questo fenomeno è la sua mirabile distribuzione in ogni Provincia, in ogni Distretto, in ogni Terra. Si scorra dal tugurioal palagio, dalla borgata alla città, e si vedrà trovarsi sempre maggiore il danaro, dove maggiore è la copia e la circolazion delle cose; nella Metropoli, più abbondante che nelle città provinciali, e in queste più che nel contado; e nel contado, più nelle castella che nei villaggi; e fra le castella, in quello dov' è più animata l'industria; e fra i villaggi, dov' è più fertile e meglio coltivato il suolo, e nello stesso villaggio, più nelle botteghe dei commestibili che nelle case; e fra le botteghe, in quella che è più fornita di copia evarietà di cose; e in tutti questi luoghi, nei giorni di mercato; fra tutti i mercati, nel più popoloso e solenne, dove grande è l'affluenza de' generi commerciabili, indigeni e stranieri.

Quali sono i codici, quali le leggi, quali le discipline, che regolano questo sì esatto, sì minuto, sì vario, e insieme costante ripartimento del danaro in tutti i mestieri, in tutte le famiglie, in tutti gl' individui, in tutti gli angoli dello Stato, in modo che la Città neabbia più della Terra, e la Terra più della Villa, e la Villa più della raunata di semplici capanne, e l'industrioso più dell' inerte, e il proprietario più del fittajuolo, e il padron più del servo, e il mercatante più dell'operajo? Quali editti, o premj, o pene, o custodie potrebbero esser valevoli a governare il corso, e la distribuzion del danaro con una si stupenda e sì costante armonia, che fosse sempre, e dovunque in proporzion delle cose? Dunque l'oro nell'uscir dalle miniere segue i prodotti, li segue nel commercio, li segue per tutti i Porti, e per tutti gli Stati dell'Europa, e dopo eziandìo ch'entrò in una Nazione, segue ancora i prodotti per le città, per le campagne, per i mercati, e corre loro dietro indivisibilmente in ogni luogo.

Che se l'oro esce da una nazione posseditrice dei prodotti, egli è chiaro indizio ch'è soverchio e nocivo, poichè ogni nazione non ha bisogno che di una certa quantità di numerario a misura della sua industria. Ella ne assorbe per dir cosi, quanto è necessario, e finchè ne sia saturata. Il di più non può ritenerlo. Crescendo soverchiamente la quantità della moneta, scema di prezzo come merce, perde la sua virtù come segno, diviene inutile come strumento di circolazione. Ora la merce và dove trova un maggior prezzo; il segno parte da un luogo in cui non rappresenta; lo strumento non rimane ove giace inoperoso. Dunque il danaro soverchio uscir deve e come merce, e come segno, e come strumento. Nè hanno forse i Principi maggior possanza sopra il corso e la quantità dell'oro e dell'argento, di quello che abbiano sopra il Pò, il Reno, ed il Danubio. Se per invidia di chi vien dopo di loro arrestar volessero il corso delle Riviere, ne sarebbero ben presto puniti. La loro prudenza consiste nel profittarsi delle acque che passano, e lasciarle passare. Non altrimenti l'oro deve uscir liberamente per entrar liberamente, quando si voglia che si mantenga da se stesso in quella proporzion che conviene alla propria industria, senza servirle d'impaccio e di peso, e senza cagionare incomodi ristagni e ingorgamenti dannosi[2].

Da ciò si vede quanto sia vana e ridicola la nostra paura sull' uscita del danaro. I medici politici e ipocondriaci dipingono una nazione, da cui credono ch'esca il danaro, come un corpo semivivo, con le vene aperte, che versa il sangue e la vita. Con queste immagini lugubri spaventano i popoli e i gabinetti, e annunziano loro la emorragia, e la morte della nazione. Quindi compongono, e vendono con gran fortuna, un numero infinito di rimedj per chiudere le sue ferite. Ma i nostri buoni medici e apoticarj politici non sanno che una nazione è come quel vecchio Rè di Tessaglia, che quanto di sangue perdeva da un braccio, altrettanto la maga gliene infondeva per l'altro. L'oro ch'esce chiama l'oro ch'entra, ed è come fiume, dove l'onda che precede dà luogo all'onda che segue[3]. I

[2] Hume Ess. Polit. Ess. V.
Locke Consid. sopra le Mon., Finan., e Commerc. P. I. Cap. 2.
Du Tot Reflex. polit. sur les Finances et le Comm. T. I. Art. 9. et. suiv.
Dechamps Exam. des refl. polit.
Carli Delle antiche e moderne proporzioni de' metalli monet. Tom. 6. Dis. 6.

[3] L'argent produit de l'argent; cette matière est un flux et réflux perpétuel destiné au commerce. Du Tot. Réflex. polit. Tom. I., Chap. I., Artic. 9.
La plûpart ont regardé comme pernicieux le transport de l'argent à l'étranger. Pensent-ils que c'est un présent qu'on leur fait? Melon Ess. polit. sur le com.
L'argent ne doit faire que passer; et la liberté de sa sortie doit être égale à la liberté de son entrée. Mercier de la Riv. Ordre nat. et ess. Tom. 2. Chap. 41.

nostri frivoli e puerili terrori di perdere il danaro, sarebbero dunque come quelli di un certo popolo, che va in ogni plenilunio a piangere, e disperarsi sulle rive del patrio fiume, sempre temendo che le sue acque finiscano di scorrere. E sono venti secoli che piange ancora sulle stesse sponde.

Che se panico e vano è il nostro timore di perdere il danaro, vane del pari e inefficaci sono tutte le leggi, con cui se ne proibisce l'uscita[4]. I Portoghesi e gli Spagnuoli la vietarono sotto pena di morte. Ma disanimata essendo presso loro l'Agricoltura, fonte delle produzioni, e madre e balia delle Arti, grande in que' Regni è la sproporzione fra il danaro e le cose. Da ciò ne segue, che soverchia trovandosi la quantità de' metalli, il valor numerario delle cose sia maggiore fra essi che nelle altre nazioni. Ma dove le derrate, le materie prime, le mercedi degli Artefici, e le manifatture siano cresciute di prezzo, si perde necessariamente la preferenza in confronto degli stranieri, che vender possono a miglior mercato. È dunque allora inevitabile che l'oro si sforzi di fuggirsene, e di andare in traccia delle merci forestiere. Tal' è appunto l'effetto del disequilibrio nel valore dell' oro, che filtra, trapela, rompe, e corre dove il pendìo del prezzo lo chiama; nè leggi o pene, nè mura o palizzate, nè vigili escubie potrebbero impedirlo, poichè non v'ha legge nè forza, che possa opporsi all' imperioso e audace interesse di tutta una nazione. Così la Spagna e il Portogallo sono come quel doglio senza fondo delle Danaidi, che sempre riempivano, e sempre era vuoto[5].

Che giovano dunque tante cure e gelosie per ritenere, o per accrescere una ricchezza si mobile ed indocile, che sorda alle leggi, sorda alle pene, invitata non ascolta, non chiamata sen viene, libera non si parte, trattenuta sen fugge, volontaria ritorna, da se stessa si sparge, si livella, e si conserva? Quanto

---

[4] Les défences de sortir l'argent ont été, et seront toujours sans effet, quelqu' attention qu'on y apporte. Du Tot Ref. polit. Liv. I. Chap. I. Art. 9.
Smith. La richess. des Nat. Liv. 4. Chap. 5.
Locke Considerazioni sopra la Mon. ec. Part I. Cap. II.

[5] Le bon marché de l'or et de l'argent, ou ce qui est la même chose, la cherté de toutes les marchandises, qui est l'effet nécessaire de la surabondance de ces metaux, décourage l'agriculture et les manufactures de l'Espagne, et du Portugal, et met les nations etrangeres ec. Smith Riches. des Nat., Livr. 4. Chap. 5 [IV.v.a.19].
Ulloa Retabiliss. des manufact. et du comm. d'Espagne Ustariz Theorie, et prat. du comm., et de la marine.

è più saggio il cercar la vera, la reale, la permanente ricchezza, la copia di prodotti proprj, le cose sempre utili per se stesse, che portano seco l'abbondanza, la prosperità, e la sicurezza di una nazione, e seco portano ancora l'oro e l'argento, ma in modo che sia veramente nostro e durevole, che più non si tema di perderlo, che non possa esserci tolto dagli stranieri; ma vengano anzi gli stranieri a tributarlo spontaneanmente alla nostra industria e fortuna!

Se dunque, come mi sembra, è provato, che il danaro è di sua natura libero e indipendente, che non va soggetto a discipline, a regole, e leggi, ma che ubbidisce a una voce più potente, ad una forza più efficace e sempre attiva, che è l'attrazione dei prodotti, ch' esso li segue nell' uscir dalle miniere, che li segue nel corso suo per tutta l'Europa, che non li abbandona quando entra in una nazione, ma che si dirama, e si diffonde in ogni parte, in ogni classe, in ogni famiglia con una gradazion portentosa, e sempre in proporzion delle cose; egli è ormai chiaro, che chi avrà una gran massa di cose proprie, avrà eziandio una gran copia d'oro e d'argento, e chi avrà la maggior possibile massa di cose proprie, avrà la maggior possibile copia d'oro e d'argento. Ma ora io mostrerò che questa maggior possibile massa di cose proprie non puo mai conseguirsi se non nella libera concorrenza o sia nella libertà di commercio, dunque mostrerò nel tempo stesso che la concorrenza è la causa delle ricchezze vere, che sono le cose, e delle ricchezze convenzionali, che sono l'oro e l'argento.

Ora parmi, se non m'inganno, che le mie idee comincino a prendere una qualche forma regolata, e a dedursi una dall'altra. Il danaro segue con forza irresistibile le cose, dunque chi sarà più ricco di cose, sarà più ricco altresì di danaro; ma per esser il più ricco di cose convien godere di una libera concorrenza; dunque la concorrenza è quella, che produce la ricchezza di cose e di danaro. Vediamo immantinente come la concorrenza procuri la maggior possibile massa di cose.

Della Concorrenza.

Il prezzo delle cose cresce sempre in proporzione della ricerca che se ne fa. Ora tanto maggiori saranno le ricerche, quanto maggior sarà il numero de'compratori, e tanto sarà maggiore il loro numero, quanto sarà più libera la concorrenza. Dunque la libera concorrenza produce il maggior prezzo possibile delle cose. Essa è che radunando insieme una gran moltitudine di compratori e nazionali e stranieri, eccita tra loro la gara, la emulazione, lo studio di acquistar le nostre produzioni, e ingenera in ciascheduno la inquietudine, l'ansietà, e la tema di restarne senza, onde nascono le offerte di vantaggioso prezzo, cosicchè il mercato si converte in una spece d'incanto, dove ogni merce si vende, dirò così, sotto l'asta.

Ma s'egli è chiaro che la concorrenza procura il più vantaggioso prezzo, egli è chiaro altresì che il vantaggioso prezzo è il solo mezzo per accrescere la quantità dei prodotti, nè sarà mai sperabile di aver abbondanza di cose, se non precede l'esca e l'invito di un vantaggioso prezzo; poichè gli uominini non gettano tempo, fatica, e spese per raccogliere ciò che non sia per rendere alcun profitto. Quindi la concorrenza coll'allettamento di un sícuro guadagno chiama tutto un popolo all' industria: ella sveglia lo spensierato e l'inerte con l'acuta voce dell'interesse: ella insegna l'amor del travaglio, la sedulità, la solerzia, l'ostinata pazienza, l'ordine, l'economia: ella inspira il coraggio delle imprese, il disprezzo de'pericoli, e tolleranza de' disagj. Alla vista del guadagno l'agricoltor si rivolge a versar sulla terra più larghi capitali e sudori, e a coltivare in preferenza quelle derrate, che gli promettono più ricca mercede, e più copiosa ricompensa: a tal vista il manifattore impiega un maggior nimero di artefici, e perfeziona gli stromenti e le macchine, che gli accrescono quasi le braccia ed il vigore de'muscoli, e rendono più equabile e regolare il lavoro: e siccome ognuno per natural deside rio tenta di giungere a miglior fortuna il più presto che sia possibile, così da questa foga e contenzion generale, e dagli affrettati e riuniti sforzi di tutti nasce ben presto l'abbondanza, e cresce prodigiosamente la massa di tutti i prodotti di natura e d'arte. Ecco come il vantaggioso prezzo genera necessariamente un rapido accrescimento di prodotti.

Si contempli ora il benefico effetto della concorrenza. Essa fa crescere il prezzo, e col prezzo fa crescere la quantità dei prodotti. Ma la maggior possibile ricchezza di una Nazione è appunto composta dal maggior possibile prezzo, e dalla maggior possibile quantità de'suoi prodotti; poichè nè il prezzo senza cose, nè le cose senza prezzo sono ricchezza; dunque la concorrenza promovendo nel tempo stesso e il maggior valore, e la maggior quantità delle cose, cagiona la maggior possibile ricchezza di una Nazione; ed essendo già provato che il danaro segue inseparabilmente i prodotti di natura e d'arte, e si proporziona sempre alla quantità dei medesimi; ne viene per illazion necessaria, che dove si trova la concorrenza, ivi si trovi eziandio e si conservi la maggior possibile copia di danaro.

[FROM] REPORT ON MANUFACTURES*
5 December 1791
Alexander Hamilton

Though it should be true, that in settled countries, the diversi-
fication of Industry is conducive to an increase in the
productive powers of labour, and to an augmentation of
revenue and capital; yet it is scarcely conceivable that there
can be any [thing] of so solid and permanent advantage to an
uncultivated and unpeopled country as to convert its wastes
into cultivated and inhabited districts. If the Revenue, in the
mean time, should be less, the Capital, in the event, must be
greater.

To these observations, the following appears to be a satisfactory answer—

1. If the system of perfect liberty to industry and commerce
were the prevailing system of nations—the arguments which
dissuade a country in the predicament of the United States,
from the zealous pursuits of manufactures would doubtless
have great force. It will not be affirmed, that they might not
be permitted, with few exceptions, to serve as a rule of national
conduct. In such a state of things, each country would have
the full benefit of its peculiar advantages to compensate for its
deficiencies or disadvantages. If one nation were in condition
to supply manufactured articles on better terms than another,
that other might find an abundant indemnification in a superior
capacity to furnish the produce of the soil. And a free exchange,
mutually beneficial, of the commodities which each was able
to supply, on the best terms, might be carried on between
them, supporting in full vigour the industry of each. And
though the circumstances which have been mentioned and
others which will be unfolded hereafter render it probable,
that nations merely Agricultural would not enjoy the same

* From *The Papers of Alexander Hamilton*, ed. Harold C. Syrett (New York,
1966), vol. 10, pp. 262–9, 285–7, 300–301.

degree of opulence, in proportion to their numbers, as those which united manufactures with agriculture; yet the progressive improvement of the lands of the former might, in the end, atone for an inferior degree of opulence in the mean time: and in a case in which opposite considerations are pretty equally balanced, the option ought perhaps always to be, in favour of leaving Industry to its own direction.

But the system which has been mentioned, is far from characterising the general policy of Nations. [The prevalent one has been regulated by an opposite spirit.]

The consequence of it is, that the United States are to a certain extent in the situation of a country precluded from foreign Commerce. They can indeed, without difficulty obtain from abroad the manufactured supplies, of which they are in want; but they experience numerous and very injurious impediments to the emission and vent of their own commodities. Nor is this the case in reference to a single foreign nation only. The regulations of several countries, with which we have the most extensive intercourse, throw serious obstructions in the way of the principal staples of the United States.

In such a position of things, the United States cannot exchange with Europe on equal terms; and the want of reciprocity would render them the victim of a system, which should induce them to confine their views to Agriculture and refrain from Manufactures. A constant and encreasing necessity, on their part, for the commodities of Europe, and only a partial and occasional demand for their own, in return, could not but expose them to a state of impoverishment, compared with the opulence to which their political and natural advantages authorise them to aspire.[1]

Remarks of this kind are not made in the spirit of complaint.

---

[1] Impediments to the institution of free trade policies, which H discusses in this and the three preceding paragraphs, had been discussed by several writers. Although Smith was critical of the corn laws, which he compared to laws of religion, he also wrote in their defense: 'Were all nations to follow the liberal system of free exportation and free importation, the different states into which a great continent was divided would so far resemble the different provinces of a great empire. . . . But very few countries have entirely adopted this liberal system. . . . The very bad policy of one country may thus render it in some measure dangerous and imprudent to establish what would otherwise be the best policy in another' (Smith, *Wealth of Nations*, II, 38: IV.v.b.39).

The following statements by Necker should also be noted:

'Tis for the nations, whose regulations are alluded to, to judge for themselves, whether, by aiming at too much they do not

'Une académie distinguée avoit proposé pour question, il y a quelque tems, d'examiner quel seroit l'effet de l'abolition des loix prohibitives à l'égard de la nation que les abrogeroit la premiere. . . .
Une société qui laisseroit entrer toutes les productions de l'industrie étrangere, tandis que les autres nations continueroient à interdire l'introduction des siennes, seroit peu-à-peu obligée de payer, en subsistances ou en argent, ce qu'elle demanderoit aux étrangers; bientôt ses richesses et sa population diminueroient. Ce que nous venons de dire, dans une hypothese absolue, telle que l'interdiction totale des marchandises d'un pays, jointe à la libre introduction dans ce même pays de toutes les marchandises étrangeres, s'appliqueroit proportionnellement aux hypotheses mixtes et tempérées.' (Necker, Œuvres, III, 260–61.)
'Un pays ne peut acheter qu'autant qu'on reçoit ses propres richesses en paiement; ainsi refuser d'acheter de lui, c'est refuser de lui vendre, c'est détruire le commerce.' (Necker, Œuvres, III, 259.)
'Doubtless if all other nations, by a general compact, would agree to abolish all prohibitions, and all import duties, France ought not to refuse to accede; for it is probable that she would be a gainer by such a convention. However, she would still have occasion to reflect upon it maturely, if either the increase of the public burthens should sensibly raise the price of labour, or if an industrious nation should spring up in the midst of a fertile country, free from those taxes which wars and the luxury of modern governments have introduced into Europe. But all those hypotheses which are founded upon a general freedom of commerce, are chimerical propositions; the powers who would lose by this freedom would never adopt it, and those who would gain by it, might in vain desire it; however, that power which should wish to introduce it, by setting the example, would imitate the folly of a private individual, who in the hope of establishing a community of effects, suffered all his neighbours to share his patrimony.' (Necker, *Finances of France*, II, 192.)
This point of view did not disappear in France with Necker's resignation. See, for example, Gaspard Joseph Amand Ducher, *Analyse des Loix Commerciales, Avec le Tarif des Droits sur les Batiments & les Marchandises dans les Treize Etats Unis de l'Amerique* (n.p., n.d.).
The difficulties in the way of inaugurating free trade policies were also appreciated by many Americans. On April 9, 1789, Madison in a speech in Congress said:
'If my general principle is a good one, that commerce ought to be free, and labor and industry left at large to find its proper object, the only thing which remains will be to discover the exceptions that do not come within the rule I have laid down. . . . Although the freedom of commerce would be advantageous to the world, yet, in some particulars, one nation might suffer to benefit others, and this ought to be for the general good of society.
If America was to leave her ports perfectly free, and make no discrimination between vessels owned by her citizens and those owned by foreigners, while other nations make this discrimination, it is obvious that such policy would go to exclude American shipping altogether from foreign ports, and she would be materially affected in one of her most important interests.' (*Annals of Congress*, I, 117.)
For the viewpoint of many American merchants on this subject, see the article by Charles Pettit in *The American Museum*, VIII (July, 1790), 28.

lose more than they gain.[2] 'Tis for the United States to consider by what means they can render themselves least dependent, on the combinations, right or wrong of foreign policy.

It is no small consolation, that already the measures which have embarrassed our Trade, have accelerated internal improvements, which upon the whole have bettered our affairs. To diversify and extend these improvements is the surest and safest method of indemnifying ourselves for any inconveniences, which those or similar measures have a tendency to beget. If Europe will not take from us the products of our soil, upon terms consistent with our interest, the natural remedy is to contract as fast as possible our wants of her.

2. The conversion of their waste into cultivated lands is certainly a point of great moment in the political calculations of the United States. But the degree in which this may possibly be retarded by the encouragement of manufactories does not appear to countervail the powerful inducements to affording that encouragement.[3]

An observation made in another place is of a nature to have great influence upon this question. If it cannot be denied, that the interests even of Agriculture may be advanced more by having such of the lands of a state as are occupied under good cultivation, than by having a greater quantity occupied under a

---

[2] On this problem Smith wrote:
'But if foreigners, either by prohibitions or high duties, are hindered from coming to sell, they cannot always afford to come to buy; because coming without a cargo, they must lose the freight from their own country to Great Britain. By diminishing the number of sellers, therefore, we necessarily diminish that of buyers, and are thus likely not only to buy foreign goods dearer, but to sell our own cheaper, than if there was a more perfect freedom of trade.' (Smith, *Wealth of Nations*, I, 456: IV.ii.30.)
'Even the regulations by which each nation endeavours to secure to itself the exclusive trade of its own colonies, are frequently more hurtful to the countries in favour of which they are established than to those against which they are established. The unjust oppression of the industry of other countries falls back, if I may say so, upon the heads of the oppressors, and crushes their industry more than it does that of those other countries.' (Smith, *Wealth of Nations*, II, 136: IV.vii.c.83.)

[3] The importance of cultivating wasteland had been suggested by Smith, (see note 127) and also by many Americans. For example, one writer stated: '. . .the opposers of American manufactures may perhaps, object,—that, as we have large tracts of unsettled country, it would be more for the national benefit, that the people should be employed in cultivating the unimproved lands, than in manufacturing goods. . .' (*Columbian Magazine*, I [February, 1787], 282). See also *The American Museum*, II (October, 1787), 331.

much inferior cultivation, and if Manufactories, for the reasons assigned, must be admitted to have a tendency to promote a more steady and vigorous cultivation of the lands occupied than would happen without them—it will follow, that they are capable of indemnifying a country for a diminution of the progress of new settlements; and may serve to increase both the capital [value] and the income of its lands, even though they should abrige the number of acres under Tillage.

But it does, by no means, follow, that the progress of new settlements would be retarded by the extension of Manufactures. The desire of being an independent proprietor of land is founded on such strong principles in the human breast, that where the opportunity of becoming so is as great as it is in the United States, the proportion will be small of those, whose situations would otherwise lead to it, who would be diverted from it towards Manufactures. And it is highly probable, as already intimated, that the accessions of foreigners, who originally drawn over by manufacturing views would afterwards abandon them for Agricultural, would be more than equivalent for those of our own Citizens, who might happen to be detached from them.

The remaining objections to a particular encouragement of manufactures in the United States now require to be examined.

One of these turns on the proposition, that Industry, if left to itself, will naturally find its way to the most useful and profitable employment: whence it is inferred, that manufactures without the aid of government will grow up as soon and as fast, as the natural state of things and the interest of the community may require.[4]

Against the solidity of this hypothesis, in the full latitude of the terms, very cogent reasons may be offered. These have relation to—the strong influence of habit and the spirit of

---

[4] This objection to the encouragement of manufactures was, of course, stated most forcibly by Adam Smith, who wrote: 'As every individual, therefore, endeavours as much as he can both to employ his capital in the support of domestic industry, and so to direct that industry that its produce may be of the greatest value; every individual necessarily labours to render the annual revenue of the society as great as he can. . . . By preferring the support of domestic to that of foreign industry he intends only his own security; and by directing that industry in such a manner as its produce may be of the greatest value, he intends only his own gain, and he is in this, as in many other cases, led by an invisible hand to promote an end which was no part of his intention' (Smith, *Wealth of Nations*, I, 447: IV.ii.9).

imitation—the fear of want of success in untried enterprises—
the intrinsic difficulties incident to first essays towards a
competition with those who have previously attained to perfection in the business to be attempted—the bounties premiums
and other artificial encouragements, with which foreign nations
second the exertions of their own Citizens in the branches, in
which they are to be rivalled.

Experience teaches, that men are often so much governed by
what they are accustomed to see and practice, that the simplest
and most obvious improvements, in the [most] ordinary occupations, are adopted with hesitation, reluctance and by slow
gradations. The spontaneous transition to new pursuits, in a
community long habituated to different ones, may be expected
to be attended with proportionably greater difficulty. When
former occupations ceased to yield a profit adequate to the
subsistence of their followers, or when there was an absolute
deficiency of employment in them, owing to the superabun-
dance of hands, changes would ensue; but these changes would
be likely to be more tardy than might consist with the interest
either of individuals or of the Society. In many cases they
would not happen, while a bare support could be ensured by
an adherence to ancient courses; though a resort to a more
profitable employment might be practicable. To produce the
desireable changes, as early as may be expedient, may therefore
require the incitement and patronage of government.[5]

---

[5] In *A Treatise of Human Nature* Hume wrote: 'By degrees the repetition
produces a facility, which is another very powerful principle of the human
mind, and an infallible source of pleasure, where the facility goes not beyond
a certain degree.... But custom not only gives a facility to perform any
action, but likewise an inclination and tendency towards it, where it is not
entirely disagreeable, and can never be the object of inclination' (David
Hume, *A Treatise of Human Nature: Being An Attempt to introduce the
experimental Method of Reasoning Into Moral Subjects. Book II. Of The
Passions* [London: Printed for John Noon, at the White-Hart, near Mercer's-
Chapel, in Cheapside, 1739], 423–24: II.S.V, paras. 3, 5).

In opposing free trade Necker emphasized the need for the central direction of a national economy in the following fashion: 'Les hommes sont
tellement gouvernés par l'habitude, qu'une nation industrieuse peut mécon-
noître long-tems ses forces, et faire un trafic continuel de ses grains contre
les manufactures étrangeres, tandis qu'avec quelques efforts ou quelques
privations momentanées, elle parviendroit à établir chez elle ces mêmes
manufactures, et satisferoit ainsi le goût de ses propriétaires sans nuire à sa
population' (Necker, *Œuvres*, IV, 36).

The apprehension of failing in new attempts is perhaps a more serious impediment. There are dispositions apt to be attracted by the mere novelty of an undertaking—but these are not always those best calculated to give it success. To this, it is of importance that the confidence of cautious sagacious capitalists both citizens and foreigners, should be excited. And to inspire this description of persons with confidence, it is essential, that they should be made to see in any project, which is new, and for that reason alone, if, for no other, precarious, the prospect of such a degree of countenance and support from government, as may be capable of overcoming the obstacles, inseperable from first experiments.[6]

The superiority antecedently enjoyed by nations, who have pre-occupied and perfected a branch of industry, constitutes a more formidable obstacle, than either of those, which have been mentioned, to the introduction of the same branch into a country, in which it did not before exist. To maintain between the recent establishments of one country and the long matured establishments of another country, a competition upon equal terms, both as to quality and price, is in most cases impracticable. The disparity in the one, or in the other, or in both, must necessarily be so considerable as to forbid a successful rivalship, without the extraordinary aid and protection of government.[7]

Again, in a discussion of Colbert's policies Necker wrote: 'Nous voyons encore des nations agricoles échanger leurs bleds...contre des travaux qu'elles pourroient encourager chez elles...car l'habitude la plus déraisonnable et la plus stupide a souvent besoin d'être rompue par un administrateur éclairé...' (Necker, *Œuvres*, III, 205).

Steuart was also concerned with the role of habit and emphasized it as a limiting condition of economic growth (Steuart, *Political Economy*, I, 117–18).

[6] The need for government encouragement of fledgling industries had been stressed by many Americans who were interested in domestic manufactures. For example, see [Philadelphia] *National Gazette*, November 24, 1791; *Annals of Congress*, I, 121. See also Moses Brown to John Dexter, July 22–October 15, 1791, printed as an enclosure to Dexter to H, October, 1791.

[7] In opposing this view, Smith wrote: 'Whether the advantages which one country has over another, be natural or acquired, is in this respect of no consequence. As long as the one country has those advantages, and the other wants them, it will always be more advantageous for the latter, rather

But the greatest obstacle of all to the successful prosecution of a new branch of industry in a country, in which it was before unknown, consists, as far as the instances apply, in the bounties, premiums and other aids which are granted, in a variety of cases, by the nations, in which the establishments to be imitated are previously introduced. It is well known (and particular examples in the course of this report will be cited) that certain nations grant bounties on the exportation of particular commodities, to enable their own workmen to undersell and supplant all competitors, in the countries to which those commodities are sent. Hence the undertakers of a new manufacture have to contend not only with the natural disadvantages of a new undertaking, but with the gratuities and remunerations which other governments bestow. To be enabled to contend with success, it is evident, that the interference and aid of their own government are indispensible.

Combinations by those engaged in a particular branch of business in one country, to frustrate the first efforts to introduce it into another, by temporary sacrifices, recompensed perhaps by extraordinary indemnifications of the government of such country, are believed to have existed, and are not to be regarded as destitute of probability.[8] The existence or assurance of aid from the government of the country, in which the business is to be introduced, may be essential to fortify adventurers against the dread of such combinations, to defeat their effects, if formed and to prevent their being formed, by demonstrating that they must in the end prove fruitless.

Whatever room there may be for an expectation that the

to buy of the former than to make. It is an acquired advantage only, which one artificer has over his neighbour, who exercises another trade; and yet they both find it more advantageous to buy of one another, than to make what does not belong to their particular trades' (Smith, *Wealth of Nations*, I, 450: IV.ii.15).

Steuart considers the problem of new nations entering into foreign trade in Book II (Steuart, *Political Economy*, I, 285, 298–99, 301–05).

[8] Interested Americans were aware of the attempts of industrial nations to frustrate the introduction of manufacturing in the United States. See, for example, *The American Museum*, III (January, 1788), 179; IV (October, 1788), 343–44; [Philadelphia] *National Gazette*, November 21, 1791. See also John Mix, Jr., to John Chester, September 30, 1791, printed as an enclosure to Chester to H, October 11, 1791, and Moses Brown to John Dexter, July 22–October 15, 1791, printed as an enclosure to Dexter to H, October, 1791.

industry of a people, under the direction of private interest, will upon equal terms find out the most beneficial employment for itself, there is none for a reliance, that it will struggle against the force of unequal terms, or will of itself surmount all the adventitious barriers to a successful competition, which may have been erected either by the advantages naturally acquired from practice and previous possession of the ground, or by those which may have sprung from positive regulations and an artificial policy. This general reflection might alone suffice as an answer to the objection under examination; exclusively of the weighty considerations which have been particularly urged. . . .

. . .There remains to be noticed an objection to the encouragement of manufactures, of a nature different from those which question the probability of success. This is derived from its supposed tendency to give a monopoly of advantages to particula⟨r⟩ classes at the expence of the rest of the community, who, it is affirmed, would be able to procure the requisite supplies of manufactured articles on better terms from foreigners, than from our own Citizens, and who it is alledged, are reduced to a necessity of paying an enhanced price for whatever they want, by every measure, which obstructs the free competition of foreign commoditi⟨es⟩.[9]

It is not an unreasonable supposition, that measures, which serve to abridge the free competition of foreign Articles, have a tendency to occasion an enhancement of prices and it is not to be denied that such is the effect in a number of Cases; but the fact does not uniformly correspond with the theory. A

---

[9] Smith mentioned the monopolistic effect of mercantile regulations in *The Wealth of Nations* when he wrote:

'In the restraints upon the importation . . . the interest of the home-consumer is evidently sacrificed to that of the producer. It is altogether for the benefit of the latter, that the former is obliged to pay that enhancement of price which this monopoly almost always occasions.' (Smith, *Wealth of Nations*, II, 173: IV.viii.50.)

'Merchants and manufacturers are the people who derive the greatest advantage from this monopoly of the home market.' (Smith, *Wealth of Nations*, I, 450: IV.ii.16.)

The argument to which H is referring was frequently used in debates in the First Congress. See, for example, the remarks of Thomas Tudor Tucker of South Carolina and Theodorick Bland of Virginia during the debate over the 1789 impost (*Annals of Congress*, I, 129, 307–08) and a speech by Andrew Moore of Virginia (*Annals of Congress*, I, 160). See also *The American Museum*, V (April, 1789), 422.

reduction of prices has in several instances immediately succeeded the establishment of a domestic manufacture. Whether
it be that foreign Manufacturers endeavour to suppla⟨nt⟩ by
underselling our own, or whatever else be the cause, the effect
has been such as is stated, and the reverse of what mig⟨ht⟩ have
been expected.[10]

But though it were true, that the immedi⟨ate⟩ and certain
effect of regulations controuling the competition of foreign
with domestic fabrics was an increase of price, it is universally
true that the contrary is the ultimate effect with every successful
manufacture. When a domestic manufacture has attained to
perfection, and has engaged in the prosecution of it a competent number of Persons, it invariably becomes cheaper. Being
free from the heavy charges, which attend the importation of
foreign commodities, it can be afforded, and accordingly
seldom or never fails to be sold Cheaper, in process of time,
than was the foreign Article for which it is a substitute. The
internal competition, which takes place, soon does away every
thing like Monopoly, and by degrees reduces the price of the
Article to the *minimum* of a reasonable profit on the Capital
employed. This accords with the reason of the thing and with
experience.

Whence it follows, that it is the interest of a community with
a view to eventual and permanent oeconomy, to encourage
the growth of manufactures. In a national view, a temporary

---

[10] After listing price increases caused by mercantile regulations, Smith wrote:
'When a landed nation, on the contrary, oppresses either by high duties or
by prohibitions the trade of foreign nations, it necessarily hurts its own
interest in two different ways. First, by raising the price of all foreign goods
and of all sorts of manufactures, it necessarily sinks the real value of the
surplus produce of its own land, with which, or, what comes to the same
thing, with the price of which, it purchases those foreign goods and manufactures. Secondly, by giving a sort of monopoly of the home market to its
own merchants, artificers and manufacturers, it raises the rate of mercantile
and manufacturing profit in proportion to that of agricultural profit. . .'
(Smith, *Wealth of Nations*, II, 186–87: IV.ix.25).
   On the other hand, in connection with the tendency of an increased
demand for Indian goods in India and a consequent price increase he wrote:
'The increase of demand, besides, though in the beginning it may sometimes
raise the price of goods, never fails to lower it in the long run. It encourages
production, and thereby increases the competition of the producers, who,
in order to undersell one another, have recourse to new divisions of labour
and new improvements of art, which might never otherwise have been
thought of' (Smith, *Wealth of Nations*, II, 266: V.i.e.26).

enhancement of price must always be well compensated by a permanent reduction of it.

It is a reflection, which may with propriety be indulged here, that this eventual diminution of the prices of manufactured Articles; which is the result of internal manufacturing establishments, has a direct and very important tendency to benefit agriculture. It enables the farmer, to procure with a smaller quantity of his labour, the manufactured produce of which he stan⟨ds⟩ in need, and consequently increases the value of his income and property.

. . . 4. Bounties are sometimes not only the best, but the only proper expedient, for uniting the encouragement of a new object of agriculture, with that of a new object of manufacture. It is the Interest of the farmer to have the production of the raw material promoted, by counteracting the interference of the foreig⟨n⟩ material of the same kind. It is the interest of the manufactu⟨rer⟩ to have the material abundant and cheap. If prior to the domes⟨tic⟩ production of the Material, in sufficient quantity, to supply the manufacturer on good terms; a duty be laid upon the importation of it from abroad, with a view to promote the raising of it at home, the Interests both of the Farmer and Manufacturer will be disserved. By either destroying the requisite supply, or raising the price of the article, beyond what can be afforded to be given for it, by the Conductor of an infant manufacture, it is abandoned or fails; an⟨d⟩ there being no domestic manufactories to create a demand for t⟨he⟩ raw material, which is raised by the farmer, it is in vain, that the Competition of the like foreign article may have been destroy⟨ed.⟩

It cannot escape notice, that a duty upon the importation of ⟨an⟩ article can no otherwise aid the domestic production of it, than giving the latter greater advantages in the home market. It ca⟨n⟩ have no influence upon the advantageous sale of the article produced, in foreign markets; no tendency, there⟨fore⟩ to promote its exportation.

The true way to conciliate these two interests, is to lay a duty on foreign *manufactures* of the material, the growth of which is desired to be encouraged, and to apply the produce of that duty by way of bounty, either upon the production of the material itself or upon its manufacture at home or upon both. In this disposition of the thing, the Manufacturer commences his enterprise under every advantage, which is attainable, as to quantity or price, of the raw material: And the Farmer if the bounty be immediately to him, is enabled by it to enter into a successful competition with the foreign material; if the bounty be to the manufacturer on so much of the domestic material as he consumes, the operation is nearly the same; he has a motive of interest to prefer the domestic Commodity, if of equal quality, even at a higher price than the foreign, so long as the difference of price is any thing short of the bounty which is allowed upon the article.[11]

Except the simple and ordinary kinds of household Manufactures, or those for which there are very commanding local advantages, pecuniary bounties are in most cases indispensable to the introduction of a new branch. A stimulus and a support not less powerful and direct is generally speaking essential to the overcoming of the obstacles which arise from the Competitions of superior skill and maturity elsewhere. Bounties are especially essential, in regard to articles, upon which those foreigners, who have been accustomed to supply a Country, are in the practice of granting them.

The continuance of bounties on manufactures long established must almost always be of questionable policy: Because a presumption would arise in every such Case, that there were natural and inherent impediments to success. But in new undertakings, they are as justifiable, as they are oftentimes necessary.

There is a degree of prejudice against bounties from an appearance of giving away the public money, without an

---

[11] Smith objected to bounties because they forced industry 'not only into a channel that is less advantageous, but into one that is actually disadvantageous: IV.v.a.24.' On the other hand, he wrote: 'To encourage the production of any commodity, a bounty upon production, one should imagine, would have a more direct operation, than one upon exportation. It would, besides, impose only one tax upon the people, that which they must contribute in order to pay the bounty. Instead of raising, it would tend to lower the price of the commodity in the home market; and thereby, instead of imposing a second tax upon the people, it might, at least, in part, repay them for what they had contributed to the first. Bounties upon production, however, have been very rarely granted. . . . But it is not the interest of merchants and manufacturers, the great inventors of all these expedients, that the home market should be overstocked with their goods, an event which a bounty upon production might sometimes occasion' (Smith, *Wealth of Nations*, II, 13–14: IV.v.a.25).

H's suggestions on bounties had been recommended by other Americans. See, for example, Barton, *The True Interest*, 27–28; *The American Museum*, V (January, 1789), 50.

immediate consideration, and from a supposition, that they serve to enrich particular classes, at the expence of the Community.

But neither of these sources of dislike will bear a serious examination. There is no purpose, to which public money can be more beneficially applied, than to the acquisition of a new and useful branch of industry; no Consideration more valuable than a permanent addition to the general stock of productive labour. . . .

ALSO AVAILABLE FROM THOEMMES PRESS

KEY ISSUES

Series Editor: **Andrew Pyle,** *University of Bristol*

The *Key Issues* series makes available the contemporary
reactions that met important books and debates on their first
appearance.
Examining the range of contemporary literature – journal articles
and reviews, book extracts, public letters, sermons and pamphlets
– *Key Issues* gives the reader an essential insight into the historical, social and political context in which a key publication or
particular topic emerged.
Each text has a new editorial introduction to supply the necessary
historical background.

On Moral Sentiments
Contemporary Responses toAdam Smith
Edited and introduced by **John Reeder,** *Universidad Complutense de Madrid*

MORAL PHILOSOPHY, ECONOMICS
ISBN 1 85506 550 9 : 256pp : Pb : £14.95 $24.95
ISBN 1 85506 549 5 : 250pp : Hb : £45.00 $72.00

Population
Contemporary Responses to Thomas Malthus
Edited and introduced by **Andrew Pyle,** *University of Bristol*

ECONOMICS, POLITICS, SOCIAL HISTORY
ISBN 1 85506 345 X : 320pp : Pb : 1994 : £13.95 $24.95
ISBN 1 85506 344 1 : 320pp : Hb : 1994 : £40.00 $72.00

Leviathan
*Contemporary Responses to the Political Theory of Thomas
Hobbes*
Edited and introduced by **G. A. J. Rogers,** *Keele University*

PHILOSOPHY, POLITICS
ISBN 1 85506 406 5 : 317pp : Pb : 1995 : £14.95 $24.95
ISBN 1 85506 407 3 : 317pp : Hb : 1995 : £45.00 $72.00

THOEMMES PRESS KEY ISSUES

The Subjection of Women
Contemporary Responses to John Stuart Mill
Edited and introduced by **Andrew Pyle**, *University of Bristol*

PHILOSOPHY, POLITICS, HISTORY OF FEMINISM
ISBN 1 85506 408 1 : 340pp : Pb : 1995 : £14.95 $24.95
ISBN 1 85506 409 X : 340pp : Hb : 1995 : £45.00 $72.00

Race: The Origins of an Idea, 1760–1850
Edited and introduced by **Hannah Augstein**,
Wellcome Institute, London

ANTHROPOLOGY, POLITICS
ISBN 1 85506 454 5 : 294pp : Pb : £14.95 $24.95
ISBN 1 85506 455 3 : 294pp : Hb : £45.00 $72.00

John Locke and Christianity
Contemporary Responses to the Reasonableness of Christianity
Edited and introduced by **Victor Nuovo**, *Middlebury College, Vermont*

ANTHROPOLOGY, POLITICS
ISBN 1 85506 540 1 : 250pp : Pb : £14.95 $24.95
ISBN 1 85506 539 8 : 250pp : Hb : £45.00 $72.00

Mill and Religion
Contemporary Responses to Three Essays on Religion
Edited and introduced by **Alan P.F. Sell,**
United Theological College, Aberystwyth

ANTHROPOLOGY, POLITICS
ISBN 1 85506 542 8 : 250pp : Pb : £14.95 $24.95
ISBN 1 85506 541 X : 250pp : Hb : £45.00 $72.00

Religious Scepticism
Contemporary Responses to Gibbon
Edited and introduced by **David Womersely**, *Jesus College, Oxford*

THEOLOGY, PHILOSOPHY, HISTORY, LITERATURE
ISBN 1 85506 510 X : 250pp : Pb : £14.95 $29.95
ISBN 1 85506 509 6 : 250pp : Hb : £45.00 $75.00